The Bowler's Art
Understanding **Spin**, **Swing** and **Swerve**

Richie Benaud in 1961. The first and third fingers are about to begin their powerful spin-ning movement around opposite sides of the ball (*courtesy of S & G Press Agency*).

The Bowler's Art

Understanding **Spin, Swing** and **Swerve**

Brian Wilkins

A & C Black · London

First published 1991 by
A & C Black (Publishers) Ltd
35 Bedford Row,
London WC1R 4JH

© 1991 Brian Wilkins

ISBN 0 7136 3448 0

A CIP catalogue record for this
book is available from the British
Library.

Typeset by August Filmsetting,
Haydock, St Helens
Printed and bound in Great
Britain by William Clowes Ltd,
Beccles and London

Acknowledgements
The author would like to thank
all those friends who have
helped to make this a better book
than it otherwise would have
been. In particular the author
would like to acknowledge
the assistance of the following:
Dick Hince
Bert Christensen
Roger Stanton
Central Institute of Technology
David Wratt
*New Zealand Meteorological
Service*
Stephen Green
Curator of the *Lord's Museum*
'Wo' Wilson
Basin Reserve Cricket Museum
Dr Colin Cook
Victoria University of Wellington
Richie Benaud.

The publishers are grateful to
the following for permission to
use copyright material:
**Methuen and Eyre and
Spottiswoode** for extracts
from *The Complete Leg-Break
Bowler* by C.S. Marriott
**The University of
Newcastle, Australia**
for figures from a project report
by A. Imbrosciano on 'The
swing of a cricket ball'
Thomas Nelson for the
illustration from *Grimmett on
Cricket*
Lord's Museum for the
photograph of Simpson-
Hayward
**The University of Notre
Dame** for the photograph by
F.N.M. Brown
**The University of
Pennsylvania Press** for the
extracts from *A Century of
Philadelphia Cricket*
George Beldam for his father's
photographs.

It has not been possible to trace
the owners of certain
photographs but proper
acknowledgement has been
made to these and to extracts
from various publications.

Notes on the photographs
The ball photographs were
devised and taken by the author.

The grip photographs were
devised by the author and taken
by **Brett Robertson**,
photographer at Victoria
University of Wellington, who
also carried out all the
photographic processing. The
grips, photographed in the
author's hand, are shown in
order to illustrate important
principles. Hands of a different
shape and size will require
modifications to the illustrated
grips shown in order to achieve
the maximum comfort and
efficiency.

*To my wife Pauline, and my
children, Jeremy, Miriam,
Damien, Sarah, Rachel, Lucy
and Emma, who have put up
with my passion for cricket for
so long.*

Contents

Preface

When the Hambledon player Lamborn first bowled off-spin, cricketers received a shock; such technical development has continued to enrich the game for two hundred years. If modern sport is any guide, cricket of the future will require human skill and endeavour to be even more firmly based on technical understanding. Fortunately, unlike many modern sports, cricket can draw upon a rich storehouse of knowledge and experience. The purpose of this book is to allow cricketers and cricket lovers to draw on the past while at the same time looking at bowling in a thoroughly modern way. A modern sport deserves something better than the vague and sometimes confusing language and ideas that frequently surround bowling. I invite readers of this book to enjoy clearing new pathways in their thinking.

Why does a ball swing? Does late swing really exist? Does humidity affect swing? What is the place of spin in medium-pace and fast bowling? Do we need another term, spin-swerve? Can swing and spin-swerve act together or against one another? What exactly do we mean by seaming? We hear that there are several types of googly; what are they? Are they all equally worthy of our attention?

Looking back at the talents of bowlers forty or more years ago one is struck by their ability to spin the ball, not only as slower bowlers, but at all speeds, fast and slow. It is generally agreed now that cricket will be a better game, both for players and spectators, when spin returns to its essential place. Poor understanding creates unnecessary barriers to our appreciation of the spinning skills available to all bowlers. One of the aims of this book is to break down these barriers.

I hope the reader is not put off by the sight of a few graphs in these pages. They are merely a simple and quick way of stating the force tending to push the ball one way or the other at various bowling speeds, and with various seam angles and spins. I will be disappointed if they cause any difficulty whatsoever; the information is really quite basic.

The television camera takes us from the bowler's fingers to the bat with each delivery, while the world's cricket experts pour out hour upon hour of frequently instructive and entertaining commentary. I hope that this book will interest the viewer, as well as the player at all levels, by supplementing that commentary and adding a little more depth to many of the topics which come up for discussion.

Batsman, know thine enemy: have I given away just enough to make you eager for the contest?

Women cricketers are probably hardened by now to the constant assumption on the part of authors that cricketers are males, and this book is no better. Bowler, fortunately, is a universal term, and when we see in one of the earliest known illustrations of cricket, or a game similar to it (c. 1340), that the bowler is a woman, a new prospect of women deploying their particular qualities of skill and insight at the crease opens up.

Unless stated otherwise, the bowlers and batsmen referred to in this book are right-handed.

It would probably help the reader to have a cricket ball at hand: grasp the ball, grasp the meaning.

Brian Wilkins

Introduction

THIS IS BOTH A WHY AND A HOW BOOK, as well as being a book which links
the present with the past; why a ball moves in the air and off the pitch, how a
bowler can get the very best from his hard work and skill.

Modern sportsmen and women have generally reached a high level of
understanding of their various techniques and coaching is on a correspondingly sophisticated level. Although cricket is not short of coaching books,
important areas of basic performance are not well served in comparison with
modern development in other sports. This book is an attempt among other
things to bridge that gap.

A cricket ball deviates in the air when the air flow around it is distorted.
This occurs because the stitching, or some other roughness, or the spin on
the ball, makes the flow different on one side of it compared to the flow on the
other side. Such a mix of influences is not easy to investigate and it is here
that the controllable environment of the wind tunnel has proved valuable.

Air driven past a cricket ball fixed in a wind tunnel is no different from the
air that rushes past a ball that has left the bowler's hand. In the wind tunnel
we can measure very accurately the various forces which push on the ball, we
can spin it at a known rate on fixed equipment and can set the seam at any
angle. This is how I and others have uncovered a good deal of the fascinating
picture of what happens to a ball in flight. Used as a starting point, this
knowledge brings new interest to the story of the game, allows us to look at
many of its aspects in a clearer light and gives us a modern basis for the
development of bowling technique.

To understand good bowling and the fascination of cricket we need a clear
and simple language to describe what a cricket ball is doing, or may do. We
won't be short of reasons why the ball won't swing, won't swerve, or won't
turn, but at least we can be perfectly clear about its direction, the spin it
carries, the angle of the seam, whether the seam appears to wobble from side
to side, and the expected direction of swing, spin-swerve and turn off the
pitch. In fig. 1 these basic facets – direction, spin and seam angle – are shown
in back views of the ball, seen by the bowler as it leaves the hand.

Cricketers use the seam for swing, for grip in spinning, and for bite on the
pitch. For every example shown in fig. 2 the seam spins like a tyre on a wheel,

which is the most common way it spins in all bowling. In all fig. 2's situations, the seam, being at 90° to the axis of spin, would appear to be moving smoothly, but bowlers frequently make the seam appear to wobble from side to side as the ball spins. To describe this we need not one illustration but a number, with the seam at different stages of the wobble – fig. 3.

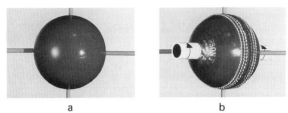

a   b

Fig. 1 *Bowler's view of the back of the ball* as it moves away from the eye in a direction in line with the point where the four rods meet. Unless otherwise stated, all of the ball photographs in this book have the ball moving away in that direction. Photo on right also shows axis of spin, direction of spin, and seam angle. Here the seam is at 45° to the direction of flight.

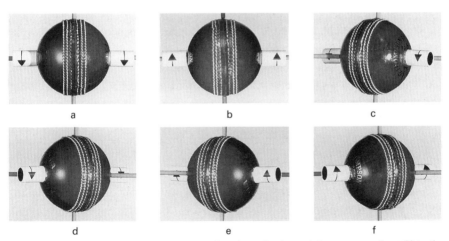

a   b   c

d   e   f

Fig. 2. *Spinning balls with the different direction of spin and the seam angle at 0° to the line of flight (a and b) or at 30° to one side or the other (c, d, e and f). Axis of spin is horizontal in all cases. Ball a is "pure" back-spin; b is "pure" top-spin; c and d are mixtures of back-spin and what, for want of a better term, can be called side-spin; e and f are mixtures of top-spin and side-spin.*

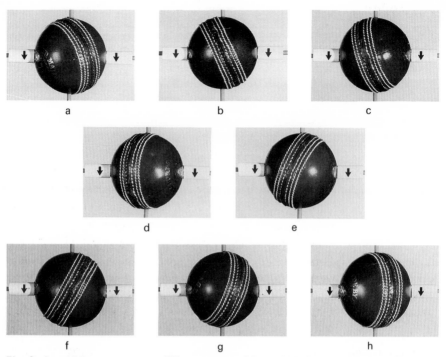

Fig. 3 *A wobbling seam seen at different stages of the wobble.* The wobble occurs because the axis of spin is not at 90° to the plane of the seam (the "tyre on the wheel"). The seam angle is seen to be constantly changing as the ball turns. Note also how the minor seam of the four-piece ball changes its alignment with the oncoming air. Although the wobbling seam offers interesting possibilities for late swing, it is generally unhelpful to swing.

Chapter 1
Under-arm to over-arm

PICK UP A CRICKET BALL, or any ball of similar size, and note the important role played by the thumb in this action. It is likely that any one of those fingers could be lifted from the ball without an appreciable loosening of the grip. But not so the thumb, which comprises almost half of the natural grasp.

Cricketers of the early centuries would not have picked it up differently. Nyren (1764–1837) writing in 1833, advises: "The best method of holding the ball to bowl is between the thumb and fingers, firmly enough to steady it yet that it may leave the hand with ease"[1]. G. H. Simpson-Hayward (1875–1936), one of the last of the under-arm or lob bowlers, is shown in a photograph (fig. 4c) taken just prior to the release of the ball leaning forwards with the bowling hand swinging through just above knee level, and the ball held with the thumb on one side and the fingers on the other, ready to impart sharp off-spin.

One of Australia's best all-rounders – medium-pacer Monty Noble (1873–1940) – embarked on a notable career in 1898 based on a devastating spin-swerve, spinning the ball from between thumb and forefinger. He learned his grip from American baseballers who toured Australia to promote their sport.

Half a century later, in 1948, Clarrie Grimmett (1891–1980) revealed his "Mystery ball" in his book *Grimmett on Cricket*[2], the driving force for that enigmatic delivery being the thumb. Emphasising this continuity through the centuries is the role of the thumb in that most misunderstood and misrepresented ball, the flipper, also a Grimmett invention, or rather a revival.

Continuing our exploration of the capabilities of the human hand grasping the ball between thumb and fingers, we may bring the ball through somewhere under the armpit, and move as if to propel it forwards along the ground. Such was bowling until about the middle of the eighteenth century. Up to then bowling was nothing more than the strict meaning of the word, i.e. rolling the ball along the ground. Under-arm bowlers then had no incentive to use anything other than speed, with perhaps a cunning eye for a lump or a hollow on the way.

Once the ball came to be delivered through the air, "pitched" to bounce somewhere near the batsman, the early records show that run-making became

a

Fig. 4 *Round-arm and under-arm: a* is Alfred Mynn, the greatest leg-break bowler of his day – from *The Cricket Field* by J. Pycroft (St James Press, 1922)

THE BOWLER.

b

c

d

Fig. 4 (cont): *b* is an unnamed round-arm bowler (from *Cricket* by John Wisden, 1873); *c* is G. H. Simpson-Hayward (MCC Collection); *d* is M. A. Noble

easier. To counter this, bowlers soon discovered the possibilities arising from "twist" (spin) to accompany their under-arm push, swing or jerk.

The transition from "bowling" to "pitching" is thought to have taken the best part of twenty-five years[3], a long period during which the importance of "length" was appreciated, and during which it was slowly realised that speed was no longer essential.

Noah Mann Snr, of the Hambledon Club, is the first recorded "under-curver", the pioneer of the ball which curves in the air, not because of shine or seam, but through spin. Mann's descendants in skill therefore include not only G. H. Hirst (1871–1954) and S. F. Barnes (1873–1967) but every single cricketer, baseball or softball pitcher, who has ever spun a ball.

The hand coming from below the armpit can easily twist one way or the other. Nyren[4], writing not long after this period, describes most of the bowlers who gave the ball spin as twisting in from the leg to off after pitching. In order words, the original and natural method of spinning the ball was leg-spin, the hand and ball coming out from under the armpit while turning anti-clockwise.

It is doubtful whether any reason based on the structure of the hand or arm could be advanced to support the idea that leg-spin is more natural than off-spin, but the early writers are in no doubt that leg-spin was adopted first. The basic action in under-arm leg-spin is no different from that of over-arm leg-spin, the hand turning anti-clockwise in both cases.

Meanwhile, another pioneer, Lamborn ("The Little Farmer") was practising a different type of delivery against gates while tending his sheep. Lamborn may well have been a good deal brighter than the somewhat slow-witted shepherd portrayed by Nyren who described him as:

> Right-handed, and he had the most extraordinary delivery I ever saw. The ball was delivered quite low, and with a twist; not like that of the generality of right-handed bowlers, but just the reverse way: that is, if bowling to a right-handed hitter, his ball would twist from the off stump into the leg. He was the first I remember who introduced this deceitful and teazing style of delivering the ball. When All England played the Hambledon Club, the Little Farmer was appointed one of our bowlers; and, egad! this new trick of his so bothered the Kent and Surrey men, that they tumbled out one after another, as if they had been picked off by a rifle corps. For a long time they could not tell what to make of that cursed twist of his.[5]

Lamborn's under-arm twist of the hand was therefore clockwise and Nyren adds that because of a general lack of intelligence ("deficiency"), and with "a comprehension not equal to the speed of lightning", Lamborn needed to be told to pitch the ball a little outside the off stump "when it would twist full in upon the stumps". Sensitive off-spinners may be glad that Nyren is not around today!

Although we will never again see the classic under-arm bowlers, Nyren's lyrical description of Harris takes us as close as we will ever get to seeing in our mind's eye the late eighteenth century equivalent of a Michael Holding or a Dennis Lillee:

> His attitude when preparing for his run previously to delivering the ball would have made a beautiful study for the sculptor. First of all, he stood erect like a soldier at drill; then, with a graceful curve of the arm, he raised the ball to his forehead, and drawing back his right foot, started off with his left. His mode of delivering the ball was very singular. He would bring it from under the arm with a twist and nearly as high as his armpit, and with this action push it, as it were, from him. How it was that the balls acquired the velocity they did by this mode of delivery I never could comprehend.
>
> In bowling, he never stooped in the least in his delivery, but kept himself upright all the time. His balls were very little beholden to the ground when pitched; it was but a touch, and up again; and woe to the man who did not get into block them, for they had such a peculiar curl, that they would grind his fingers against the bat: many a time have I seen blood drawn in this way from a batter who was not up to the trick.[6]

The first bowler recorded as having stretched out his arm horizontally, at least to some extent, to bowl round-arm, was warned against persisting with it. This was Tom Walker in the 1780s. Having once experienced the satisfying full swing of the extended arm, cricketers were not to be denied.

The reaction of bowlers to changing batting methods was an important factor. One of the Hambledon men, Tom Seuter, is the first batsman recorded as leaving his crease, a technique which came to be used more frequently early in the century, particularly against the high-tossing slow lob bowlers.

An attempt to ban round-arm by a law change in 1816 failed. After a period in which it was widely tolerated unofficially, a new Code of Laws legalised round-arm bowling in 1835. But the tide was unstoppable and by this time over-arm was already employed when umpires allowed it!

Old methods were not forgotten however, and the first of many fine exponents who revived under-arm was William Clarke, a star of the mid-nineteenth century, who achieved "a consistent spin from leg".

The new breed of round-arm bowlers maintained the skills discovered by their under-arm predecessors. However, the round-arm technique involved a significant change in the position of the hand at the moment of delivery. Whereas the under-armers generally delivered the ball with the palm facing upwards, the round-arm delivery used a downward-facing palm at least for a good part of the action, hence the alternative name "over-hand" which was used at the time.

Hillyer in the 1840s had a tremendous "curl" (assumed to be a curve), as well as a "quick sharp break" from the leg to off, "often uprooting the middle or off stump"[7]. Willsher, a crack left-hand bowler of the 1860s, was described as:

> fast and ripping with a twist from the leg to the off . . . [he] came up to the wicket with a quick-march kind of step, raised his hand high above his head, bringing it down to shoulder level at the last moment with a quick jerky movement which seemed to put spin and impetus on the ball that caused it to rise like lightning from the pitch.[8]

Willsher was surely the true begetter of another famous, pacy, left-hand spinner from Kent – Derek Underwood.

The revolutionary bowler of the round-arm period was Alfred Mynn (1807–1861), tall and powerful, who bowled a ball which generally broke in from the leg to off and rose rapidly at a speed described as greater than anything previously seen on the cricket field. One of the only batsmen to master him was Nicholas Wanostrocht, alias 'Felix', who needed the help of practice against a bowling machine, the "catapulta", to become accustomed to such speed.

Although it is more difficult to bowl straight using round-arm than with under- or over-arm, Alfred Shaw (1842–1907) had no problem. With an easy, slow-medium round-arm action he could turn the ball both ways, particularly from the off, bowling 24,700 overs in first class cricket, conceeding 24,107 runs and taking 2,051 wickets (average 11.75).

When the Marylebone Club eventually legalised over-arm bowling in 1864, the roughly semicircular eighty year journey of the hand from near the armpit, to the sideways extended arm, to high above the head, was complete. The maximum height at delivery, which under-arm bowlers had sought by bowling as high up under the armpit as possible, was now achieved in a more natural and spectacular way. Pace, flight, spin both from leg and from off, and spin-swerve, were all well established before over-arm came on the scene.

A century of over-arm was bound to bring new developments. Some are not as new as we might think – the flipper, for example; others were made possible by the use of shiny balls and prominent seams.

Early in the century, Nyren had written a dire warning to young cricketers.

I cannot approve of his [Lambert's] recommending a young player to give a twist to his balls: for in the first place, there are a hundred chances against his accomplishing the art and ten hundred favour of the practice spoiling his bowling altogether.[9]

In spite of Nyren, the great bowlers of the mainly round-arm era were those who did indeed impart a goodly twist.

REFERENCES

1 John Nyren, *The Young Cricketer's Tutor* (David-Poynter, 1974), p. 31   **2** C. V. Grimmett, *Grimmett on Cricket* (Thomas Nelson and Son, 1948), p. 42   **3** R. Bowen, *Cricket, A History of its Growth and Development Throughout the World* (Eyre and Spottiswoode, 1970), p. 77   **4** John Nyren, *The Young Cricketer's Tutor*, p. 62   **5** ibid., p. 62–3   **6** ibid., p. 80   **7** E. Parker, *The History of Cricket*, The Lonsdale Library of Sports and Games, Vol. 30 (Lonsdale, 1950), p. 231   **8** ibid., p. 234   **9** John Nyren, *The Young Cricketer's Tutor*, p. 32

Chapter 2
Spin-swerve

NOAH MANN'S "UNDER-CURVER" was not the first spinning ball recorded as curving through English air. Benjamin Robins (1707–1751) was a British mathematician and military engineer who laid the foundation for modern field artillery theory and practice. In 1742, thirty-five years before Mann joined the Hambledon Club, Robins published a book, *New Principles of Gunnery*, in which he describes how he investigated the reason why musket balls and cannon balls, even on windless days, are frequently driven off their course by some force other than gravity. His results were the beginning of understanding one of the forces controlling the behaviour of a cricket ball in flight.

The musket balls were lead spheres fired from unrifled (i.e. ungrooved) rifle barrels. Robins thought that the off-target curving might be caused by the spinning of the lead balls in flight. He set out to test his idea by firing from rifles, the last 3–4 in (7–10 cm) of the barrels of which he had deliberately bent slightly to one side. The balls therefore pressed hard against the side of the barrel as they passed through the bent portion, and were slowed down on that side, thus emerging with a side-spin.

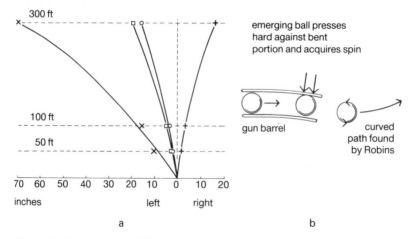

Fig. 5 *Spin-swerve in 1742: a* shows Robins' arrangement of two sheets of tissue paper through which he could trace the curved path of musket balls fired with side-spin in different directions from point *0; b* shows bent gun barrel and direction of spin.

8

Figure 5 shows Robins' arrangement with sheets of tissue paper at 50 ft (15 m) and 100 ft (30 m), and a wall of 300 ft (91 m). The holes in the paper and a mark on the wall showed the curved path taken by the ball[1]. His hypothesis was thus proved correct; when the barrel was bent to the right the ball curved to the left and when bent left the ball curved right.

This phenomenon is usually, but not always, called the "Magnus Effect", named after H. G. Magnus, a German physicist and chemist, who did not publish his work until 1853, more than a century after Robins. Magnus, in any case, has no real claim to association with ball games, since he failed in his work with spheres and obtained his results from rotating cylinders. Robins will be accorded his due honour throughout this book.

Present-day sports people are constantly reminded of the Robins Effect in ball games like tennis, golf, baseball, soccer and softball, but nowhere is it more marked than in table tennis, where the lightness of the ball, in comparison to the Robins Force on the surface, gives rise to quite dramatic effects. The topspun ball will dip sharply downwards; the underspun (i.e. backspin) ball will perhaps climb a little or at least not fall so rapidly under gravity, then drop quickly as it slows down (a "stall"); the ball given a sideways hit will curve to the side opposite to the direction in which the bat is moving across behind it.

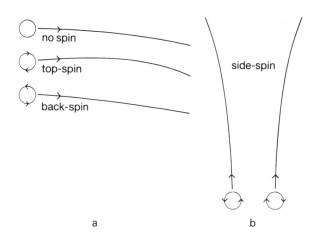

no spin

top-spin

back-spin

side-spin

Fig. 6 *Spin-swerve resulting from the Robins Force.* The effect of spin on the flight path is shown in side view (*a*) and top view (*b*). These are all *positive* Robins effects. Under certain conditions the force is in the opposite direction – the *negative* Robins Force.

a   b

The basic Robins movements, applying to any ball, are shown in fig. 6. These take place vertically (fig. 6*a*), or horizontally (fig. 6*b*), but a combination of the two is both possible and common in sport.

Before the reader gets the idea that Robins' work told it all, we must note that Briggs[2], two-hundred years later, found that while spinning baseballs behaved like Robins' musket balls, smooth spheres sometimes gave a deflection in the opposite direction as a result of what can be called a "negative Robins Effect". The negative effect has also been demonstrated with smooth experimental golf balls without dimples. A topped drive with one of these would follow a flatter path than an unspun ball.

Sports books are often misleading when attempting to explain the Robins Effect. One simple but incorrect description states that if the top side of the ball rotates against the oncoming wind it will experience a stronger wind force on the curved surface facing the wind than on the bottom side rotating away with the wind, and that this force will push the ball downwards.

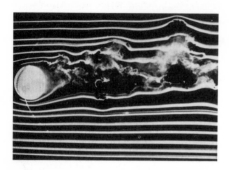

Fig. 7 *Smoke photograph of air flow over a spinning baseball* showing diverted wake. Flow is from left to right at 47 mph. Spin is counter-clockwise at 15 revs/sec. *(Photograph taken by F. N. M. Brown, courtesy of the University of Notre Dame.)*

Smoke photographs of spinning balls such as the excellent one by F. N. M. Brown[3] (fig. 7), show a diverted wake to one side of the ball. As we will see later when looking at swing, this is what happens when the seam affects the air flow. The basic features of swing and spin-swerve are therefore the same.

In Chapters 3 and 4 we will see that the turbulence caused by the air passing across the seam enables the air stream on that side to remain close to the surface of the ball for longer. This results in a diverted wake and a pressure difference between one side of the ball and the other. Without any seam at all, spin alone has this effect and can likewise delay the separation of the air stream on one side compared to the other. A positive Robins Effect is illustrated in fig. 8a.

The side spinning towards the air stream is thus seen to be acting in the same way as the smooth (non-seam) face of a swinging ball, and the side spinning away from (i.e. with) the air stream is acting in the same way as the stitching, i.e. providing minor additional turbulence near the surface. The negative Robins Force, although it is relatively uncommon, originates from the oncoming side acting as the rough (seam-like) side and the away-spinning side acting as the smooth side.

While published studies of the Robins Force on tennis balls, dimpled golf balls, baseballs, softballs and table-tennis balls all show positive Robins behaviour, my own work has shown that cricket balls at particular speeds,

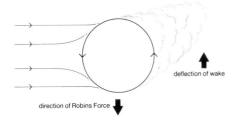

direction of Robins Force

deflection of wake

Fig. 8 *Air flow around a spinning ball* for a positive Robins effect. The surface spinning against the oncoming air acts in the same way as the smooth side of a swinging cricket ball.

spin rates and angles to the wind, will, as Briggs found with smooth plastic balls, and as Macoll[4] found with wooden balls, "go negative". This "mixed" behaviour of cricket balls is explainable since they possess both rough and smooth areas, each quite large in extent, more so than on baseballs. In various positions of spin these will influence the air stream in different ways.

Because swing and Robins behaviour are basically the same phenomenon, it follows that atmospheric turbulence which reduces swing will also reduce the Robins Force. The conditions of low turbulence discussed in Chapter 9 as favouring swing will also favour Robins spin-swerve.

Fieldsmen and wicket-keepers will be very aware of the Robins Force. A fast, low return from the out-field will normally carry a good deal of side-spin, but the direction of the spin-swerve will depend on which side of the ball the hand curves around as the ball is let go. Against the wind, returns could swerve well off-line.

REFERENCES

1 H. M. Barkla and L. J. Auchterlonie, J. Fluid Mech. 47 Part 3 (1971), p. 437–47
2 L. J. Briggs, Am. J. Phys (1959), p. 589–96 3 F. N. M. Brown, 'See the Wind Blow', Dept. Aerosp. Mech. Eng. Rep. (University of Notre Dame, 1971). *The photograph, taken by the late Professor Brown, has been kindly supplied by his old department.* 4 J. W. Macoll, J. Roy. Aeron. Soc. 32 (1928), p. 777–98

Chapter 3
Understanding swing

THE WINNING BALL in many sports is the spun ball, spun to make it curve through the air. But cricket is unusual; the cricket ball will curve in flight without any applied spin whatsoever – behaviour which demands a new name, swing.

More correctly we should say that the ball *may* swing and let Bernard Hollowood, writing in *Cricket on the Brain*, help bowlers keep their feet on the ground:

> I have watched Trueman on numerous occasions, but only once or twice has he been able to bowl his famous outswinger *consistently*. The radio and TV commentators (some of them, anyway) are ever ready to ascribe marvels of cut and swerve to a successful trundler. "That was his outswinger," they say. "A beautiful ball – it swung late and then cut back off the pitch." Well, yes, it happens. Not often though. There would be few batsmen with averages of thirty and more if bowlers were able to achieve the miracles of flight and turn claimed for them. In my experience the vast majority of fast bowlers deal chiefly in straight stuff and achieve cutters and swervers only rarely.[1]

Nevertheless, many a batsman has had to watch helplessly as the swinging curve takes the edge, or worse, finds nothing at all blocking its passage to the stumps.

There are reasons why a ball swings and there are reasons why it does not. First we will look at the situation, nothing more than a dream for most bowlers, where the ball can be swung at will to one side or the other, all under good control. Not quite the dream however: in the dream the swing occurs late in the flight, just when the batsman thinks he has it nicely lined up.

Unlike the latest in sleek motor cars whose low air resistance (drag) is a major selling point, the cricket ball is a blunt object, pushing through the air, leaving a turbulent wake behind it wider than the ball itself.

To understand swing we must look back to the days when the invention of the aeroplane stimulated scientific investigation into the behaviour of air flowing over wings and surfaces of all shapes. In 1914 a German aircraft engineer[2] published photographs showing how a wire hoop tied around the front of a sphere influenced the shape of the wake behind it (fig. 9). The hoop

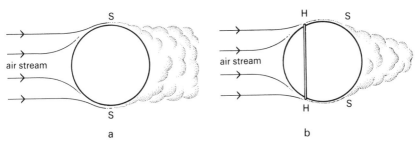

Fig. 9 *Air flow past a sphere,* based on wind-tunnel photographs and using smoke to make the flow pattern visible: *a* is a smooth sphere; *b* is a smooth sphere fitted with a hoop, *H.* The smooth flow separates from the surface at point *S.* The smoothly flowing air stream leaves the ball later in *b* because the hoop creates a shallow turbulent layer which clings to the surface between *H* and *S.*

had the opposite effect to what might have been expected; instead of causing the air stream to fly off the surface of the ball and form a wider turbulent space behind the ball, it narrowed the wake. The hoop in fact made the ball more streamlined. This was because the hoop delayed the separation of the air stream from the ball. Stated another way, the hoop caused the air stream to go around the ball a little further before leaving the surface. Dimples on a golf ball have exactly the same effect and therefore allow a shot to go much further.

There is no such thing as a perfectly smooth solid surface; all solids viewed under a powerful microscope are more or less rough. Air molecules passing over the supposedly smooth surface of a cricket ball would resemble a cloud of fine dust blowing across a series of mountain ranges, colliding with them and swirling around in eddies. This means that there is no such thing as smooth air flow, close to a solid surface. Across a cricket ball therefore, all flow is turbulent. But the turbulent layer varies in thickness from one surface to another. Across the smooth area of the ball the turbulence is shallow, but across the seam it is deeper, and across a worn patch it is something between the two. This extra turbulence resulting from the stitching or from worn leather hangs on to the ball a little longer than the smoother air streaming off the ball on the other (non-seam, or less worn) side. Not a difficult picture to grasp once we realise that the turbulent air has lost some speed and therefore has less tendency to fly off the surface. The result is a deflection of the wake to one side behind the ball. The ball having deflected the air, must itself be deflected in the opposite direction, i.e. it will swing to the side (fig. 10).

Forty-one years after the experiments with wire hoops, J. C. Cooke, in the first published scientific account of swing[3], applied to the cricket ball the discovery that a wire hoop increases streamlining. He pointed out that the seam could, as I have just described, act in the same way as the wire hoop. If

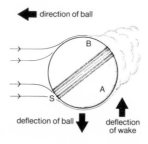

direction of ball

B

A

S

deflection of ball

deflection of wake

Fig. 10 *Top view of an outswinger with the seam pointing towards the slips.* The seam at *S* increases the thickness of the turbulent layer of air and delays the separation of the air stream from the surface until it reaches *A.* On the other (smooth) side there is no increase in turbulence and the air stream leaves the ball a little earlier at *B.* The result is a deflection of the wake, behind the ball, to one side. The ball must therefore be deflected in the opposite direction.

the seam is on one side of the ball facing the air flow, then, as Cooke stated, the delayed flow separation will take place on that side only (fig. 10).

Cooke did not carry out any experiments with cricket balls; his work was nothing more nor less than speculation. But all the work done by others since that time has shown what a fine piece of speculation it was. Numerous photographs and measurements of the flow and pressure patterns around cricket balls have fully supported his general idea.

Two years after Cooke's paper, R. A. Lyttleton published an article[4] repeating the wake diversion idea, but still without testing it experimentally. Lyttleton went much further than Cooke, discussing related topics such as late swing and the effect of weather on swing. But speculation had gone too far and his assumption that flow around a cricket ball changes at a certain critical speed, and that this may account for late swing and swing in a humid atmosphere, has not been supported by subsequent work.

Don Bradman published part of a talk given by Lyttleton on the BBC at that time, in his classic *The Art of Cricket*[5]. I wonder whether cricketers gained much by grappling with those dense pages. Although limited in scope and incorrect in parts, it was nevertheless the best discussion of the subject then available.

REFERENCES

1 B. Hollowood, *Cricket on the Brain* (Eyre and Spottiswoode, 1970), p. 62   **2** C. Wieselsberger, "Der Luftwiderstand Von Kugeln" Zeitschr. f. Flugtchn. u. Motorluftschiffahrt, 5 (1914) p. 142–4   **3** J. C. Cooke, Math. Gazz. 39 (1955), p. 196–9   **4** R. A. Lyttleton, *Discovery* 18 (1957), p. 186–91   **5** D. Bradman, *The Art of Cricket* (Hodder and Stoughton, 1958), p. 139

Chapter 4
The wind tunnel

EXPERIMENTS MUST BE CARRIED OUT IN THE MIND before they are carried out in the wind tunnel. But it takes more than creative scientific musing to produce the wind tunnel – a costly piece of equipment, more than likely to be in great demand for all sorts of paying projects such as the design of a new aeroplane, a building, or a better yacht sail.

A few cricket enthusiasts, lucky enough to have access to a wind tunnel, have carried out useful work in their leisure time. In other cases the projects have served to train students in the techniques of investigation. I spent nearly every weekend and holiday for six months making thousands of measurements in pursuit of my own work.

To N. G. Barton goes the credit for publishing the first measurements of the swing force[1]. He used two methods, one involving a ball skewered on a pendulum hanging at the exit air stream of the wind tunnel (fig. 11a). From

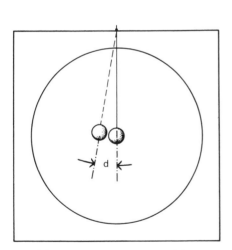

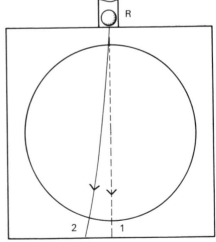

Fig. 11a *Ball skewered on pendulum at mouth of a wind tunnel.* The sideways (swing) force was measured from the amount of deflection (*d*) of the ball to one side.

Fig. 11b *Front view of wind tunnel with the ball* dropped across the air stream after rolling down a ramp. Dotted line shows path if there was no sideways force. Solid line shows actual path. The distance between points *1* and *2* indicates the swing force.

the amount of sideways deflection of the pendulum with the seam at a few different angles to the wind, he could calculate the swing force. The other method (fig. 11*b*), which had been used 23 years earlier in a study of base-balls[2], involved dropping balls through the emerging air stream with the seam at various angles and measuring the position where they landed. If there was no swing force the balls would drop straight down. But in actual fact the falling balls found themselves, for the fraction of a second that they took to drop through the air stream, in the same situation as a ball hurtling through the air towards the batsman. The air pushing past the ball was no different from the situation in which the ball was bowled through the air. The result was that the falling balls were diverted sideways by an amount which was measured from the mark they made hitting the floor. The swinging balls were of course pushed ahead a little as well, because of their drag, but the sideways deflection was easily measured. In fact the balls were not just dropped, but rolled down a ramp set at various angles to the air stream. In this way the back-spin, applied by the bowler as the fingers travel down the back of the ball during release, is imitated. However, the rolling ball had forward-spin, but since the spin was regarded as stabilising like a gyroscope the position of the ball in flight, spin in the opposite direction would have the same effect from this point of view.

Barton found swing forces increasing from 10% to 40% of the weight of the ball as the air speed was increased from 34 to 67 mph, and the seam angle held at 30° to the air flow. Swing forces on the free-falling balls were found to be somewhat lower than for the fixed balls. As well as having to cope with a certain amount of uncontrollable seam wobble as the balls rolled down the ramp, Barton had no way of knowing what fraction of a second it took for the diverted wake flow pattern to develop around the ball as it fell through the moving air.

The photograph he published showing a cricket ball held in the wind tunnel with the wake made visible by smoke, nicely confirmed the diverted wake explanation of swing. Seventeen balls were used in the study. Worn balls, as expected, generally gave lower swing force values, but not always. Slight surface roughness often caused a large reduction in swing force. Quite large fluctuations in value were found during repeated measurements on the same balls. Unstable behaviour was common, a reminder to cricketers that plenty of surprises are in store when they get involved with swing.

These methods were effective in establishing very approximate values for a few of the situations encountered in swing bowling, but there were many features of the behaviour of cricket balls, including spin-swerve, which were of great interest to cricketers but which were not capable of being studied in that way.

The wind tunnel

Shortly after Barton published his pioneering work, a study was published by a group from Imperial College London[3] which used the same rolling and dropping technique that Barton had employed, but dropped the balls into the interior of the wind tunnel rather than into the exit stream. A new type of measurement carried out by this group was to find the pressure differences around the surface of a fixed ball. For this they inserted tubes into the ball connected with small holes on the surface. Their results fitted in very well with the air flow required by the diverted wake pattern discussed earlier. The fast-moving air stream which clings longer to the ball on the rough (seam) side creates a low pressure area which is not matched on the opposite side of the ball. This pressure difference causes the ball to swing towards the rough side. The process described here and illustrated in fig. 12 adds more detail to the diverted wake picture.

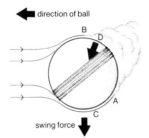

Fig. 12 *Origin of the swing force showing flow pattern* as in fig. 10 and the pressure differences it causes. Because the air stream separates later on the rough (seam) side of the ball (point *A*) than on the smooth side (point *B*), there is a faster air flow across region *C* than across region *D* which is under the highly turbulent wake. Daniel Bernoulli, a Swiss scientist, noticed in the eighteenth century that the pressure is least where the flow rate is greatest. This means that the pressure at *D* is greater than the pressure at *C*, thus causing the swing force.

About this time, Sherwin and Sproston[4] in Liverpool carried out a brief study of a ball mounted on a column at the exit of a wind tunnel, and, using strain gauges, measured the forces on the column. The drag and swing forces on the ball were compared to that of a sphere fitted with a trip wire, and shown to be similar. The swing force at 54 mph with the seam at 30° was found to be about 30% of the weight of the ball.

For my own work in New Zealand I had access to a high quality wind tunnel[5] and was able to develop methods which were sensitive and versatile.

The basic equipment for swing force measurement is shown in fig. 13a. The balls were mounted on the end of a rod coming up into the wind tunnel through a hole in its floor. The rod was pivoted on a ball race and joined by another rod at 90° (i.e. horizontal), the end of which rested on the pan of a sensitive electronic balance. A sideways (i.e. swing) force on the ball thus registered as a change of weight on the balance pan. No actual movement of

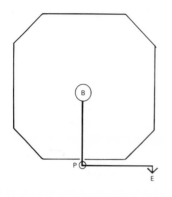 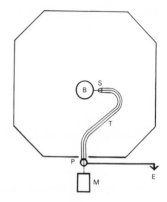

Fig. 13 *Cricket balls in the wind tunnel.* Imagine the wind as travelling from your eye along the tunnel to the ball: *a* shows the view along the inside of the wind tunnel of a ball mounted on a rod connected to point *P* and electronic balance *E; b* shows similar view of mount for studying the spinning and swinging ball. The ball is mounted on a thin shaft (*S*) at the end of a metal tube (*T*) through which passes a flexible cable to convey rotation from a variable speed motor (*M*).

the ball or the balance pan was visible, but the force changes could be read on the digital display down to one hundredth of a gram. Considering that forces were measured up to about half the weight of the ball, i.e. half of 156 g, it can be seen that the method used was well adapted to uncovering detailed behaviour in many different circumstances connected with both static and spinning balls.

To study spinning balls they were mounted on a hollow column through which was inserted a thin flexible cable turned by an electric motor to supply the spin (fig. 13*b*).

Imagine a fast bowler coming in to bowl with the ball cupped in his fingers and delivering it merely by pushing it straight ahead without any of the normal final downward flick of the fingers. This would not be his fastest delivery because that final wrist and finger action is known to be the source of 5% or more of the ball's speed. However, it is an uncomplicated delivery and for that reason was the first type I studied in the wind tunnel.

New four-piece balls of Test match quality[6] were used and the wind speeds matched the normal range of bowling speeds – 33 to 81 mph. Fast men have been timed at 95 mph or more, but the few bowlers capable of such awesome speed appear to use it sparingly. The secondary or minor seam crossing the smooth leather hemispheres was in line with the air flow on the smooth (non-seam) side of the ball as in fig. 18*b* (page 25).

A shiny red ball skewered on the end of the thin metal rod had already shown, in a few quick preliminary runs through a range of wind speeds, that it would give interesting results. The seam angle could be changed simply by twisting the rod and ball around on its axis. That Sunday morning, turning up the wind and calling out the force figures to my son Damien, who wrote them in a notebook, was an exciting time. Some days later, everything was ready for a full series of tests over the whole range of wind speeds and seam angles.

The wind tunnel is somewhat more than half a cricket pitch in length and makes quite a noise. Air flung out of one end by a powerful fan flows back through the large room and is sucked into the other end. A seam angle of zero is chosen; the seam points straight down the pitch. The knob is turned, the wind builds up; slow, slow-medium, medium, fast-medium, fast – name your hero appropriate to the pace. The rising howl of wind and machinery drowns all conversation. But inside the working compartment of the tunnel, behind strong plastic windows, the air flow is known to be beautifully smooth, the hallmark of a good instrument. We are now at the top of the range, the returning air scatters paper from the table.

Inside the tunnel the ball may well have just left the hand of a warmed-up fast man letting it go at a lively pace. But what's happening? Ball and rod begin to vibrate uncontrollably, the readings on the electronic balance fluctuate wildly, making no sense at all. Quick, turn down the wind – slow-medium, not much improvement. Stop; start up again at two other seam angles – 2.5° and 5°. (You must be mad; bowlers don't carry protractors!) The same problem, but less at 5°. This can't go on; our equipment will fly to bits. A quick look at the results of the early trials. Ah ha; we didn't try these very small seam angles before? Try 7.5°; yes that's much better. Now everything settles down, no more problems all the way to 90°. Well, no problems with this ball, but with other balls, old and new, some spectacular collapses, reversals of swing force and unstable regions were encountered, and not only at low seam angles.

Much later I came across work by a German[7] and a Japanese[8] who had seen it all before. Flow around spheres, they found, was basically an unstable phenomenon. Their published smoke photos showed wakes oscillating in all directions behind the spheres and creating a wavy pattern.

Our cricket ball at low seam angles had been experiencing a similar rapidly changing force. In this case, because the seam lay at or near the middle of the ball as it faced the on-rushing air, the force was first to one side and then to the other, hence the violent vibrations. Nothing new here for the observant bowler, I'm sure. Most bowlers are candid enough to admit that the ball can do strange and unpredictable things. Maurice Tate, one of the great medium-pace bowlers, noted for his late swing, confided many years after his retirement that he was unsure of which way the ball would move in the air because he held the seam bolt upright.

Ray Lindwall has said that one of his chief joys in England was to wait and see which way the ball moved after he had bowled it.[9] Mike Proctor, in a well known photograph by Ken Kelly, is shown with his arm high at the moment of release and the ball emerging with the seam perfectly upright[10]. No wonder he achieved great success. The fact that it was achieved with an unusual action where he gave the false impression of appearing to bowl off the wrong foot, should give coaches something to think about. If confirmation of this was needed, it comes from motion pictures taken by Imbrosciano who used high speed photography to study the Australian left-handed swing bowler Garry Gilmour.[11] Close examination of the pictures indeed showed sudden changes of direction, where loss, gain, and reversal of swing had occurred.

The wind tunnel incident, repeated deliberately with other balls, should remind bowlers that the benefits to be gained from pointing the upright seam straight, or more or less straight, down the wicket, do not necessarily stem from the moment when the ball hits the ground. Useful, unpredictable swing, including late swing, may be there for the taking.

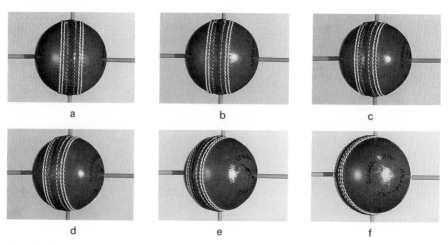

Fig. 14 *Seam angles as they appear to the bowler: a 0°, b 7.5°, c 15°, d 25°, e 45°, f 70°.*

Before discussing the rest of the work on swing, it is worthwhile looking at how the various seams angles would appear to the bowler (fig. 14). Protractors are not needed on the field, but there is no harm in having some idea of where the seam should be placed for the various angles.

The results of the first work I carried out showing how the swing force changes with speed and with seam angle are set out in fig. 15. These and each of the other swing force diagrams summarise more than 2000 separate measurements. The swing force is stated as a fraction of the weight of the ball

(156 g) and is on a scale of 0–1. A great deal of information is contained in the lines of fig. 15 and from the results on other balls, and the various topics suggested by it will now be discussed.

The faster the delivery, the greater is the swing force (except around 70°, which is an impossible angle for a medium or fast bowler to use). The reason for the collapse of swing at 70° will be clear from fig. 14*f* which shows the seam to be so far around the ball that the air stream is beginning to "see" this roughness on the previously smooth side. This has been shown to be the rule right throughout the study of new balls, at all usable seam angles, and at all speeds and rates of back-spin. Only in those cases where the surface was seen to be rough through wear (or because of some variation in the manufacturing process) was the above rule violated at certain speeds and certain seam angles.

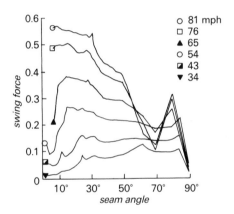

o 81 mph
□ 76
▲ 65
o 54
◪ 43
▼ 34

Fig. 15 *Swing force on a new four-piece ball at various seam angles and wind speeds.*

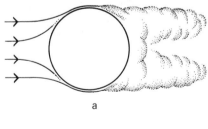

Fig. 16 *Wake reduction at different speeds: a low, b high.*

Writers on the subject have wrongly assumed that cricket balls above a certain speed would experience a sudden drop in swing force. Lyttleton first proposed this idea, basing it on the fact that a perfectly smooth sphere about the size of a cricket ball experiences at 120 mph a sudden lessening of drag. At this critical speed the sphere is shown to have a much smaller wake since very fast air travels further around the ball before it leaves the surface (fig. 16). If the wake is diminished at high speeds, according to Lyttleton, the swing force is also diminished.

Lyttleton also speculated that since hoops or trip wires around these spheres allowed low drag to appear at lower wind speeds, then, because the seam of a cricket ball is quite extensive and quite prominent, low drag and a narrow wake may occur within the range of fast bowling speeds irrespective of its position. The swing force would then be lost because the air streaming smoothly past both sides of the ball would not be able to provide the diverted wake required for swing.

Late swing, according to Lyttleton's proposal, was explainable by assuming that the bowler initially delivers the ball too quickly for it to swing, i.e. at a speed above the critical speed. As it travels towards the batsman, the remaining drag, according to Lyttleton, might slow it to a speed where the diverted wake *can* form. At this point it would suddenly begin to swing. But when this idea was tested by means of precise measurements on cricket balls, I found no evidence of a general and sudden reduction in drag or swing force at any speed.

Sherwin and Sproston obtained a similar result to mine at the speeds lower than the highest I employed. These findings showed that scientific speculation on the similarities between smooth spheres fitted with trip wires, and cricket balls, although it explained swing very satisfactorily, had gone too far. We must therefore look for other possible explanations of the mystery of late swing, a subject we will return to later.

Why do the fastest bowlers swing less if the swing force in a faster delivery is greater? For a ball to swing it needs both a swing force and sufficient time for that force to have its effect in pushing the ball sideways. Since the faster ball arrives at the other end sooner, it has less time in which to feel that effect and will therefore show less sideways movement than we might expect. But there is more to it. If we take this to be the only factor, some simple calculations show that all bowlers will swing by about the same amount. However, this can't be true: we know that fast bowlers swing less.

The effective length over which a ball swings between the bowler's hand and the bat is probably no more than about 19 yds (17.4 m). In Table A, using the average swing forces for seam angles of 10° to 30° taken from fig. 15, are shown the results of calculations of the amount of sideways deviation seen by the batsman. But since it is impossible for the air flow pattern which provides the swing force to develop instantly, there must be a delay at the beginning of its flight during which the ball is not swinging at all. No one has been able to measure this delay, and it would be difficult to do so, but I have included in the table figures to show how the amount of final deviation would be affected by delays of one tenth and by one quarter of a second.

Table A   *Sideways movement in the air*

Bowling speed (mph)		Time in air for 19 yds flight (secs)	Calculated sideways movement (inches)*		
			No time delay	Delay 0.1 sec	Delay 0.25 sec
33	Slow	1.18	14	11	9
43		0.92	22	17	11
54	Medium	0.72	24	18	10
66		0.59	25	17	8
76	Fast	0.52	25	16	7
81		0.48	24	15	6

*Using the relationship between the sideways deviation ($\triangle$), the acceleration (a) and the time (t): $\triangle = \frac{1}{2}at^2$

With no time delay, all of the bowlers in the fast and medium range, say down to 43 mph, achieve about the same amount of swing. As the delay increases, the fast men achieve less swing in comparison to the medium-pacers, until a delay of 0.25 sec reduces their swing to nearly half as much. Although swing will vary tremendously, depending on the state of the ball, the atmosphere and the skill of the bowler, the common experience of cricketers indicates that the results of the time delay concept agree with the real situation.

The curves plotted by Imbrosciano from the photos of Gilmour's bowling show little or no curvature at the beginning of the flight paths. Those that do show some curvature may have been delivered at a slower pace. Other aspects of this subject will be discussed in Chapter 6.

Baseball pitchers use this combination of increased speed, and consequently later curve, in the slider ball, probably the most effective ball in their repertoire. Although the stitching pattern around a baseball differs from that around a cricket ball, the forces causing baseballs and cricket balls to curve or to swing in the air are essentially the same.

Which is the best seam angle to use in order to achieve the maximum swing? What are you trying to bowl? Are you going for the unpredictable, the delivery that leaves everybody, including the wicket-keeper, stranded, aghast at your brilliance? With a swinging ball, that sort of bonus may drop into your lap every so often, no matter what you attempt to do. If you decide to take this approach, and seek the unpredictable, then use low seam angles, 7.5° or less.

But first a few words of warning. Remember that the swing force only which way the seam is lying. Some of these "useless" tilted seam angles are shown in fig. 17.

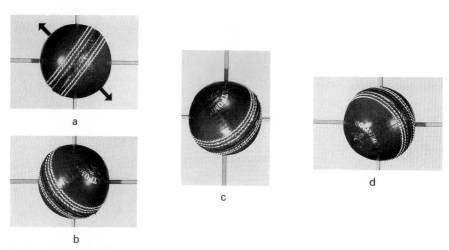

a

b

c

d

Fig. 17 *Some relatively "useless" seam angles.* Ball *a* represents seam pointing at batsman but tilted to one side. Swing force will be wasted by acting partly up or down as well as to one side or the other. Likewise, *b, c* and *d* will produce up or down swing forces. All of these positions give the bowler a poor return for his efforts.

The ball in fig. 17*a*, being at a zero seam angle to the line of flight, can swing either way, as shown by the two arrows. If it swings to the left some of the swing force is manifest as a lift force, and may therefore cause it to over-pitch. On the other hand, if it swings to the right some of the swing force acts downwards and the ball, while swinging less to the side, will dip into the ground earlier and therefore be of shorter length.

The same considerations apply to the other balls in fig. 17. None of the angles are favourable for sideways swing and a good deal of the swing force will be manifest as an upwards or downwards force. In an extreme case where the plane of the seam is tilted well to one side, as well as being pointed at an angle to achieve maximum swing, the ball could drop short or over-pitch.

The round-arm slinger tends to be an erratic type of bowler. We have now pin-pointed one of his difficulties. The arm swinging around rather than over makes it difficult in any case to avoid spraying deliveries across the pitch, but the up-or-down swing factor adds to the problem by affecting the length as well. All swing bowlers have this tendency and should be conscious of its consequences.

The accuracy of returns from fieldsmen to the wicket-keeper is also at the mercy of swing and spin-swerve. The problem from swing, but not necessarily from spin-swerve, can be eliminated by gripping the gathered ball across rather than along the seam.

Grip and action only make sense if seen in the light of these basic factors. The next time you are looking at a photograph of a ball leaving a fast bowler's hand, apply the test. Is the seam vertical as in fig. 18? Not all photographs are taken at an angle allowing you to be sure in your assessment, but many are and the results are interesting.

Assuming that you opt for a type of swing that offers at least some chance of control, you need a seam angle greater than 7.5° to one side or the other. Beyond that my results show that it does not matter what angle you use, up to about 30°. Very high angles are normally impossible for fast and medium bowlers where their final contact with the ball is mainly a downwards movement of the fingers behind it or slightly to one side or the other. However, if the final contact with the ball involves a cupped hand rather than the downward finger flick, then the ball can be sent on its way in any position.

If a very large seam angle, say above 60°, is used, the swing force drops (fig. 15); at that angle the seam has come around far enough to "see" the oncoming air on the smooth side (fig. 14*f*), thereby beginning to convert the smooth side into the rough side.

Curving flight after pitching is one of the more intriguing sights revealed to television watchers. Spin-swerve is a factor, but change of seam angle as the stitching catches the ground unevenly on one side of the contact area is another. A fuller discussion of this behaviour is to be found in Chapter 25.

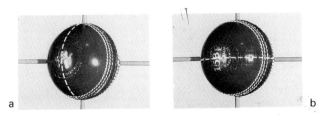

a   b

Fig. 18 *The two types of alignment of a four-piece ball with respect to the air flow.* Assume for the sake of a clear representation that the air is flowing from the viewer to the page. (This is in the opposite direction from that normally used in this book but it allows the minor seam to be seen.) In *a* the minor seam lies *across* the air flow on the smooth (non-seam) side and will decrease swing. In *b* it is *in line* with the flow on this side.

Swing collapses and goes through the floor. A moderately worn four-piece ball, which had been used for 40 overs on a grassy wicket, gave the results shown in fig. 19. Two sets of results were obtained because the secondary (or minor) seam which runs around the smooth hemisphere can lie in two possible positions with respect to the air flow (fig. 18).

The ball, although worn, was generally quite smooth, with no shredded leather, yet not shiny except for a few limited areas. In fig. 19*a* the minor seam lies across the air flow on the smooth (non-seam) side as in fig. 18*a*. In fig. 19*b* the minor seam is in line with the air flow as in fig. 18*b*: this alignment is seen to be a major factor. When the air stream has to cross this minor seam the swing force collapses and reverses over an extensive range of seam angles and speeds. The wear on the ball appeared to be fairly even over its surface, but uneven wear cannot be ruled out as a contributor to the spectacular collapse shown in fig. 19*a*. This also illustrates the great sensitivity of swing to quite minor surface irregularities. The minor seam is a tiny groove the sides of which lie quite flush with the surface. However, in some worn balls it opens up somewhat.

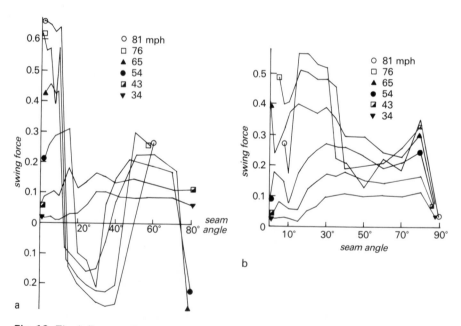

Fig. 19 *The influence of wear and the minor seam:* swing forces on a worn (40-over) four-piece ball at various seam angles and speeds. In *a* the minor seam is *across* the air stream on the smooth side, with the additional possible influence of uneven wear, causing collapse of the swing force at medium pace and faster speeds at seam angles greater than about 10°. In *b* the minor seam is *in line* with the air stream on the smooth side, giving a different pattern of swing forces on the same ball.

Although worn, the ball is still capable of generating a swing force as large as that from a new ball, but it is negative swing over much of the range. Numerous steep portions of the curves indicate extreme instability with sudden changes.

"Going the other way" becomes the rule rather than the exception in fig. 20 where extensive regions of negative swing force show up in a well-worn four-piece ball used for 100 overs. Although in fig. 20*a* the minor seam lies across the air flow, and in *b* in line with it, this factor, which was seen to be important in the 40-over ball, makes little difference here compared to the effects of wear.

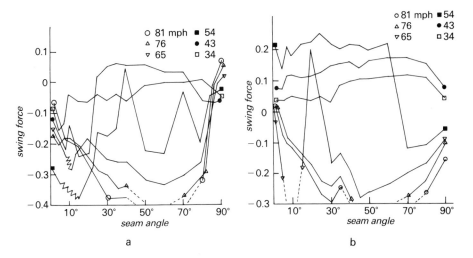

Fig. 20 *Swing forces on a well-worn (100-over) four-piece ball: a minor seam across air stream on smooth side; b minor seam in line with air stream on smooth side.*

Further evidence for the great sensitivity of the air flow on the smooth (non-seam) side to almost imperceptible surface roughness, comes from the behaviour of two apparently identical new two-piece balls (fig. 21*a* and *b*). One showed a sudden collapse of swing force between 10° and 30° seam angle at fast and medium speeds. Close examination of this ball showed it to be made from leather of somewhat coarser texture on one side than on the other. Fig. 21*a* shows that beyond 10° the seam angle is not critical up to about 40° for the two-piece ball. This is a wider range than that for a four-piece ball.

Finally, two worn two-piece balls were studied. The results in fig. 22*a* and *b* show the different behaviour caused by 40 overs of wear as compared to 100 overs; in the latter the swing force has virtually disappeared for all situations.

To find out more about the effect of surface roughness on swing, I deliberately roughened the new four-piece ball which had given the results in

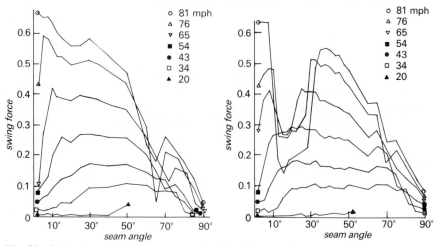

Fig. 21 *Swing forces on two apparently identical two-piece balls.* Close examination revealed slight differences in the texture of the leather surfaces.

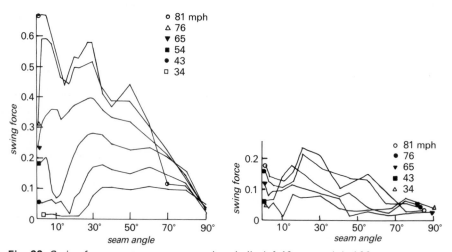

Fig. 22 *Swing forces on two worn two-piece balls: left* 40 overs; *right* 100 overs.

fig. 15. This was done in two ways, using droplets of water in one experiment, and a small lump of material stuck to the ball in the other.

My "rain" came from a thin stream of water which I released from a narrow tube upwind of the ball in the wind tunnel. A rapid and drastic loss of swing force occurred, both when the ball was static and when it was spinning. As long as water droplets were visible on the ball, the swing force remained at only 10–30% of its original value. The return to full force, when the water evaporated, was equally dramatic. The fact that none of the droplets were big is another illustration of the great vulnerability of the air stream on the smooth side of the ball. This interference was not caused by wetness as such, but by small dome-shaped blobs of water interfering with the smooth air flow. A very wet ball with a continuous film of water may in fact swing well, simply because the film is smooth. In the unlikely event of a heavy water-logged ball retaining a smooth surface on one side, it would swing rather less simply because it is heavier.

Allegations have been made that certain teams have interfered with the ball by soaking one side of it in water. This could be a very effective method of cheating, not through a change of weight but because it would reduce the smoothness on that side. It would also make the wet leather more vulnerable to roughening in normal use or through attack by finger-nails or other means.

My second experiment on surface irregularity was designed to answer the question: where exactly on the ball is roughness likely to cause the most interference with swing?

Your cover fieldsman, in a valiant save on the boundary, manages to put his metal sprig into the new ball in the first over. You wonder whether four runs might have been preferable to the deep little tear and the shred of leather hanging from it. I imitated this tear, in a less expensive manner, by attaching to the ball a small disc of soft plastic material ("BLUTACK"), 2 mm in diameter and 1 mm in thickness. The ball was made to spin in the wind tunnel and the spot of plastic was removed and replaced in ten different positions for ten swing force tests. Fig. 23a shows how the spot would move around and present to the wind as the ball spins.

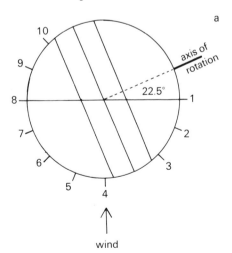

Fig. 23a *Arrangement for finding which areas on a ball, when damaged, are most likely to reduce swing force.* Lumps of interfering material were placed in turn at positions *1–10*. Dotted lines show their path around the ball as it rotates.

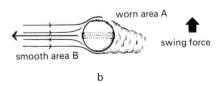

Fig. 23b *The influence of wear.* A ball with wear on one side at *A*, but delivered with the seam at zero angle to the wind, will swing towards the worn side.

The results were highly informative. In most positions the lump had no effect whatsoever. But lest your cover fieldsman regard this as a licence to indulge in more tricky footwork, it must be added that when the lump is placed on or near the outside (equatorial) bulge on the smooth (non-seam) side, the swing force dropped to about half. This large effect by one small lump moving around a particular part of the ball shows yet again how sensitive swing is to roughness. The area encompassed by *6*, *7* and *8* was the vulnerable area, and it looks as if those bowlers who polish any area other than the sensitive outside bulge on the smooth (non-seam) side are wasting their time.

Swing reversal, as shown by several of the cases we have discussed, results from the worn areas having more effect than the seam (fig. 23*b*). This may seem surprising because one seldom sees wear looking rougher than the seam. But when it is realised that the amount of wear is only one factor, and that its position on the ball is just as critical as its roughness, this swing reversal is quite logical. Wear on or near the equatorial bulge is what matters. This situation is aggravated when the seam becomes less significant through wear, flattening, embedded dirt, or merely by being at the front of the ball and some distance away from the critical bulge area.

Since useful swing is sideways movement, air flow causing swing must be diverted sideways off the ball. The further away on the surface of the ball we move from the outside bulge, the less the air is being diverted sideways and the more it is diverted up or down. In this case we get the less useful up or down swing. At the extreme end of the bulge, i.e. at the top or bottom of the ball, the air can *only* be diverted up or down. Herein lies the explanation for the results of my experiment. Worn areas high or low on the mainly backward-rotating ball can have little effect on swing.

Bowlers have known for many years that balls can swing "against the seam". For instance, an attempted outswinger with the seam pointing towards the slips may become an inswinger. My results confirm the existence of such behaviour as well as measuring the amount of it. Low seam angles, natural wear, worn or dirty stitching, the orientation of the minor seam to the wind, and almost imperceptible variations in the surface texture of new balls (see fig. 21), can all lead to large and unexpected changes in swing force.

In other words, the seam is only one of the numerous possible areas capable of affecting air flow around the ball. At a low angle as in fig. 23*b* the seam is so far away from the critical bulge *B* that it does not make the air stream cling to the ball as much as does the worn area at *A* which lies on the critical bulge. What would normally be the shiny side is now effectively the rough side, and what is normally the rough or seam side is acting as the smooth side: the ball "goes the other away". All the bowler needs to do is keep the seam side shiny! The so-called "reverse swing" is therefore simply explained.

Since, in the situation just explained, the seam has no effect on swing, there is no need for the bowler to deliver the ball at any particular angle, provided that the seam is upright and pointing either straight down the pitch or at some fairly low angle. For the inswinger the rough side is on the leg; for the outswinger it is on the off.

This delightfully simple approach to swing both ways has induced certain players to break the laws of the game and deliberately damage one side of the ball. Australian umpires inspecting the ball in the interval of a game between Victoria and Pakistan in 1990 discovered "unnatural marks", as if it was prepared for a game of noughts and crosses, on one side of the ball, whereas the other side was bright and shiny.[12]

Water is another entry in the list of tricks tried by swing bowlers. One side of a ball which has been used for about twenty or more overs is watered in some way or other. Take your pick – sweat, saliva, the drinks bottle. With a new ball it won't work because of the waterproof lacquer. But in an experiment with a moderately worn four-piece ball with the entire leather hemisphere, excluding the stitches, immersed for five minutes, I found that it took up a little more than 1 g of water, whereas one side of a new ball under the same conditions took up only about a third of this amount.

It has been claimed that the ball will swing towards the wet side because the water, by making it heavier, gives that side a bias. Leaving aside any wonderment about what exactly is meant by bias in flying missiles, I would hope at least that readers are by now in no doubt about the cause of swing. Swing results from different air flow on the two opposite sides of the ball. Being a surface effect it has no direct relation to anything below the surface. For example, a leather ball filled with lead would experience the same swing force as a cricket ball. But it wouldn't swing as much. If it was say ten times the weight of a cricket ball, it would swing only one tenth as far. Increased weight therefore reduces swing, surface properties being equal. As for bias, it is a term which has no meaning and therefore no place in our discussion. A cricket ball won't fall over sideways or twist in the air merely because one side is slightly heavier than the other; even if it did the swing force would then be up or down rather than sideways. In the next chapter I show that the force causing a ball to twist in the air does exist but it is a very small one and derives from the air striking the seam. A little water in the leather would have less effect than the seam.

Cricketers using water say that after wetting one side they shine it and the ball will then swing to that side. Since all the research on swing, by myself and others, tells us that swing is always to the rough side, what are we to make of this apparent contradiction? The crucial question is to decide whether the wet side really is the shiny side, as some bowlers claim. First I would ask readers to look again at fig. 21 where two apparently identical balls differing only slightly in the texture of the leather surface gave quite different swing forces. The ball in my wetting experiment gave me a clear answer. Not only was the wet leather rougher, but more importantly it showed the effects of water having entered the area of the minor seam. Above each of the totally hidden stitches there now appeared a pronounced little ridge which remained even after the outside of the leather had dried. Anyone who has tried to shine a pair of wet boots will not be misled on this.

Cricketers cunning enough to use water to accentuate swing have proved to be even more cunning by invoking a suspension of the laws of aerodynamics in order to bluff law-making authorities into thinking that wet leather is shinier than dry, and that rather than breaking the Law which says that the ball must not be damaged in any way, they are actually improving the ball!

My wetting experiment also showed that the leather, while it was still wet on the surface, became soft and easily roughened by the finger-nails as it would also be by normal wear. Yet another trick used in first class cricket and recently revealed to me by an international umpire, is the picking up of the leather along the minor seam. The finger-nail pushed into the narrow groove where it passes across the outside bulge is quite capable of causing sufficient roughness, which incidentally can be pressed down again at the end of the over. There are some problems here for umpires; they can't get too dogmatic about surface texture but they should ban any form of wetting, as well as keeping an eye out for deliberate mutilation.

Now that we know that even one small tear on leather can affect swing, will bowlers be encouraging batsmen early in the game to hit the ball into the boundary fence or even over it? A nicely-placed area of damage on the ball could well be worth six runs.

REFERENCES

1 N. G. Barton, Proc. Roy. Soc. London A 379 (1982), p. 109–31 2 L. J. Briggs, Am. J. Phys. 27 (1959), p. 589–96 3 K. Bentley, P. Varty, M. Proudlove and R. D. Mehta, Imperial College Aero Tech. Note (1982), p. 82–196, Nature, 303, June 30 1983, p. 787–8 and R. D. Mehta, "Aerodynamics of sports balls" (Ann. Rev. Fluid Mech 17, 1985), p. 151–81 4 K. Sherwin and J. L. Sproston, Inst. J. Mech, Eng. Educ. 10 (1982), p. 71–9 5 Central Institute of Technology, Heretaunga, New Zealand 6 Kookaburra brand balls manufactured by A. G. Thompson Ltd, Victoria, Australia 7 E. Achenbach, J. Fluid Mech 62 Pt 2 (1974), p. 209–21 8 S. Taneda, J. Fluid Mech 85 Pt 1 (1971), p. 187–92 9 A. G. Moyes, Australian Bowlers (Angus and Robertson, 1953), p. 172 10 Ken Kelly, Cricket Reflections (Heinemann, 1985), p. 104 11 A. Imbrosciano, 'The swing of a cricket ball', Project Report, Newcastle College of Advanced Education, Australia, 1981, p. 54 12 P. Smithers, Melbourne Age, 17 November 1990, p. 32

Chapter 5
The fast bowler's natural spin

THIS CHAPTER IS NOT ABOUT LEG-CUTTERS, OFF-CUTTERS or those hopeful flirtations with spin which sometimes drift down the wicket just before the fast man finally takes his pullover from the umpire. It is about the spin which nearly all bowlers impart naturally as the fingers pull the back of the ball down at the moment of release, i.e. back-spin. So far we have dealt with balls fixed at various angles to the air stream. Much valuable information was revealed but it was necessary to come closer to the real situation and study spinning balls. I studied the effect of back-spin using motor-driven balls on the mount shown in fig. 13b. Later, using another type of mount, I studied other spins.

It has been claimed that back-spin is good for swing bowling because, like the spinning top that will not fall over, the backward spinning ball will be better able to remain at a fixed angle as it travels through the air. Why would it change its angle? If it was a perfectly smooth sphere it would not. But the seam gets in the way of the air and changes its flow pattern as we have seen in our discussion of swing. The seam side of the ball must therefore tend to be pushed around, twisted, by this frictional effect of the air stream. Since a few authors have mentioned the probable existence of this twisting ("torque") force, and since no one had ever measured it, I decided to do so with the aid of a delicate lever system connecting a new four-piece ball to the sensitive electronic balance.

Fig. 24 shows the basic twisting process and the results of the torque measurements. It proves that there is torque and that it varies markedly with the angle of the seam to the air flow. At seam angles where the wind "sees" no difference in roughness between one side of the ball and the other, there is no torque, i.e. at 0°, 90°, 180° and 270°. Between these positions the torque force rises to a very moderate 3–7 g (i.e. the amount of push around the equator), depending on wind speed. However, at the seam angles used by medium and fast bowlers – up to about 30° or 40° – these forces are halved.

Small torque forces such as those found are unlikely to twist the ball around during flight, even if it had no spin whatsoever to stabilise it. Even if the seam angle did change a little during flight, the results need not be all bad since it might blunder into a region where swing is better, or where catastro-

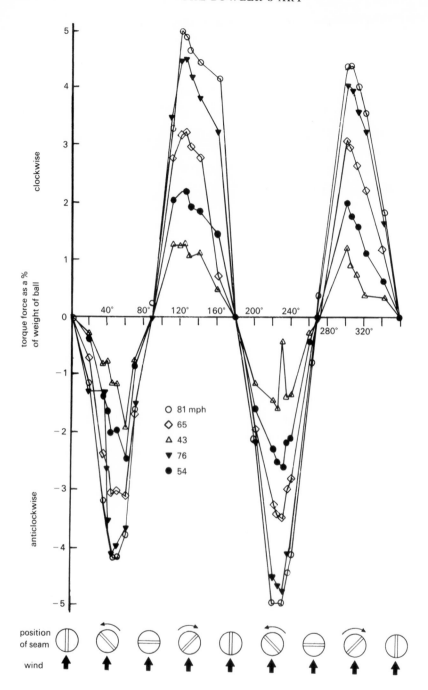

Fig. 24 *Torque on a new four-piece ball,* measured over a range of seam angles and wind speeds. Arrows over balls show whether or not there is torque and in which direction it is twisting the ball.

phic collapse and reversal of swing force may yield an unexpected bonus when it "goes the other way". My results show that for new four-piece balls the swing force is fairly constant over a wide range of seam angles above about 10°.

Another oddity that has been mentioned by writers is the possibility of the spinning and twisting ball behaving like a spinning top and displaying a sort of slow, weaving, circular movement known as gyroscopic precession. A calculation on this gives a time of 12 seconds for one complete rotary motion of the axis. The ball, by this time most likely back in the bowler's hand for the next delivery, would unfortunately not be able to complete this complex dance to nature's tune.

We are discussing back-spin as in fig. 2a, c and d, but only a is "pure" back-spin, a type of spin which normally will not cause any sideways movement off the pitch. However, all of the other possible back-spins (e.g. c and d) carry a degree of side-spin; we have entered the area where fast men have common ground with spinners.

Jack Massie (1890–1966) must have been one of the best Australian bowlers never to play for his country. In the years just before the First World War he was one of the best in the game but was wounded in the war and played no more first class cricket. In 1926 he wrote a coaching booklet full of good practical advice.[1] Unlike many earlier writers he recognised the difference between swerve and swing. But, limited by the knowledge of those days, he thought that if more back-spin was applied to a ball it would swing more.

Does back-spin affect swing, and if so what is the optimum amount to use? Two earlier workers, using the rolling and dropping method, came to differ-

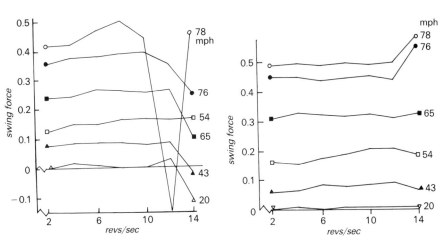

Fig. 25 *Effect of back-spin on swing.* Seam angle is 5° *(left)* and 10° *(right)* for various wind speeds and rates of spin.

ent conclusions on this. Barton found that a back-spin rate of about 5 revs/sec was best for swing[2], but Bentley's group found 12 revs/sec to be best[3]. My own work, carried out under more controlled conditions, showed that it did not matter how much back-spin was on the ball. At spin rates of up to 14 revs/sec, which seem to be around the highest which cricketers are capable of imparting, it can be seen in fig. 25 that except for the fastest delivery at a 5° seam angle, the swing force was virtually unchanged right up to this rate. Nor did the spin reduce the overall swing forces significantly.

REFERENCES

1 R. J. A. Massie, *Bowling* (NSW Cricket Association, 1926), p. 10   **2** N. G. Barton, Proc. Roy. Soc. London A 379 (1982), p. 109–31   **3** K. Bentley, P. Varty, M. Proudlove and R. D. Mehta, Imperial College Aero. Tech. Note (1982), p. 82–196

Chapter 6
Late swing

THE BALL THAT SWINGS LATE IN FLIGHT is the Holy Grail of the medium and fast crusaders. But, as Bernard Hollowood reminded us earlier, such an awe-inspiring gift is more the stuff of legend than cricket in the flesh. However, enough unusual swing behaviour has been revealed in the preceding pages to provide a rational foundation for it, and it is just possible that the reader is now ready to come to grips with this fascinating delivery.

In a sense, nearly all swing is late swing, simply because the path taken by the ball generally increases in curvature the further it goes. Like the bend in a fishing rod pulling in a small fish, the parabola of a swinging cricket ball is usually of an unspectacular kind; J. B. King called his inswinger "The angler" after its hooked curve.

The final amount of deviation varies tremendously from a frustratingly common nothing, to the "big banana" or "cartwheel" which are most often wind assisted. Many factors affect the outcome of every delivery; the skill and pace of the bowler, the state of the ball and the atmospheric conditions. Also spare a thought for the unfortunate bowler who is forced to bowl right through a spell in a one-day game under strong discouragement against swinging because of the restrictive ruling on wides, which unfortunately is sometimes mistakenly applied by player-umpires in other grades of cricket as well.

Assuming that the ball follows a smooth parabolic path, most of the deviation – i.e. more than 50% of it – occurs in the last 30% of the flight, as shown in fig. 26 which is drawn from high speed photographs of Garry Gilmour. A

Fig. 26 *Parabolic path of a swinging ball* bowled by Australian left-hander Garry Gilmour (A. Imbrosciano, "The swing of a cricket ball", Newcastle College of Advanced Education, 1981): an outswinger delivered from over the wicket.

good batsman makes an early assessment of this curve, but a less able bats-man not picking it up until later, and embarrassed by the resulting disaster, may describe this perfectly normal ball as a late swinger. The genuine late swinger needs, for proof of its existence, an impartial judge. In the absence of a top-class batsman, a well-placed observer or a video or cine camera would be required.

We have previously ruled out the existence of a critical speed beyond which swing was thought impossible, but below which the ball, slowed by drag, suddenly begins to swing. No practical evidence exists for this explana-tion of late swing, although it has been favoured by some authors. Looking elsewhere for explanations, we have the well established instability assoc-iated with air flow around smooth spheres, which has been discussed earlier. Cricket balls at low seam angles show this behaviour, which was dram-atically demonstrated by the violent vibration observed in the wind tunnel. Such changes could occur anywhere in flight except very early, since the diverted wake as pointed out previously is unlikely to develop instanta-neously. Imbrosciano plotted the flight paths of these wobbles from the cine photographs of Gilmour.

However, an additional possible cause, also deriving from the discovery of unstable regions, is seen at other seam angles in the swing force diagrams of figs 15, 19, 20, 21 and 22. Every steep part of the curves means a region of instability where the swing may suddenly increase, or decrease. In most cases it needs only quite a small change of seam angle to bring about these large changes of swing force.

Wind at ground level, frequently variable in direction, can as a result effectively change its angle to the seam as it swirls about. The resulting change of swing force is just as dependent on this as it is on an angle change effected by the bowler. For example, in fig. 19a a small increase or decrease of seam angles in the region of $7°$–$15°$ will take the ball through a region where the swing may drop to zero and even "go the other way". As with all four-piece balls, a major influence here is the minor seam lying across the air flow on the smooth side, or aligned with it. Imbrosciano's photographs of Gil-mour's bowling showed unexpected changes of direction.

Bowlers, particularly upwind bowlers, should be experimenting with vari-ous seam angles so as to enter these regions where wind-seam angle changes during flight can lead to sudden changes in direction.

A bowler can bring about both of the critical unstable situations described above. He can deliver the ball with a slow wobble (fig. 3) of the seam, so that at some late stage of its flight the wobble happens to place the seam at a very favourable angle for swing. The same slow rotation, with or without seam wobble, may take the minor seam from a position where it lies across the air stream on the smooth side of the ball and interferes with swing, to a position where it is aligned with the air flow, and therefore allows swing to take place, late in flight. A slowly wobbling ball will in fact tend to spiral through the air, but it won't show any upward movement against the force of gravity. The batsman may be fooled by an accentuated downward movement as well as being in trouble to the sideways parts of the spiral.

To achieve either or both of the above late swing situations, the bowler must ensure that the rate of back-spin applied to the ball is not too great. If it is, then the seam angles or minor seam positions which are likely to cause or prevent swing may come and go too rapidly for the swing to develop.

Baseball and softball players pitching the knuckle ball rely on exactly the same principles as outlined for the slow seam wobble as a cause of late swing. The knuckle ball is pitched with only a small amount of rotation and flutters unpredictably in various directions during flight. The effect of pitching with only a small amount of rotation is to bring the complex line of stitching into various different positions facing the air stream. Variable swing forces result.

Bowlers attempting this technique should try releasing the ball with more of an outward push than a sharp downward flick of the fingers. Merely holding the ball more in towards the palm of the hand will go a long way towards achieving the desired result. Such a grip is often seen in old coaching books. In the light of the present discussion there may be more to such grips than merely obtaining a change of pace. Spofforth's "small portion" grip (*see* Chapter 14), released with the seam at various angles, is worth a trial as a slower ball with late swing.

Another method for minimising imparted rotation is to release the ball from a grip where the fingers are splayed wide out on either side of the seam. In the context of reducing cut or turn off the pitch, the technique is discussed in Chapter 8 and Chapter 14.

A possible source of late swing, resulting from slow back-spin but not requiring seam wobble, derives from uneven flattening of the stitching, or the presence of uneven dirt deposits in the stitching, or both. The matter is discussed more fully in the next chapter. Flattened stitching on a worn ball will be less capable of providing the minor turbulence necessary for swing. If the flattening is uneven the swing force will change as the different parts of the seam reach the front of the ball as it rotates. Similarly with a partially dirt-filled seam, since dirt affects swing. Such partially-filled stitching would be common when a bowler is in action on a moist pitch; the dirt would only fill those parts on which the ball had landed.

Slow rotation may also take a worn spot away from a position where it has been preventing swing to one where it interferes less. In this case the ball may suddenly begin to swing.

If we regard all unpredictable swing as a potential source of late swing, then we must look on the modern fixation with shining one side of the ball as bad for late swing. Lindwall's delight, mentioned earlier, is less and less likely to materialise the more the two sides of the ball become different.

Wind can play a part in late swing; not that one must conjure up a sudden hurricane, but in a rather more subtle way. The situation to be described would apply to an upwind bowler, with the wind coming from somewhere between the slips and fine-leg, who swings it enough to change the angle of the flight to the oncoming wind. A cascade of effects begins to occur. As the ball curves a little the wind appears to come more from the side, which in turn gives it a push from the side and makes it curve more, and so on. What began as a head wind has now become much more of a side wind, and the ball has ducked smartly into the leg stump, or gone the other way, and taken the outside edge with a late outswinger.

As we will see in Chapter 9, smooth non-turbulent air conditions favour swing. Here is yet another possible cause of late swing: the ball leaving a turbulent body of air and entering a smooth swing-favouring region of air nearer the batsman. Valuable indeed is the upwind swinger who has a reasonable degree of control, but the discouragement of such skill, arising from the wide ruling in some one-day cricket, is regrettable.

Finally we come to the effect of spin alone. During wind-tunnel work I found some quite sudden force changes associated with off-spin and leg-spin carrying varying amounts of side-spin. It is possible for a fast or medium bowler to enter this area which we shall discuss in the chapters on spin bowling.

Since most of the situations described in this account of late swing are reversible, they can just as easily give rise to situations where a ball which begins to swing may straighten up or go the other way.

Chapter 7
Stitching

THE FOUR ROWS OF EXTERNAL STITCHING, and frequently the seam that encircles the ball, are raised approximately 1 mm above the surface. Swing, at least in any predictable form, will not take place without them. Nor is it possible for the fast or medium leg- or off-cutter, or the slower spinner, to grip firmly the frequently quite shiny ball, unless they are prominent. Thread is easily flattened.

A ball struck by the bat, or landing on hard ground, will not retain the full seam height for long. The bowler cannot apply the same amount of spin (or cut), and bite or grip of the ball on the surface of the pitch is also reduced.

Soil picked up by a ball landing on a moist wicket lies alongside the raised stitching and to some extent lessens its effect on the passing air stream. In order to find the extent of this effect, I smeared wet soil over the stitching of a new ball and measured the new swing force in the wind tunnel. Instead of protruding sharply, the stitches now showed a rounded profile, illustrating the situation when bowling on a moist wicket.

For a new four-piece ball at seam angles of less than 10°, the swing force was reduced by 30–50%. But at angles of 15–35° it was increased by about 20%. If swing is the only consideration therefore, this result is inconclusive. But since it is certain that a clean seam at full height will grip the earth better, then there should be no doubt that cut, lift, and every other type of anti-batsman behaviour that the ball may display (except perhaps the low shooter), will benefit from constant attention to cleaning and raising that stitching. Neither operation is contrary to the laws of cricket, which allow the stitching to be cleaned, and the ball (and this includes the stitching) may be returned to its original condition. The latter provision implies that the flattened stitching may quite legally be unflattened, sharpened or raised back to its full height. It would be impossible to raise it above its original height without the aid of a sharp-pointed instrument. The widespread notion that raising the seam is illegal is of course correct, but only where it applies to the leather on either side of the major or minor seams. That leather can with some effort be raised considerably above its original smooth bulge. But the stitching and the seam are different parts of the ball; cleaning and raising the stitching has nothing to do with the seam.

All bowlers should therefore restore and maintain the stitching. For spinners and cutters it is vital. For fast and medium bowlers, it is quite as important as attempting to maintain shine. Bowlers, fast and slow, are not getting the best possible results unless their thumb-nails are worn down by this essential activity.

Chapter 8
The moment of release

HOW ONE SHOULD GRIP THE BALL has always fascinated cricketers. Their particular hero, photographed with fingers curling on either side of, along, or slightly across the seam, reveals the secret of his fame. Other photographs and diagrams may show his arm and body swing; different for the outswinger and the inswinger. But, as many a cricketer and coach have discovered, it is not as simple as that. Even more frustrating is the sudden loss of the ability to swing, a not uncommon problem among cricketers at all levels.

These problems arise because we have focussed too much on grip, and aspects of action, which in themselves do not guarantee that the ball begins its flight in a state capable of giving the best results. Instead, we should start with a clear picture of the ball on its way, and, by careful experimentation and observation, adjust all the other complex movements of body, arms and hand, to achieving that end. It is said of the great F. R. Spofforth that his hand action was a very poor guide as to how the ball would behave.

A useful start is to realise how a flexible action can deliver the ball at all sorts of angles, even though the grip is unchanged. Grip the ball with the seam running straight out between the first and second fingers. Merely by cocking the hand to one side or the other, the ball can be delivered at angles identical to those in frequently published photographs for the inswinger or outswinger. This does not mean that the usual grips are wrong, but it does mean that they are not in themselves a guarantee of success. Neither is the arm action any guarantee. It is possible to swing the arm down across one side of the body, while at the same time having the hand cocked so that the ball leaves the hand facing the opposite way.

Finger action is another variable. Precisely how do your fingers come off the ball at the instant of release? While supporting the ball in one hand, bring your other (bowling) hand down off the ball in the various possible ways. Do your fingers come off to one side or the other and is the seam tilted away from the vertical or not? Does one finger tend to dominate the final push?

A stranger to the game of cricket may well describe the task we are undertaking as impossible. At the same time as propelling the ball straight down the pitch, the fingers must ensure maintenance of a steady angle during flight, with the ball upright, but with the seam pointing to one side.

Gripped between the thumb and fingers, the ball can be brought up to full speed at any angle. Then, just before the moment of release, the thumb comes off the ball, and in the final push, the fingers, which previously lay at least partly to one side, pull that side down just as the ball moves away from the touch. Whether the downward moving fingers should both be on the seam, or one on the seam and one on the smooth leather, or even both on smooth leather, depends to some extent on the success or failure of your own experimentation, but also on your intentions.

If your intentions extend to cutting the ball off the pitch, with or without swing, then the backward spin carrying a significant amount of off- or leg-cut, as in fig. 2c and d respectively, must be the best obtainable. In that case the more grip or friction the fingers obtain as they move down, the better. At least one finger should therefore be on the stitching.

If swing is the sole intention, with a minimum of cut-back off a gripping pitch in the opposite direction, then fingers on smooth leather are called for, provided you don't lose control on the slippery surface. An extreme form of this grip involves the fingers splayed wide on either side of the seam and propelling the ball from points near the outside bulges. Very little back-spin of the type involved in fig. 2c and d will result from this technique.

There is no such thing as a correct grip which will apply to every bowler. Even a finger-across-the-seam grip may finally deliver the ball with the seam vertical, as a consequence of the body, arm, wrist and finger action of a particular bowler. Success for the swinger therefore hinges entirely on the final instant which is the climax of the whole delivery. No one type of body action can itself guarantee success, but the high arm coming more or less straight over the top clearly offers better launching than that of the round-arm slinger whose problems we discussed earlier.

We saw that variable seam-wind angles can lead to unpredictable late swing. A bowler wishing to change the angle of the seam needs to do more than merely point the seam in a different direction as gripped between the fingers. If, for example, the angle is changed from 5° to 30° without a change of action there will merely be more seam wobble. To deliver a non-wobbling ball at a greater angle the bowler must change his release action so as to bring the fingers down more to the side. Practice with an observer or the use of a video will be necessary. We will return to grips in Chapter 15, but before then it is better to understand ball behaviour uncomplicated by the presence of fingers.

Valuable information has been collected in Australia in recent years pinpointing aspects of fast bowlers' actions which lead to injury and premature breakdown[1]. Most back troubles seemed to stem from raising the front leg to, or above, a horizontal level during the delivery stride. This is also a cause of shin soreness. Opening the shoulders and falling away early was another problem for the back, as was the production of much rotational movement of the back, and bending the lower back during the time of peak force. Shin soreness also arose from landing on the ball of the front foot, and from allowing the front leg to collapse during ball release. Groin injuries resulted from longer delivery strides and collapsed front knees.

Desirable features, according to this work, are a small backward lean prior to delivery, minimal fall away, the front foot raised but not up to the horizontal, the front arm bent and raised in front of the body, the head aligned with the plane of the arm, the front foot to land on the heel, the knee to be bent slightly to absorb some of the force, then straightening during delivery to produce a pivot with height, and finally the shoulders to open late by the front arm moving on the line of the delivery.

It is necessary to practise and experiment with an observer present. The visibility of the position and behaviour of the ball in the air must be increased in some way. Perhaps a thin white line painted around the circumference where the two leather hemispheres meet between the lines of stitching is the best. No matter what seam angle is used, that line should always be seen to be vertical if swing (and not spin-swerve) is the sole objective.

Needless to say, all contact with concrete or wire or any other hard abrasive material such as crushed limestone on run-ups, must be strictly avoided. Modern practice facilities are decidedly unfriendly to swing and to the development of swing bowlers. If indoor facilities must be used, some ingenuity and careful choice of soft materials can overcome the problem. The banishment of batsmen from the scene will remove some of the danger. Make stumps from soft plastic piping. Repainting of worn balls can also help.

If practising outdoors, a still, cloudy day is best for swing. A readily accessible and ball-friendly location is a grassy field, away from fences, with a simple back net, a few feet high and supported by two poles. The surface need not be perfect, since it is movement through the air, not off the pitch, that is the purpose of such practice. Regular cleaning of the stitching with the thumb-nail will be necessary.

Coaching books often underestimate the powers of young bowlers to learn. I see no reason why a bowler learning swing should not, from the beginning, learn the different actions required for bowling both inswingers and outswingers. The sooner the better; there are plenty of other skills to get on with.

REFERENCES

1 P. Spence, "Bending the back", *Australian Cricket*, January 1990, p. 48

Chapter 9
Swing and the atmosphere

EVERY CRICKETER KNOWS that there are periods when swing is rampant and periods when straightness rules. If weather is to be implicated, other possible explanations must be ruled out: better bowling, a better ball, less wear on the ball, less impact of bat to flatten the seam. With all of these out of the way, what about the cloud blocking out the sun for an over? "I could swear it swung more in that over".

Whoever first suggested that increased atmospheric humidity increases swing must have been pleased with the lasting power of their idea. An idea satisfying the need to explain genuine experience, and not under threat of being supplanted by a better idea, will not be discarded merely because a scientist or two say that it cannot work. So it is with humidity and swing.

No great knowledge of science is required to appreciate that there is no way in which a change in the moisture content of the air can affect swing. Humid or damp air, often described as "heavy", is in fact slightly less dense than dry air. But the fact that this has been pointed out by several authors seems not to have lessened the popularity of the humidity idea one iota.

Part of the reason for its persistence may stem from the account of Daish[1] who, while dismissing the idea for the reasons given above, gave humidity a reprieve by suggesting another way in which it could influence swing. This was by means of the possibility of the stitching around the ball swelling in highly humid conditions, and thereby increasing the swing force. Not until ten years later did Bentley and others actually carry out the necessary experiment.[2] They placed two balls in a chamber at 75% relative humidity for 48 hours, before measuring the swing force and the thickness of the stitching. No change was found in either.

Before that work was published, two papers appeared reporting wind-tunnel tests carried out in different humidity conditions. Neither showed any effect on the swing force. Sherwin and Sproston did not report actual measurements, but merely stated that "Although relative humidity values of between 61% and 100% were recorded, no noticeable change in value was apparent."[3] Barton repeated some of his own measurements under different weather conditions (50–70% relative humidity); although he found some differences, he did not regard them as significant.[4] Since neither of the above workers used equipment as sensitive as that which I developed for my own work, I decided to carry out the most rigorous test yet undertaken.

A passer-by observing my antics of hanging wet laboratory coats on chairs and liberally splashing water around the wind-tunnel room, may have been forgiven for thinking that they had stumbled across some ancient rite. Liquid water rapidly became airborne water vapour in the windy surroundings. Carrying out regular and accurate chemical analysis, I measured the humidity when it had settled to a steady figure. Temperatures and barometric pressure were checked and the swing force was measured precisely at three wind speeds. The results given in Table B show that humidity has no influence whatsoever on swing.

Table B Swing forces

Wind speed	**Relative humidity (%)**					
(mph)	**46.7**	**54.0**	**65.1**	**68.8**	**79.6**	**80.3**
81.0	**0.592**	**0.577**	**0.591**	**0.576**	**0.577**	**0.574**
	0.0124	0.0113	0.0124	0.0096	0.0092	0.0162
65.2	**0.397**	**0.371**	**0.397**	**0.390**	**0.391**	**0.380**
	0.0062	0.0154	0.0063	0.0065	0.0054	0.0087
42.5	**0.117**	**0.114**	**0.115**	**0.115**	**0.117**	**0.109**
	0.0052	0.0078	0.0085	0.0090	0.0079	

Note Swing forces are expressed as a fraction of the weight of the ball. Each force value is the mean of 10 balance readings; the figure in italics is the standard deviation. Values are for a new four-piece ball— Kookaburra Turf— mounted with the seam at 15° to the wind in the wind tunnel. All measurements were taken at temperatures in the range 23–25°C and a barometric pressure of 759–760 mm of mercury

Is it too much to hope that the flat-earthers in the commentary box and elsewhere will finally erase humidity from the book of cricket terminology? Perhaps I could attempt to entice them away from error towards an alternative explanation. Sherwin and Sproston in a few brief lines at the end of their paper on trip wires and seams, suggested that enhanced swing under cloud cover may be due to lowered atmospheric turbulence which would interfere less with the smooth flow around one side of the ball.[5]

Such an attractive idea needed evidence to support it, and with the help of a local meteorologist my search uncovered a most informative review by

Ibbetson of the subject of atmospheric turbulence.[6] Ibbetson described what happened two metres above a field when the sun shone. Using sensitive instruments, which could respond extremely rapidly to changes of wind speed and temperature, he measured both vertical and horizontal air currents and how they fluctuated with temperature. The picture uncovered was one of rising air currents fluctuating rapidly, within a fraction of a second. These coincided with local and rapid fluctuations in air temperature resulting from the sun's radiation and causing local hot spots on the ground. Superimposed on this rising air was a moderate breeze of about 9 mph which did not obliterate the micro-turbulence.

Here then is a highly satisfactory explanation of at least one aspect of our subject – the sudden ability to swing when a cloud crosses the sun. Less solar heating; less micro-turbulence; less interference with the smooth flow required on the shiny side of the ball, and therefore more swing – no other explanation deals with the rapidly changing series of events in a way which matches the experience of cricketers.

Support for the idea that micro-turbulence destroys swing also comes from wind-tunnel work. Although Bentley and others were not investigating alternative explanations to replace humidity, they found that turbulence deliberately introduced into the air stream reduced the swing force markedly. A cross wind can blow a ball off course and magnify quite a small amount of swing into something significant. Under these conditions the wind has a gross effect which more than off-sets the loss (of swing force) due to turbulence. But that is not the situation we are discussing.

Now the way is open to relate the necessity for non-turbulent flow, on the smooth side of the ball, to the false idea of humidity. The word "humid" is often used along with "heavy" or "oppressive", to describe the uncomfortable feeling associated with a lack of air movement or poor ventilation. In other words it describes the state of being in an environment of low air turbulence. Mist at sea level is normally associated with relatively windless conditions. When the mist rises from a river near a cricket ground, e.g. the Trent in Nottingham, cricketers have always regarded the swing as being due to moisture. Since that is impossible, we must focus on the "windless" aspect rather than on the moisture.

The "close" morning atmosphere at the beginning of a game of cricket often described as "humid" can be quite correctly described as "still" and therefore non-turbulent.

In the light of all this, can we expect good swing on a sunny day? Putting the question another way, can we expect to get smooth, swing-favouring air on such a day? Yes, we can, if the following conditions apply: the wind should not be strong or gusty; the sun should not be able to heat the ground to a temperature much above that of the air; a damp soil following rain will also aid cooling by evaporation and reduce the likelihood of hot spots as sources of turbulence.

Seaside grounds have a reputation for favouring swing. Since, under windless conditions, they are also frequently covered with a heavy dew early in the day, the cooling effect on the grass as this moisture evaporates offers a plausible explanation for the removal of hot spots at least during the early part of the day.

All these conditions describe exactly the first day of the New Zealand vs. Australia Test at Wellington on March 15 1990. The New Zealand bowlers swung the ball unusually well throughout the entire innings in the bright late-season sunshine as a light breeze moved steadily across the sodden outfield, and Australia, floundering on a slow pitch, were all out for 110 in less than four hours.

The height of the sun in the sky is not only related to the season but to the time of day and the distance from the equator. All other factors being equal, we would therefore expect the lower sun earlier or later in the day to interfere less with swing. On this basis captains should give more serious consideration to taking the new ball late in the day.

It is tempting to develop this idea to explain why England, the cricketing nation furthest from the equator, places more emphasis on swing than does the West Indies, the closest. But the emergence of high class swing bowlers in Pakistan serves to bring out another important factor, the need for the turbulent rising air above the hot spots to be hotter than the surrounding air. In a climate such as Pakistan, where the surrounding air tends to be warm, the necessary temperature difference will be less, resulting in less turbulence and therefore more swing.

The sun shines, the wicket is friendly, the ball is showing a little wear and the opening bowlers, relying on swing, are merely bowling the batsmen into form. The great pioneer of inswing, J. B. King, helps us realise that swing on its own has not much of a future:

> We must always remember that the ball that curves is just an adjunct to the stock in trade of a good bowler. It is a very valuable weapon; but first the bowler must be able to hit the wicket with a good length ball, to turn it from the pitch, and at times to send it down with a deceptive change of pace. When the bowler has equipped himself with these skills he may try to develop the swing. If he *always* curves, a good batsman will find him just as easy to play as the man who bowls perfectly straight.[7]

C. G. Macartney (1886–1958), the dominant Australian batsman of the early twentieth century, dismissed mere swingers:

> Since its introduction, bowlers have sacrificed the natural spin for the swing, and nowadays we find ourselves possessing more of the straight up and down type of performer than the clever bowler of former days.[8]

The rise of the swinger is linked to the decline of the spinner and a set of circumstances, only one of which has been removed, i.e. the 55 over new-ball rule. More needs to be done; hard wickets on which the ball will grip are a priority. But even now, using a ball polished in the out-fields of most countries by soft green grass, and bowling on ball-friendly, non-abrasive wicket surfaces, the swinger *per se* is rarely a match-winner.

Famous deliveries, made so by famous participants, can be an inspiration. In the context of a discussion on what makes the total fast or medium bowler, no better example can be cited than the ball with which Alec Bedser bowled Don Bradman in 1947. Bedser tells the story:

> A turning point in my career was to bowl Don for a duck in the Fourth Test at Adelaide with a ball which he generously described as the finest ever bowled to him. It started on the line of the off stump, swung late to hit the pitch on or about the leg stump, and came back to hit the middle and off stumps. My stock was boosted sky high and I gained considerable confidence. I had discovered my so-called leg-cutter, in which I actually spun the ball, during the Bradman-Barnes record fifth wicket partnership of 405 in the Second Test at Sydney. I was bowling to Barnes, who knew all about my inswing. To tempt him into error, I tried to make the ball go straight through without deviation. Allan Peach had taught me how to stop the new ball swinging by holding it across the seam in a leg-break grip. To my surprise, and that of Barnes, the ball went away from leg to off after pitching. Barnes' first reaction was to study the pitch with suspicion, and when he found it to be totally without blemish, he stared at me in disbelief and called out, 'What the hell's going on?' From that moment I knew I could spin the ball at a good speed, a considerable addition to my armoury.[9]

Note that Bedser's description of the ball as a "so-called leg-cutter" reveals an interesting link with the great S. F. Barnes. At a somewhat slower pace than Bedser, Barnes's best ball was an in-curving leg-spinner.

Here we are discussing the common ground where fast and slow, spinners and cutters, meet. It is likely that Bedser's historic inward curve originated from spin (*see* Chapter 11), a movement we call spin-swerve to distinguish it from seam-induced movement.

Swing and the atmosphere

All fast and medium-pace bowlers aiming to be something other than batsmen's fodder, unless they have exceptional pace, must enter this world. How often do we see a bowler's lack of real skills cruelly exposed on a good pitch? The often-quoted comment that spinners take a long time to develop probably applies to all bowlers, fast and slow, who acquire these skills. Alec Bedser was well established in his career before he achieved confidence with his leg-spinner. How many fast or medium bowlers are complete with these skills today?

A young bowler thrust into a high grade of cricket must attempt to reconcile two potentially incompatible lives: in one he seeks consistency, using a modest range of variations; in the other he experiments, practises, and unveils new variations in less important matches, until such time as these are fit to parade at large. Coaching books which convey the impression that the arts of spinning are in any way extras, or merely desirable additions to the armoury of fast and medium bowlers, are selling the game short.

REFERENCES

1 C. B. Daish, *The Physics of the Ball Games* (English Universities Press, 1972), p. 72 **2** K. Bentley, P. Varty, M. Proudlove and R. D. Mehta, Imperial College Aero. Tech. Note (1982), p. 82–196 **3** K. Sherwin and J. L. Sproston. Inst. J. Mech. Eng. Educ. 10 (1982), p. 71–9 **4** N. G. Barton, Proc. Roy. Soc. London A 379 (1982), p. 109–31 **5** K. Sherwin and J. L. Sproston, Inst. J. Mech. Eng. Educ 10 (1982) **6** A. Ibbetson, *Weather* 33 (1978), p. 369–82 **7** J. A. Lester (ed), *A Century of Philadelphia Cricket* (University of Pennsylvania Press, 1951), p. 165–6 **8** C. G. Macartney, *My Cricketing Days* (William Heinemann, 1930), p. 46 **9** A. Bedser, *Twin Ambitions* (Stanley Paul, 1986), p. 43

Chapter 10

A closer look at spin-swerve

L. J. BRIGGS STUDIED THE EFFECT OF SPIN on the flight of baseballs by dropping them across the horizontal air stream of a wind tunnel.[1] When I began my work, Robins measurements on cricket balls had never been recorded, as far as I was aware.

Along with all cricketers I was, of course, familiar with the many situations where spin-swerve adds an element of great interest to the game; the outward drifting off-spinner or off-cutter; the dipping top-spinner; the inward-curving leg-break or leg-cutter; the frequently strange antics of the ball in the air after pitching; a list not complete without the greatest of all excuses of the slippery-fingered fieldsman, "It just drifted away from me in the air".

Balls to be studied were mounted in the wind tunnel (figs. 13*b* and 27*e*) and spun by means of an electric motor connected to a flexible cable, leading to the end of a steel shaft (diameter 2 mm) inserted into the ball. Spin rates were varied up to 12 revs/sec, a rate which has been recorded for cricket balls in play. A few old balls which were difficult to mount symmetrically, because of slight distortions of shape, vibrated too much for measurements to be made at the higher spin rates.

The first ball studied (fig. 27*a*) was a fairly smooth one prepared from a shiny plastic imitation cricket ball by carefully removing the imitation seam and lacquering the surface to produce a shiny but not perfectly smooth finish; in fact, a fair imitation of a new ball's leather surface. This ball did not show the negative forces found by Briggs for smoother balls, but gave a relatively uncomplicated pattern of positive Robins Forces, generally increasing both with spin rate and wind speed. It therefore served as a reference with which to compare the results obtained from proper cricket balls, new and used.

In general, the Robins Forces found for this ball are not much less than the swing force results on a new ball. As mentioned earlier, the air flow resulting from spin-swerve is no different from that produced in swing. Put another way, if the surface air stream separates differently on the two sides of the ball, a certain force is produced and it does not matter whether that separation is caused by spin, or by the seam, or by wear, or any combination of these.

The new four-piece cricket ball (fig. 27*b*), spinning like a wheel on its side

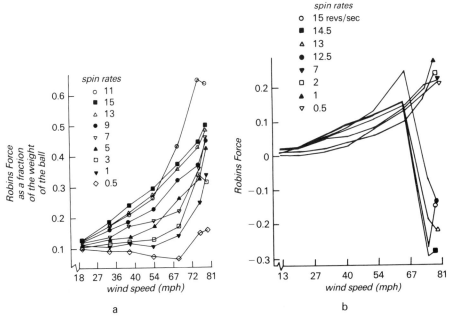

Fig. 27 *Robins spin-swerve forces on balls spinning* as in *e*: *a* is a smooth plastic ball the size of a cricket ball; *b* is a new four-piece ball; *c* is a new two-piece ball. George Hirst, a pioneer of spin-swerve, is shown in *d* about to bring his fingers around the right-hand side of the ball (as you look at the photograph) to produce side-spin which makes the ball swerve from off to leg. His spin is therefore the opposite to that in *e*, remembering that the latter is moving away from the eye.

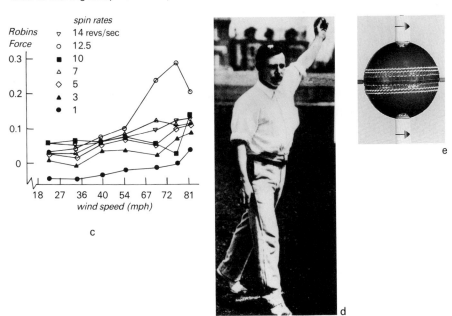

with the seam as the tyre, gave moderate Robins Forces which usually increased only slightly with wind speed and showed a variable response to spin rate. The most striking feature is the line for 12.5 revs/sec spin rate, a rate within the capability of a good spinner. At a speed of 54mph, i.e. in the slow-medium range, the force increases sharply to fast-medium speed, then drops off again at top speed.

The surprises associated with the Robins Force are best demonstrated in fig. 27c in which a new two-piece ball goes strongly negative at the higher spin rates and at speeds above about 60mph. Most of the larger Robins Forces have shown up only in the high speed range and this should serve to remind fast and medium-pace bowlers of their usefulness. However, in case the reader should regard this range of speed as being unattainable by a slow spinner, it is worth remembering that a ball delivered at, say, 40mph straight into a 20mph wind is experiencing a wind speed of 60mph. To be fully effective with his devastating side-spin-swerve from leg to off, Monty Noble needed a wind which was, at least to some extent, against him.

George Hirst, a good fast-medium left-armer, became a truly great bowler when he learned how to swerve the ball late in flight from off to leg. Bowling with side-spin, into a head wind, he was at his best exploiting the upper limits of the Robins Force. One bemused batsman demanded: "How the devil can you play a ball that comes at you like a hard throw-in from cover point?" Recognising another of the characteristics of spin-swerve, Hirst was modest and candid enough to admit its unpredictability: "Sometimes it works," he said, "sometimes it doesn't"[2].

It was probably the spectacular curves sometimes associated with spin-swerve which prompted Jack Massie[3] to conclude, wrongly, that although swing starts from the moment the ball leaves the bowler's hand, spin-swerve occurs only as the ball is dropping near the end of its flight.

When Arthur Mailey (1886–1967) spun his top-spinners, leg-breaks and googlies to a tantalising height against the wind, everyone, including Mailey himself, was guessing the final outcome. Mailey built a spectacularly successful career on upwind bowling. But such a love affair, especially in the light of the present discussion of the variability of the Robins Force, involves a measure of potential for failure and we will need to return to it later.

The well-worn, 100-over, four-piece ball gave results shown in fig. 28. The forces increased rather more with increasing spin and speed than for a new four-piece ball. A pronounced reversal to negative force, in the speed region of 27–40mph for the higher spin rates is the most striking difference compared to the new ball. Such a reversal from a downward force on a top-spinner suggests a possible cause of erratic behaviour late in flight, when the ball is slowing down, or when a gusting wind of variable speed and

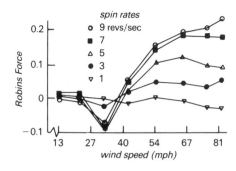

Fig. 28 Robins spin-swerve forces in a worn (100-over) four-piece ball mounted as in fig. 27e. Above 34 mph the force generally increased with speed and with spin above the minimum rates.

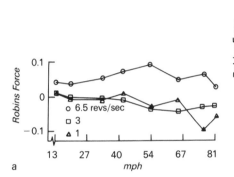

a

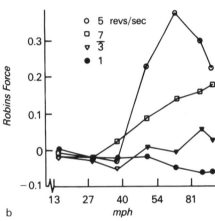

b

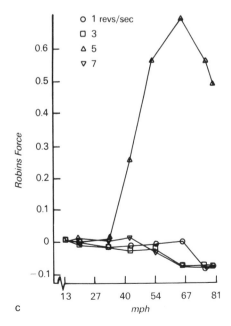

c

d

Fig. 29 The "pure" types of spin have the axis of spin at 90° to the plane of the seam, but a, b and c have the axis *through* the seam, i.e. in at one stitched area and out through the stitching on the opposite side as in d. Graph a is a new four-piece ball, b is a worn (100-over) four-piece ball and c is a new two-piece ball.

direction suddenly produces conditions identical with the dipping region of fig. 27c. Top-spin bowlers are not unfamiliar with the frustrating sight of their flightier deliveries failing to come to earth. Perhaps we can join with Mailey and Benjamin Robins (in his negative mood, in this case) and no longer regard such aerobatics as a personal failure. A new two-piece ball showed a strong reversal of force at high spin rates, but only at speeds faster than 60 mph.

So far we have been discussing balls spinning about the "axle of the seam wheel", i.e. all the situations illustrated by the balls in figs 27 and 28. But bowlers do not always deliver such "pure wheel spin", and instead may spin "across the seam," as in fig. 29d. Any spin between "pure wheel" and "pure across" would produce a wobbling seam delivery.

Three balls were studied with the axis *through* rather than across the main seam, i.e. spinning "across the seam" (fig. 29a, b, and c.) A new four-piece ball (fig. 29a) spun that way will not show very much spin-swerve at all; at least it offers the bowler a choice, and a method for delivering an uncomplicated ball. There may be some variable swing as the seam comes around into various positions if the spin is slow enough, but spin-swerve has been virtually eliminated. A worn, 100-over, four-piece ball (fig. 29b) showed a marked increase in force in the upper half of the speed range, and at quite moderate spin rates. The new two-piece ball (fig. 29c) showed little evidence of a Robins Force except for the startling rise at 5 revs/sec spin rate. "Across the seam" spinning, where the axis of spin is through the plane of the main seam, i.e. through the seam, is therefore not a very effective way of obtaining spin-swerve, but may surprise occasionally.

REFERENCES

1 L. J. Briggs, Am. J. Phys. (1959), p. 589–96 2 A. A. Thomson, *Hirst and Rhodes* (The Epworth Press, 1950), p. 37 3 R. J. A. Massie, *Bowling* (NSW Cricket Association, 1926), p. 16

Chapter 11

Swing and spin-swerve join forces

We have seen that when the ball diverts the air stream it will experience a force in the opposite direction. This diversion can be caused by the seam or other surface roughness or by spin. A combination of effects is possible. For example, in fig. 31a the outswing results from the air being diverted to the right behind the ball, in addition to which the top-spin diverts the air upwards. The combination results in air being diverted upwards to the right and the ball being pushed down to the left.

Downward force is of great potential worth in the bowler's armoury, since it makes the ball drop shorter than expected. Upward *movement* could never occur against the force of gravity, although the upward *force* is present. The upward Robins Force on a ball curving down under gravity is, in fact, the most subtle of all Robins Effects. It is worthy of close attention from the bowlers, and, because of its effect of making the ball carry on further before landing, even closer attention from the batsman.

How much does the Robins Force cause the ball to deviate in the air? The forces shown in figs 27, 28 and 29 appear fairly small compared to swing forces. However, since spin is more often applied to slow or medium-pace deliveries which therefore have longer flight times, the Robins Force has more time in which to produce an effect. Taking the behaviour of the new four-piece ball in fig. 27b as an example, and selecting a spin rate of 12.5 revs/sec, the calculated sideways movement, assuming a delay of 0.1 sec before the force operates, is approximately 9.1 in (23 cm) for a speed of 45 mph, 9.8 in (25 cm) for a speed of 67 mph and 5.9 in (15 cm) for 36 mph. These figures apply to a ball carrying "pure" side-spin as in fig. 30a and d. It is not an easy delivery to bowl as it requires the arm to be near vertical, and the hand bent back at the wrist at the moment of release with a leg- or off-break type of action.

A much more likely version of the side-spun ball is the one in fig. 30b or e. Here the axes of spin, instead of being vertical, are tipped over to one side. The force acts in the directions of the arrows. For the leg-break action, a and b are producing side-spin-swerve and c has the addition of dipping top-spin. For the off-break, d and e produce away-serve and f represents part away-swerve and part floating back-spinner.

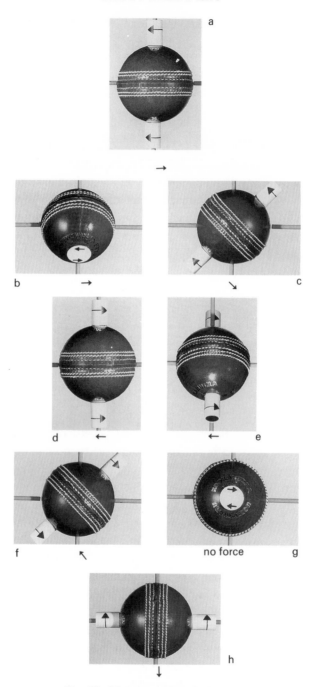

Fig. 30 *Directions of the Robins Force*
causing spin-swerve for various directions
of spin. Arrows show direction of force.
Balls *b* and *e* will also swing downwards.

It would be futile to attempt calculations of the amount of swerve and dip associated with these deliveries, because the possible angles and spin rates can vary so much. However, the underlying principles are not difficult to grasp. Any bowler neglecting them will be denied access to one of the most fascinating and productive areas in the art of bowling. Rather than complaining at having to cope with wind, bowlers should learn to exploit the increased possibilities it makes available both for Robins Effects and swing.

When the axis of spin is horizontal, there is no sideways Robins Force; but even without it there remains swing, dip and turn – potentially a most useful combination. The ball carrying top-spin to make it dip, but not "pure" top-spin (since the tyre on the wheel is pointing towards the slips), is an example. This means that a certain fraction of the spin will go towards making the ball break from leg to off when it lands. Added to this, the delivery is an out-swinger since the seam is pointing in that direction. We therefore have an outswinging, down-dipping leg-break. Although this ball is not widely known and not recorded in any of the literature that I have read, I have noticed it occurring with my own leg-breaks occasionally. Fig. 31*a* tells the story.

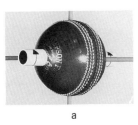

Fig. 31 Photo *a* is an *outswinging leg-break with top-spin,* causing it to dip downwards; *b* is an *inswinging off-break, also with top-spin.*

a   b

If an off-spin bowler, or more easily a left-hand chinaman bowler, delivers his version of that ball as in fig. 31*b*, it is an inswinging, down-dipping off-break. This is an exact description of Ian Peebles's googly which is recorded as having both *swung* in and *turned* in from off to leg.

Each of these two interesting deliveries has three barbs with which to sting the batsman. If, for any reason, one of the barbs is missing – say for instance, the wicket is not taking much spin – the other features remain to provide interest.

The pair of deliveries discussed above combine swing, Robins dip and turn. Another interesting pair, well known to bowlers of all speeds for a century or more, but not now developed as a skill by modern bowlers, is similar. This second pair differs in the sense that it carries the back-spin normally associated with medium and fast bowling, and has inward or outward Robins swerve to accompany the swing.

Fig. 32*a* is an inswinging leg-break which will "carry" a little further up

a   b

Fig. 32 *Left:* an *inswinging leg-break with back-spin. Right: an outswinging off-break with back-spin.* The Robins Force is upwards in both cases.

the pitch before landing as a result of the upward Robins Force. Fig. *32b* is an outswinging off-cutter which also experiences upward Robins Force. Whereas the first pair (fig. 31) swing in the same direction as their turn off the wicket, the second (fig. 32) swing one way and turn the other, making a more deadly pair.

In actual practice it is unlikely that any of the four deliveries discussed is quite as "pure" as depicted in the diagrams. All four are likely to have received a certain amount of side-spin at the moment of delivery. The axes, instead of being horizontal, are all tipped over a little as in fig. 33. Applying the basic principles, we can describe why each of these deliveries is a worthy

Fig. 33 *Off-breaks and leg-breaks.* Off-breaks: *a* with top-spin, *c* with back-spin, both with a certain amount of side-spin. Leg-breaks: *b* and *d* similarly carry top-spin (*b*) and back-spin (*d*), both with a little side-spin.

addition to the bowler's art by consulting the table below which outlines the way in which the deliveries in fig. 33 behave.

	a	b	c	d
Swing	In and down	Out and down	Out and down	In and down
Robins Forces	Out and down	In and down	Out and up	In and up
Turn on landing	In (off-break)	Out (leg-break)	In (off-break)	Out (leg-break)

The results from swing are best appreciated if it is realised that the wake in all the four cases is diverted upwards and therefore the swing is always downwards. Inswing (*d*) and outswing (*c*) is aided by the Robins in-swerve or out-swerve in both cases; but in *a* and *b* the Robins Forces oppose the sideways swing.

The relative strength of the swing force compared to the Robins Force depends on the state of the ball, the angles used and the amount of spin. With a new ball the swing would predominate, but the great S. F. Barnes, using the types of delivery shown in *a* and *b*, with the axes of spin probably tilted further back than shown in these photographs, was effective with any ball, old or new. All four balls illustrated in fig. 33 have the axes of spin tipped down at the back to obtain sideways Robins swerve, but it must be realised that if tipped over to any great amount, the ball will be less likely to land on the stitching than on the smooth leather, in which case the valuable turn off the pitch will be lost. Swing and Robins swerve on their own are useful of course, both as variations and as stock balls. In practising these it is useful to look at the mark on the ball after each delivery to find out its position on landing.

As counsel for the defence, pleading on behalf of those legions of batsmen, victims of the inswinging, in-swerving (no difference if you are on the receiving end) leg-break, or the out-moving off-break, none would be more convincing than Alec Bedser and Don Bradman, as described earlier, at the Adelaide Oval in 1947. Bradman, bowled by Bedser for a duck, describes this ball – which was delivered towards the off stump, swung late to pitch on the leg stump, then spun back off the pitch to take the off stump – as the best he ever received. Only the great are allowed to get away with tales like that, but what better example than this famous delivery for every bowler to study and master?

Of the deliveries illustrated in fig. 33, which one matches Bedser's famous ball? Since it turned from leg to off on pitching it must be either *b* or *d*. Was the inward curve in the air from off to leg, the result of swing or spin-swerve or both? If it was *b* then we would need to assume that the Robins Force inwards was stronger than the outswing. We know that Bedser spun that ball as for a leg-break. Ball *d*, although nicely positioned to swing in and swerve in, would be impossible to bowl with that type of action. Ball *b*, perhaps with the axis of spin tipped a little further down at the back than shown here, must be more likely. If this analysis is correct, Bradman was beaten not by inswing and leg-spin, but by in-swerve and leg-spin.

Fred Trueman, with characteristic frankness and in perfect agreement with Bernard Hollowood, vividly underlines the uncertainty as to whether all, some or none of the potential deviating influences associated with the delivery illustrated in fig. 32*b* will actually take effect:

> Time and again I have pitched what I believed to be the perfect out-swinger on the leg stump only to see it whisked away for four as the ball went straight through. At other times, with equal certainty, I have aimed that same outswinger at the off stump only to see it come nipping back off the pitch to hit the leg stump while the batsman shakes his head in astonishment and the fielders congratulate me on bowling the unplayable ball. And all the time I am wondering how it happened! That is how I have come to develop a fireproof philosophy about cricket. I take whatever comes my way as my due right, for I have discovered over the years that the unexpected is commonplace.[1]

In this chapter we have unravelled the way in which swing, spin-swerve and turn off the pitch, those wonderful servants of the skilful bowler, can act together. Such a fascinating story shows up the commonly used term "seaming" as little more than a cloak for ignorance of what is really happening.

REFERENCES

1 F. Trueman, *Freddie Trueman's Book of Cricket* (Pelham Books, 1964), p. 37

Chapter 12

Coming to terms with over-arm

AS A RESULT OF THE LEGALISATION OF OVER-ARM BOWLING IN 1864, scoring runs generally became easier. A similar peak in run-scoring accompanied the change from under-arm to round-arm in the 1820s. Perhaps batsmen adjust more readily than bowlers.

An historian[1] of the period regards the low scoring in the later round-arm period as due to the high number of deliveries wide of the wicket being difficult to score from, or at least difficult to score from with safety. The hand coming across the line of flight during delivery is a natural problem with round-arm bowling in any case, particularly since round-arm bowlers usually bowled around the wicket to avoid hitting the umpire. Over-arm, although it posed the additional problems of greater pace and bounce, at least involved an arm action which was more or less in line with the path of the ball.

If bowlers needed any stimulus to come to terms with their newly granted powers, a certain gentleman named W. G. Grace (1848–1915) was there in 1865 and still there in 1908, during which time he must have given at least those bowlers determined enough to fight back plenty of reasons to look for better ways of plying their trade. W. G. himself played a not insignificant role in this development by means of his own bowling, as we shall see later.

Effective spinning from above the head took some time to develop. Spin bowlers, fast and slow, commonly take years to learn to control a new delivery. They will understand the problems which faced bowlers of the 1860s and 70s.

Nevertheless, some outstanding bowlers played during that period. Cambridgeshire was one of the strongest counties during the 1860s. Its greatest bowler and one of the best in the country, who played for them in the years 1857–61, was W. (Billy) Buttress (1827–1866) who bowled vicious leg-breaks at medium pace, and has been called the father of leg-break bowling.[2] Since generations of under- and round-arm bowlers had already demonstrated great skill in turning the ball from the leg, it would be more correct to nominate Buttress as the father of over-arm leg-break bowling. Brown ale got the better of Buttress and death ended his career when he was only forty-one.

Tom Emmett (1841–1904) of Yorkshire, another bowler of the 1860s, who bowled a ball round-arm that whipped sharply from leg to off, was a left-hander, inaccurate at times, but often unplayable.

Over-arm bowling came of age at the hands of Frederick Spofforth (1853–1926). Spofforth, an Australian, was an under-arm bowler as a boy but changed when he saw George Tarrant bowling for George Parr's visiting English team in 1863–4. He experimented with various types of spin in his twenties, and consulted a university professor about the reason for the ball "curling" in the air, only to be told it was impossible!

As well as bowling off- and leg-spin at pace, he bowled what was described as "vertical spin", which must have been the ball we describe today as a top-spinner. He also bowled a ball which dropped far shorter than the batsman expected. Although this is how a top-spinner would behave, it is described as an additional ball and therefore most likely the result of a clever change of pace.

Spofforth is generally credited with having introduced true, high, over-arm bowling into England in 1882. His pace was the subject of a good deal of argument. Some said he was medium or even slow-medium, but the truth was that although he was capable of real pace, he often modified it in order to get the best out of the prevailing conditions, and employ his other skills.

George Lohmann (1865–1901) was inspired by Spofforth. For eight years he was the most successful bowler in England, capturing over 200 wickets in each of the three seasons 1888–90. H. S. Altham describes him as follows:

> We have the testimony of both W. G. that C. B. Fry that Lohmann was the best medium-paced bowler they had ever met, a combined verdict, it will be noticed, that embraces half a century. In an age still wedded to the formalism of length, he was the first English bowler really to master the revolutionary lessons of Spofforth, and to make length the handmaid of variety in pace and spin and flight. He was on the slow side of what we now call medium; he could break the ball back as he chose from the off, could bowl a leg-break at will, and always had in reserve the ball that looked like spinning but went straight on. But subtlety of flight was his greatest asset; with his very high delivery he was always dipping short of what the batsman expected; he could suck him out with his held-back slow ball, or get him driving at the half-volley which somehow "swam" on into a yorker.[3]

In one respect however, Lohmann may not be the best model for a bowler aspiring to a long life at the crease. In Altham's words: "His whole heart was in the game, which indeed, he loved not wisely but too well, crowding into thirteen years more work than even his magnificent physique could stand".[4]

Another medium-pacer who could spin the ball both ways was H. F. Boyle

(1847–1907) who had good length and flight, and played in 10 Tests between England and Australia in the period 1878–85. On his first tour of England he took 250 wickets at very low cost. His figures for twelve Tests are 1,732 balls and 32 wickets at an average of 20.03; first class by any standard.

Schoolboy leg-spinners, collecting a rich harvest from among their fellows, are not uncommon. A. G. Steel (1858–1914) was one of the few who carried on with spectacular success into first class cricket. In his first year out of school (1878), he took 164 wickets at 9.60 apiece, and was described as:

> slow, yet fast enough to make jumping out to him a matter of great difficulty, he could alter it at will, and had quite a fast ball in reserve. He was a master of the short half-volley, the slow bowler's best length ball, and he could spin the ball either way, though favouring the leg-break.[5]

"Short half-volley" is a term not used these days, but one which aptly describes the ball carrying enough top-spin to make it drop a little shorter than expected.

Pitches were not as well prepared as today. As a truer measure of a bowler's ability it is preferable to use Test match performances, which generally take place on better surfaces. Steel played thirteen Tests, bowled 1,404 balls and took 29 wickets at an average of 20.86; excellent figures. His effective career was no more than eight years and by 1885 he was a spent force. Whatever the reasons for his decline we can be sure that batsmen were learning. The English batsmen certainly had no trouble with the Australian leg-spinner Harry Trott who in 24 Tests (1888–98) took only 29 wickets.

Two notable fast bowlers of the period were the Surrey pair, T. Richardson (1870–1912) and W. H. Lockwood (1868–1932). Richardson, with splendid physique, a high action, sheer pace, and an off-break produced by body turn with a cross sweep of the arm to the off side, showed a great sense of fair play in moderating his pace if the wicket was dangerous or when he had hit a batsman. The reader should be reminded that the "sweep of the arm" referred to in the literature is not necessarily a guarantee of any particular result. As discussed earlier, it is the final release process that matters. Lockwood was less consistent, but an inspired bowler on his day, with a great break-back, bounce and control of a well disguised slow ball. Arthur Mold was another fast man at that time with a devastating break-back, who after eleven years in Test and county cricket was banned as a thrower. Prominent slow bowlers were the left-handers Briggs, Peate, and Tyler, and Flowers who was an off-spinner.

In terms of the technical evolution of bowling, the latter years of the century were something of a mixture. Right-hand leg-spin had been on the scene since Buttress in the 1860s, and its left-handed mirror image – the chinaman – was first bowled by Edward Barratt (1844–1890) in the 1870s. But in spite of the success of Charles Townsend, leg-spin was almost a forgotten art. Leg-spin of the fast and medium variety had declined with the departure of Spofforth and Lohmann. The leading fast bowlers appear to have relied only on break-back from the off. However, some fine exponents of non-chinaman left-hand leg-spin were on the scene, and some even more famous exponents were about to appear.

John Barton King (1873–1965) was perfecting the inswinger. King, whose career coincided with the prominence of Philadelphia in the cricket world, was better known by sight in England than any other American. He was fast and accurate, keeping his good form for twenty years from 1893 to 1912 against touring teams, including Australian national sides in the USA, and on three tours with Philadelphia in England.

If faster leg-spin had declined, a figure capable of filling a proud place in the lineage of this the most effective of all bowling skills was about to emerge: he was Sidney Francis Barnes. Exploitation of the Robins Force, following experiment at the hands of George Hirst, a true over-arm successor to Noah Mann, was about to bring spin-swerve to the fore again. Barnes and Hirst were soon to display the fine fruits of their labours, and in a sense, the labours of all bowlers from the time the ball was "pitched" rather than bowled along the ground.

REFERENCES

1 R. Bowen, *Cricket, A History of its Growth and Development Throughout the World* (Eyre and Spottiswoode, 1970), p. 104   **2** H. S. Altham, *A History of Cricket*, Vol. 1 (Allen and Unwin, 1962), p. 102   **3** ibid., p. 173   **4** ibid., p. 173   **5** ibid., p. 146

Chapter 13

Hitting the turf: for better or worse

THE PITCH – GOOD, BAD OR INDIFFERENT – makes cricket the game it is. Earth – bare or grassy, hard or soft, crumbling or sticky, rough or smooth, wet or dry, cracked or continuous, constant or changing – is something that plastic, the synthetic brew from the chemist's pot, will never be. A major part of cricket's fascination comes from the soil. On any other surface cricket acquires an element of predictability, ceasing to be the unique game it has been for more than two centuries.

Players of a game which is founded in turf and lives on turf, cannot avoid the task of deciding what they want from turf, and ensuring that they get it. Turf culturists can select soil and grass, groundsmen can attend seminars, use fertilisers, cut and roll, kill weeds and worms, monitor and control moisture; but in spite of all this expertise, the results too frequently disappoint.

Lord's, by 1876, had ceased to be kept in order by weekly flocks of sheep, and the playing area was described as being "in faultless condition". W. G. Grace was by then well into his stride and the mainly single digit scores of the Hambledon men began to be replaced by large numbers all over the world. Australia made 551 against England in the Oval Test in 1884 and England replied with 346, no less than eighteen bowlers being used in these two innings. We can be pretty sure that the wicket was "good" but unless we know more details, which would allow us to decide whether or not it allowed all concerned to exercise the whole range of skills which are possible in cricket, "good" is meaningless.

What is a "good" pitch and how do we go about making one? I am not at all sure that we agree on the first part of the question and I am certain that if the pitches we play on at all levels these days are the measure, then we know little about the second. The present discussion addresses both of these factors. Good cricket is the aim.

The great English captain and batsman A. C. MacLaren (1871–1944), interviewed in his later years, was in no doubt about pitches:

> I feel very much that the bowler has been badly treated ever since the groundsman has taken to doping the wicket. That robs the bowler of fifty per cent of his skill. There is no life in the wicket, it's as dead as it

can be; the batsman has only got to keep his bat straight, the ball comes off slowly; if it turns it's just as easy to play a slow-turning ball as a straight one. I'd like to see a return to the natural wicket and shorter Test matches – where it forces the batsman to play a more lively game.[1]

The book *Great Bowlers and Fielders*[2] gives us a close look at the methods of the leading English, Australian and South African bowlers of that era. Of the thirteen right-hand medium-pacers, ten broke the ball from the off, seven broke it from the leg and six broke it both ways as well. The terms off-break and leg-break have been omitted from the previous sentence because we have got into the habit of using them in a somewhat rigid way which is unhelpful to the present discussion. Fry's categories, incidentally, were fast, fast-medium, medium, slow-medium and slow. Among these was displayed an impressive range of skills – left- and right-hand, swing, swerve and spin.

We must assume that all of these various bowlers chose, learned and perfected their particular style because it brought them success. Today's bowlers seek success by different means, success in this case being partly redefined by limited-over cricket as not necessarily requiring the bowler to take wickets! If we agree that bowlers of all types, displaying the entire range of skills, will make cricket a better game, then the past can teach us that it is not only slowish bowlers who should be using spin as one of their main weapons.

The misunderstanding of spin at pace is widespread. Derek Underwood saw fit to write in italics the statement *"I am not a cutter."*[3] Alec Bedser likewise drew attention to the fact that the famous ball with which he bowled Don Bradman in Adelaide in 1947 was *not cut* but *spun* with his fingers.

We are wrong therefore to lament the decline of slow bowling and ignore the decline of spinning skills in faster bowlers. The destinies of slow spin and fast spin are inextricably linked; where one has gone in the past fifty years, so has the other; conditions unfriendly to one are also unfriendly to the other; wickets unhelpful to slow spin bowling have profoundly affected a major proportion of the entire range of bowling arts.

And why have we meekly accepted the notion that wickets must not take spin early in a game? Do batsmen run the game, and if so, don't they want a contest? Chris Cowdrey, captain of Kent and England, discussing the possibility of increasing the power of umpires over the quality of pitches, chose as a hypothetical situation the following example: "If the pitch is so obviously devoid of grass that the ball might turn excessively on the first day, they should authorise a new wicket to be prepared".[4] Coming from a country where the skill of spin at all paces is in sad decline, and where spin plays little part in the game at any stage, early or late, such remarks from one of England's leading cricketers may be giving us a valuable insight into a particular way of thinking, and one of the very reasons for that decline. The established practice today is probably better described by omitting the word "excessively" from Cowdrey's description. Even the most cursory reading of cricket history tells us that spin has played a part, right from the first hours of many of its more memorable games.

Vic Marks, another Englishman, appears to have capitulated completely in a book curiously titled *A Guide to Better Cricket*: "Spinners are a vulnerable breed. Their best deliveries can be hit to the boundary, and it is important to come to terms with this sad fact".[5] Fortunately there are signs that the cricket world doesn't accept such a defeatist attitude and its not too subtle implication that spin may now be nothing more than an embarrassment, any more than they are prepared to believe another statement Marks makes in the same publication: "The advent of so much limited-overs cricket has not altered the bowler's main aim, which is to dismiss the batsman".

When Norman Gifford says "You can't afford to leave the ball hanging in the air these days"[6], his remarks are interpreted by some as a tribute to modern batting ability. Other explanations include the wish of batsmen to get a few runs during a respite from fast bowling. I would doubt that Gifford himself would indulge in this kind of reasoning because he, like all spinners and all batsmen, knows that when the hanging ball lands on many modern pitches it does little to worry even the most mediocre slogger. If it did spin and bounce, the heavy bat, which is one more "explanation" sometimes trotted out to explain the demise of spin, would become a distinct liability when adjustment was called for. Bradman used a very light bat.

Bishen Bedi, the great Indian left-hand spinner, interviewed in 1990, blames one-day cricket for the dearth of class spinners in modern-day Test cricket. Even in India and Pakistan, the traditional strongholds of spin, standards have been adversely affected by "this one-day rubbish".

> In one-day cricket spin bowlers bowl flat, rather than use flight and spin. There is very little skill involved, just containment. It is difficult for spinners to adjust from one-dayers to Tests, though some can do it. But most use the same tactic – containment – in Tests as in limited overs.[7]

Bedi lamented this trend: "Spin bowling in Test cricket should be about skill and a battle of wits with the batsman." Another drawback of one-day games, he said is "if a bowler gets five wickets, he doesn't get any credit. They say the batsmen got themselves out. One-day cricket has always been a batsman's game".

When we read that pitches are "doubtful", "suspect", "deteriorating", "substandard" or "minefields", it is worth reserving a little scepticism and allowing for the possibility that those writers are rather too well conditioned into accepting as normal the current anti-spin environment. A similar mind automatically takes the view that a country providing pitches that take spin indulges in somewhat unfair tactics to suit their own bowlers. Should not a well balanced team sent to tour that country possess bowlers able to exploit pitches of all sorts?

What are we to make of the widely held view that a good pitch should help the new ball bowler a little early in the game, become fairly plumb in the middle stages, and take some spin towards the end? Cricket history fortunately refuses to capitulate to such a restricted view. Pitches responding early at least to some spin encouraged not only slow bowlers, but also the great medium and fast spinners, to display their skills. Good batsmen rose to the challenge and the contest was played at a level of intense interest.

Perhaps this modern view succumbs to the influence of technology, demanding a uniform, standardised and certified product. Perhaps professional batsmen making runs for a living have had a greater influence on the game than we realise.

The one-day professional game extends the production-line philosophy even further. No progressive alteration of the pitch whatsoever is allowable, with two beginnings, two middles, and two ends, all on the one day! Acceptable conditions for the one-day game, as defined by the commercial backers, are so critically narrow that the use of a totally predictable artificial surface has been suggested.

A bowler hoping to put "real work" on the ball must grip it firmly with the fingers and increase the pressure on it as the arm comes over. Many bowlers grip a worn ball better during this action than they do a shiny ball. Balls wear less today both on pitches and on out-fields which are generally regarded as being less abrasive than in the early years of the century. However, for some the stitching compensates and supplies an adequate grip, provided it is not flattened. At least in this respect the greater height at which the threads are said to stand out from the modern ball is appreciated by spinners, fast and slow, in spite of its role in also aiding those with more modest skills such as the so-called "seamers".

Although an adequate hold on the ball is an essential prerequisite to the application of spin, there is another even more important factor which can considerably reduce the powers of a Hadlee or a Qadir, and, for lesser bowlers, make the task not even worth attempting. I refer to the grip of the ball on the pitch. Unless the ball and pitch can lock together to some extent during their fleeting contact, much of the sweat and courage that goes into putting a spinning cricket ball into the air is wasted. The Robins Force on its own may promise a little consolation but spin-swerve, because it usually sends the ball in the opposite direction, will always work best in combination with turn off the pitch.

Friction is the word; or more correctly, *kinetic friction* – the grip of one surface for another moving relative to it. Just as the friction of tyres on the road allows us to turn without sliding off at corners, so does the friction between ball and pitch allow the ball to change direction off the pitch in response to the skill of the bowler.

"Friction", "grip", "bite", whichever word is chosen, is therefore one of the basic physical processes determining whether or not the bowler is adequately armed in his duel with the batsman. Since all bowlers, strictly speaking, apply spin of one sort or another to the ball, we are closing in on a factor of profound significance for the entire game, and one which will repay examination.

High speed photographs[8] of cricket balls on impact with the ground show deformation, not only of the ball, but also of the ground, even though the pitch was hard. The ball is seen to produce a saucer-shaped depression somewhat elongated in the direction of travel (fig. 34). The bounce is not from a flat surface but from the sloping face, nearest the batsman, of this shallow depression. All other things being equal, the faster the ball, the deeper the depression and the greater the area of contact of ball with pitch. For this reason, the fast and medium-pace so-called "seamers" get more turn from their spin on damp pitches.

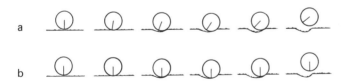

Fig. 34 *The ball in contact with the pitch: a with grip (high friction), b without grip (low friction). In a the ball acquires forward-spin during contact but in b it merely slides.*

In fig. 34 two situations are illustrated: balls bowled without spin on two pitches, one supplying high friction and the other none. The diagrams can be taken as applying both to resilient surfaces, where the only sign of the ball's contact is perhaps a red mark, and to soft pitches where a shallow indentation remains.

In fig. 34*a* (high friction), the ball comes off with top-spin, because its bottom has "caught" on the pitch while the top rolls over it. The acquired spin is the source of the unusual behaviour sometimes exhibited by cricket balls after bouncing. This torment of wicket-keepers, and a source of error for batsmen playing shots off the back foot, will be discussed later.

In fig. 34b the ball skids throughout with no change of spin. Friction is a two-way affair. If the high friction surfaces make the non-spinning balls spin forwards, then spinning balls will push at some angle against the surface, and in turn themselves experience a push at some angle. Nature says that action and reaction are equal and opposite. If the bottom of the ball is spinning towards the leg (off-break) and is gripped by the ground, the ball will turn towards the leg. If the bottom is turning towards square-leg (leg-break), the ball will turn towards the off. If the ball carries top-spin, the bottom of the ball is moving back towards the bowler and the ball will experience a push forwards. But this does not mean that it will necessarily come on to the batsman quicker; top-spin, especially against the wind, makes the ball approach the ground at a steeper angle due to drag and the Robins Force, thus reducing the forward momentum. Since it nosedives into the ground, we must also consider the effect of this on the bounce.

If the bounce of the pitch is poor, then the dipping top-spinner will not only have lost its forward momentum, but also its upward momentum, and will die without a whimper. Bowled with the wind however, where the trajectory will be flatter, a top-spinner will come on to the bat quicker than an unspun ball. This is one way in which a spinner, though being required to discard the wind which is an ally on bouncy pitches, can bowl with the wind and fight back to some extent against the slow pitches on which we play most of our cricket these days.

If the bottom of the ball is moving forwards (back-spin) the ball will experience a backward push. Here again we must not assume that it will come on to the batsman slower. The Robins Force, for back-spin especially against the wind, encourages a jet-fighter-type landing rather than the helicopter-type landing of the top-spinner. But the back-spinner, if delivered at a slow pace and flighted to drop near the batsman, may, on pitches that grip, have less forward momentum after landing than a top-spinner. Nevertheless, back-spin at any pace can sometimes produce quite gratifying (for the bowler!) kicks as the backward pushing friction fights against the forward moving ball. The frequency and severity of these kicks will depend on the state of the surface, a subject which will require us to look more closely at friction and bounce. Since back-spin, pure or angled, is the spin not only of flippers but of seamers, left-hand leg-spinners and much off-spin, we are discussing a very widely used effect.

It would be wrong, however, to attach too much importance to applied spin when discussing how quickly or slowly the ball leaves the pitch. A little simple arithmetic tells us that the surface of a spinning ball (say, 10 revs/sec) is moving around the circumference at 5 mph, which is small compared to the speed of the ball through the air. Nevertheless, the effect does operate and, in the sideways direction, is in fact the very source of turn.

A medium-pace delivery travelling at 56 mph and making a mark on the pitch which is, say, 1.6 in (4 cm) in length, is in contact with it for only 1.6 thousandths of a second. A number of events take place during that time, which we can list as follows.

1. The ball begins to push downwards and forwards on the surface. Frictional forces gripping the bottom of the ball slow it down and increase the forward-spin relative to the spin which was applied to it. It may not be spinning forwards (yet) because it may have arrived with back-spin, but the back-spin will be decreased. If it arrived with forward-spin, that spin will be increasing. If it arrived with side-spin, then that spin will be decreasing because it is giving up its energy towards pushing the ball sideways.

2. The ball begins to flatten somewhat at the impact point.

3. The surface of the wicket begins to spring down (strongly) and forwards (less strongly) and, in the case of leg- or off-spin, to the side (less strongly).

4. If the surface is soft due to dampness, then at least some of the early events involve flow of material away from the point of impact to the sides and the front of the ball. Flow may then be followed by spring if the moist layer is a thin cover over harder material.

5. The ball pushes forwards and downwards into the deepest part of the temporary or permanent depression it is forming. Friction forces are increasing and reach a maximum when the ball is at the bottom and pushing against the wall of the depression nearest the batsman. Flattening of the ball itself is also at maximum at about this point.

6. Both the compressed ball and compressed soil now begin to spring back and push the ball up into the air, a process greatly helped by the ball glancing up off the sloping face of the depression.

What can we take out of all this that will improve cricket? Two factors operate which can make or break the game; friction and rebound. Friction is a surface property; oil on lubricated surfaces may be only a few molecules thick. Spring or rebound, which for our purposes must be as quick as possible, is the property of quite a depth of material lying below the surface. Moisture affects both properties.

Common experience tell us that certain combinations of materials exhibit low friction, i.e. a shoe on a banana skin. But I am not so sure that bowlers are alert to those surfaces that bring them equally catastrophic results. New Zealand and Pakistan played a Test at the Basin Reserve in Wellington in 1989. The pitch was well rolled and quite hard. The damp weather prior to the game had affected preparation and the pitch may have been a little slower than intended. In other words, it shaped up as a normal pitch, except on one count, beside which all the others paled into insignificance; it was completely covered by a thin carpet-like layer of grass recently growing on the pitch, but now dead-looking and brown in colour, not thick enough to affect the feel of it as a hard wicket, but fatal to any hope that the ball might grip on that surface. The result was a boring draw, in which bowlers – fast, medium or slow – on neither side were allowed to demonstrate their skills, a game which is widely regarded as having done harm to the popularity of cricket in New Zealand.

Shortly after this match the teams played a one-day game on an adjacent strip which was covered with dead brown grass as for the Test. In the sense that the surface provided all the conditions that suit batsmen – it was flat and what little grass there was was dead – this one-day pitch was ideal. The time is past when under these conditions we can deceive ourselves that the skill of spin – fast, medium or slow – plays a significant role in any but a small proportion of the many games of commercial one-day cricket. Sadly, by accident or design, this philosophy spilled over and ruined a Test match.

When India toured New Zealand in 1990 this same type of brown grass surface mat was seen on most pitches. Fifteen hundred runs were made for the loss of only twenty-five wickets during the five days of the last Test at Auckland. Some spectacular batting was seen, but in the end it resembled nothing so much as five one-day games in a row. Spin, fast or slow, played no part in the game. The admirable skills of the Indians in swinging the ball both ways and the hostility of New Zealander Danny Morrison were ulti- mately ineffective. The bowlers, who included Hadlee and Hirwani, were unable to play a significant role. Media commentators, unaware of the real problem, criticised the New Zealand captain John Wright, already one up in the series, for not contriving a close finish. Given the conditions, there was no reason why runs could not have been churned out for another week. A year later Sri Lanka played New Zealand on the Basin Reserve. Apart from the first day – when grass stems and soil were a little damp – the bat domi- nated totally and run records galore were broken. Aravinda da Silva, John Wright, Andrew Jones and Martin Crowe batted admirably but such a pitch requires that our praise for them be somewhat muted.

One way leading to such a dismal surface is regular rolling without cutting the grass and without finally removing the thin carpet of dead-looking grass that remains. Congratulations to groundsmen for having produced, by this method, a hard pitch with good wearing properties, are sadly misdirected. Only the removal of most of this gripless covering will help bring about at least the surface quality of a good pitch. The image of a billiard ball being bowled onto an oil slick suggests the reality underlying much of today's cricket.

It is instructive to rub a cricket ball over the surface of a pitch, while pressing down fairly hard on it; a simple test which separates the "slippers" from the "grippers". Grass, normally present on pitches, plays a number of roles. In binding soil, it plays some role in rebound, as well as preventing break-up. Deep-rooted living grass can draw moisture out of the pitch from considerable depths and thus influence its mechanical properties. Under dry conditions grass dries out quickly, as seen on summer lawns and cricket pitches, but the apparent death is quickly revived by watering. Such "dead" grass, with most of its stems lying out flat through rolling, is like an efficient lubricating bed under a cricket ball.

In spite of their best intentions, turf culturists working on cricket pitch research have recommended procedures not in the interests of good cricket. Good work on obtaining bounce and pace is nullified by the following advice given by one such practitioner.

> Living or dead leaves and grass clippings are good for the surface because they reduce evaporation. A good grass sward is necessary. On match day the grass cover should be incorporated into the pitch surface to produce a glazed shiny surface.[9]

No need to dope the pitch, as was done in 1938 at the Oval to nullify Bill O'Reilly's spin; turf culturists may be on the way to making it official policy!

Friction great enough to satisfy the needs of good cricket will only exist when every particle of the top material is rigidly linked to the ground. Any movable or slippery material – soft or hard – such as grass, stalks in "dead" grass, grass cuttings, living grass in certain forms, sand, wet or not well consolidated soil, destroys grip. For that fraction of a second when the ball is in contact with the ground it merely slides over them or pushes them aside; since they have no firm connection with the ground, these moving materials are unable to return the push and change the direction of the ball.

Living grass should be servant not master. Green grass blades or stems, pressed under the impact of a ball on to a hard pitch surface, are as fatal to grip as anything else: the harder the pitch the worse the effect. Once it has served its desired purpose in binding soil and influencing its moisture content, there is no reason to allow it to remain on the surface and ruin the whole show. Grass, cut very short indeed, with no rolling stems or slippery blades under the ball, and pitches raked to raise flattened grass stems for recutting, and swept clear of all loose material, are an immediately attainable minimum, while we tackle the problem of what lies underneath. If the root structure is healthy, the grass will quickly revive when the strip is spelled. A healthy strip, with good root and stem structure, also implies good wearing qualities which in turn lessens maintenance problems.

Friction also depends on the strength of the soil; there is no point in growing a network of roots and stems only to have them swept aside on impact. The soil therefore needs a good set of properties of its own.

Today's "seamer" depends heavily on delivering a ball so that the stitching catches on tufts of coarse grass growing near small, frequently soft, bare patches. Hitting the front of a tuft facing the bowler, the ball lifts; worse if the soil in front of it is soft enough for it to dig in deeper. Hitting the back of it gives a shooter. Hitting the side produces a seamer-for-no-effort. Such bowling requires less skill than anything else in the repertoire.

The ball itself, being one of the two partners in friction, must not be overlooked. The grip of the stitching on any surface is greater than that of the smooth leather; worn leather is somewhere between. A worn ball, in spite of the bowler's legitimate efforts to maintain the stitches in the original upright condition, often has rather flattened stitching, which will have less grip on the ground than when new. This assumes that the new ball was not one of those in which the stitching was partly submerged under a film of lacquer: such balls are to be avoided.

Bowlers, not only slow bowlers, but all who wish to use real skill, as well as relying on pitches which grip, need also to grip the ball well. When using an old ball it is better that the leather is not shone over its whole area as it merely reduces both of these grips. Captains and others who instruct bowlers to keep shining the ball right through an innings, may in fact be harming the interests of the team if it is shone anywhere near the seam. Only in a limited area in the equatorial bulge on the smooth (non-seam) side of the ball is it worth maintaining shine. A different approach is not to shine the old ball at all and opt for the unpredictable rewards of erratic swing, associated as we saw earlier, with wear.

Balls themselves can affect bounce because they are not all manufactured in the same way. Batsmen should be interested in this because good bounce means good speed off the bat as well. Bounce is an easy property to measure and simple tests can be carried out by dropping the ball from about 10 ft (3 m) and comparing the heights of rebound. Firing balls from a bowling machine is another way. From the batsman's point of view a good paced pitch will be one on which the ball comes on to the bat well, and where he can play strokes.

This is taken to mean that there is a consistency not only in bounce but in the relationship between the pace of the ball through the air and the pace off the pitch. In other words, the pitch must be fairly fast.

No bowler should quarrel with the above criteria. On a fair wicket he has the opportunity to change these various relationships, not by some sort of chance mechanism, but as part of a duel of skills.

Bounce can be a misleading property. Two solid wood table-tennis tables can look identical, yet one may give a good, quick bounce, while on the other it is slow and low. In cricket as in table tennis we look for materials which will store the energy of impact and release as much of it as possible, and as quickly as possible, to send the ball back up again. Bowlers know only too well that a great deal of the energy they put into spin and pace is either dissipated in the soil never to reappear, or else, in the case of spin, it is never applied to the soil in the first place because of lack of friction. Hardness, though obviously required to a reasonable degree, is not the same as springiness.

If we don't seem to have done much to help groundsmen in their task, the reason may be no more than our own confusion about what exactly we want from them. The so-called rollers we provide for them are, in many cases, nothing more than heavy lawn-mowers. We then complain about having to play on what can only be described as unconsolidated earth. Cost conscious organisations should realise that time-economical effective rolling is only possible if rollers are at least as heavy as those which were pushed or pulled across cricket pitches for a hundred years or more.

Why do we admit defeat by accepting that a pitch may only take spin in the latter stages of a game? We want bounce at pace and we want grip. One of the effects of low bounce pitches in England has been to increase the use of the sweep shot. Under proper cricketing conditions such a stroke is a tense and exciting event in the duel between bat and ball, and offers a fair division of rewards for the skills of each party. On a bounceless pitch it is nothing more than a safe round-the-corner slog.

It is not difficult to jot down an agenda for research: find what soil or combination of soils, moisture, grass growth, and what treatment of these, including rolling, gives cricketers what they need. Start from scratch. Soil scientists will be able to say what the various soils are in any locality, but they are likely to be pretty vague about mechanical properties such as bounce. From the cricket point of view, which is a lot more subtle than road building or investigating foundations for buildings, it would be safer to assume that they know next to nothing. Likewise the agronomists: they can grow grass, but the rebound properties of the network of stems and roots are a complex matter.

Nothing said in these pages should be taken as supporting the notion of a uniform type of wicket. Soils and grasses differ throughout the world. I would hope that there will be as many solutions to the problem as there are cricket grounds. I would also hope that if groundsmen are made to cater for the demands of the commercial one-day game, then they must also be given the opportunity of preparing strips, with different grasses and perhaps different soil, for main-stream cricket. Such a remedy, in combination with the particular qualities of local climates, will ensure a fine degree of individual flavour in keeping with the best traditions of the game.

REFERENCES

1 D. R. Allen (ed), *Cricket on the Air* (BBC, 1985), p. 81   2 G. W. Beldam and C. B. Fry, *Great Bowlers and Fielders* (Macmillan, 1906)   3 D. Underwood, *Beating the Bat* (Stanley Paul, 1975), p. 29   4 Chris Cowdrey, *The Cricketer* (October 1988), p. 11   5 Vic Marks, *The Test and County Cricket Board Guide to Better Cricket* (Octopus Books, 1987), p. 66, 96   6 P. Murphy, *The Spinner's Turn* (Dent, 1982), p. 147   7 G. McIvor, Interview with Bedi, *New Zealand Tablet*, February 21, 1990, p. 20   8 C. B. Daish, *The Physics of the Ball Games* (The English Universities Press, 1972), p. 95   9 S. Cameron-Lee and K. W. McAuliffe, "Principles of Pitch Preparation", New Zealand Turf Management Journal, February 1989, p. 18

Chapter 14
Cutting, rolling and spinning

TO READ A RESPECTED SPIN BOWLER AND AUTHOR, Ian Peebles[1], describing Bill O'Reilly's leg-break as having been "rolled" may come as something of a surprise. Perhaps every bowler, written off as "just a roller", will now emerge to stand proudly alongside "The Tiger", especially as Peebles goes on to attach the label "superlative quality" to those same leg-breaks.

We ought to look at some of the other terms used to describe various types of bowling. Does it matter if the language of cricket lacks precision? If Richie Benaud writes a chapter[2] on the "over-the-wrist" bowler, comparing him with one who "merely bowls with his fingers", we all think we know what he means.

Fast bowlers bowl cutters, so we are told; people who had been watching Derek Underwood bowl for twenty years said he bowled cutters too. But as we saw earlier, he himself said he did not bowl cutters. Besides, spinning over the wrist is anatomically impossible. Nearly all bowling is done from above the wrist; some spinners deliver a ball from below the wrist, while others deliver it from alongside the wrist. As for the so-called finger-spinners, are we to assume that off-spinners and "orthodox" left-handers would bowl just as well with their wrists encased in plaster of Paris?

The reader need not fear an extension of this critique into a pedantic excursion through the entire terminology of cricket. I merely wish to point out that bowling is difficult enough without being burdened with language which obscures its true nature. These unnecessary blockages start with a tendency to seal off various types of bowling into separate compartments, when in fact an infinitely more interesting and productive standpoint is to regard all bowling as one basic technique, upon which numerous possible variations may be grafted. If language obscures the methods used by bowlers, then a barrier has been placed between today's cricketers and those of the past, the very best of whom have so often defied categorisation. Why confuse cricketers when clear principles can guide them on any of a thousand journeys of discovery across our sterile boundaries?

There are only two basically different methods for spinning a cricket ball; either it is spun out of a grip involving two opposite sides of the ball, or it is pushed away, as the fingers on one side only move down and/or around the ball against its own inertia (fig. 35). If we are to give names to these, I suggest Nyren's "twist" for the former, and "cut" for the latter.

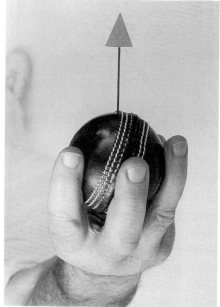

a   **Fig. 35** *Fast and medium-pace off-cutter (left)* and leg-cutter (*right*).   b

Fig. 35 illustrates the fast and medium-pace off-cutter *a* and leg-cutter *b*. In its "pure" form, cutting involves finger movement against one side of the ball without any twist being applied from the other side. Viewed from more or less directly above the hand, we see that the bowler's task is to pull the fingers down off the back of the ball, to the right for an off-cutter, or to the left for a leg-cutter, while at the same time sending it straight off in the direction of the arrow. In *a* the first finger along the stitching will apply most of the back- and side-spin, while in *b* it is the second finger. The angle of the seam to the flight may not appear to be very great in the photos, but it is about 30°. Any larger angle adds to the difficulties of control, since the fingers cutting down along the seam would be required to come down more to the side, while at the same time delivering the ball straight. The two balls are also potential outswingers *a*, and inswingers *b*.

Clarity will be served if these terms are confined to what the bowler does to the ball, rather than what the ball does in the air or on landing. Used that way we are better off than with a phrase such as "He cut the ball from the leg to the off", which is clear on the result but uncommitted on the method. I doubt whether many who make such a statement would be sure that the ball was cut as defined above, rather than twisted. All they could be certain of was that it was spun.

The hand-to-wrist joint is scarcely capable of twisting at all. Press your forearm firmly down on a flat surface with the aid of your other hand, and try to twist the free hand. The limited rotation you obtain is not generated to any significant extent by the wrist, but by the long bones of the forearm moving up and down. The principal movement of the hand at the wrist is not a twisting but a hinged movement in a forward or backward direction. Sideways movement is also possible, but to such a limited extent that it could not play much part in bowling.

What then should the bowler do with the wrist-hinge when preparing to deliver the ball; cock it forwards in a cripple-like inward curl, or bend it back with the palm of the hand facing the sky? Bowlers in fact do both. But whichever they employ, the hand always hinges forwards towards the batsman at the final flick, cunningly concealed slower balls excepted. Therefore, if the inward curl is used, the back of the hand will tend to face the batsman as the hand comes over while unhinging at the wrist, sometimes called "snapping", to give forward momentum during the act of finger movement and forearm hand rotation. This wrist snap is one of the movements that bowlers must now allow to slow down as they become tired. But if the hand is initially bent back at the wrist it must come over with the palm facing the batsman while it flicks forwards in delivery.

The major differences which we have been describing are easily discernible when one watches a bowler in action. They form the basis for the common but erroneous classification of some bowlers as wrist spinners of the leg-break or chinaman type. But such a label is no better than many of the others, because among slow to medium-pace spinners there is a whole spectrum of actions ranging from extreme wrist curling to no curling at all. The faster spinners don't need the inward-coiled hand to gain pace, although some may use it.

Bending the hand back but with the palm now facing the batsman is of course mainly associated with fast bowlers or off-spinners, as an examination of action photographs will show. There is no reason why such a bent position should be adopted at the beginning of the swing as is done by some faster bowlers. More freedom may be experienced if the wrist is bent back nearer the end of the delivery. The inward hand curlers, however, find it easy and convenient to adopt such an attitude early in the swing.

C. S. Marriott recommends the inwardly-cocked wrist to fast bowlers as well as slow.

I strongly recommend crooking up the wrist as you run up. It hides the ball from the batsman, and it will increase the effect of any natural wrist flick you possess as your arm goes over, a most valuable gift because it makes pace off the pitch, not only for spin bowlers, but for fast bowlers as well. E. A. McDonald, who ran up to bowl with his wrist bent up, had the most gorgeous wrist flick at the top of his delivery. There lay the secret of his terrific pace off the wicket. Wrist flick has evidently worked in the same striking way for many of the greatest bowlers: in 1963 we saw a magnificent example of Charlie Griffith, the West Indian. Keith Miller, who himself bowls with a pronounced flick of the wrist, wrote admiringly of Griffith's tremendous pace and lift off the pitch, which he rightly ascribed to his bowling with a "full flick of the hand", which is the same thing exactly.[3]

Marriott's advice as applied to faster bowlers is understandable only if we see three stages in the process; an inward curling, followed by an uncurling prior to but part of the wind-up for a vigorous final flick in which the palm faces the batsman.

Finger movement, combined with the forward hinging of the wrist, would not be capable of generating the amount of spin obtained by the best bowlers were it not for the extensive rotation provided by the forearm and upper arm. The hand, held out, palm upwards in front of the body, should be capable of rotation through at least three-quarters of a circle ($270°$).

When the fingers come down the back of the ball, or somewhat to one side or the other, there are various consequences for swing, swerve and break, which we examined earlier. We have defined this type of action in its purest form as "cut". Spofforth describes "cutting" as "the force that propels the ball on its journey from one side without any twisting action of the fingers", and uses the example of a billiard player cueing the ball on one side to obtain break from the cushion. He goes on to say the "cutting is certainly the more difficult method [than finger-spinning] as without a great deal of practice one is apt to be very inaccurate; but the advantage over finger-spin will repay all those who take the trouble to conquer it".[4] Coming from one of the great thinking bowlers in the history of cricket, this advice which seems to run counter to the modern idea that cutting is easier than spinning by other means at speed, will repay close consideration. Firstly it should not be taken as belittling "finger-spin". On the contrary, Spofforth says that "spinning" the ball, or what is commonly known as break, is the principal means of getting wickets a first class bowler uses, and no one can possibly be a crack bowler unless he can turn the ball.

The fact that Spofforth also regards spinning as easier than cutting must remind modern fast and medium-pace bowlers that, without well developed spinning arts, they are not up to the standards set by the best bowlers of the past. However, Spofforth was not unconscious of the difficulties when he said:

> A certain amount of break is easily acquired. In fact nowadays every bowler, no matter how bad, breaks from both sides, but few do it properly or effectively: the reason for this is that the spin is not in the right direction.[5]

Spofforth's attraction to cutting is undoubtedly connected with his use of it in the more subtle art of concealing change of pace. Speaking of variation he says:

> It is not the slightest use unless you learn to hide it. The sole object of variation is to make the batsman think the ball is slower or faster than it really is. The way to do this is most difficult to put down in writing but very easy to show or acquire. I have always considered the best plan is to hold a small portion of the ball and get the impetus that sends the ball forwards from one side. By doing this your arm will go through the air just as swiftly for a slow ball as for a fast one, which is very apt to mislead the batsman, and it is another advantage that the ball is likely to break.[6]

The "small portion" grip so brilliantly employed by Spofforth and commonly used by modern bowlers (the "half-ball" grip) is never likely to encase much less than half of the ball. Since the ball now lies closer to the wrist than in the normal grip and because there is no way that the fingers can flick down across the back of it at release, the escape route can only be by means of a relatively slow roll out from under the left side of the forefinger. Other grips for change of pace involve holding the ball in or near the palm or, in a version of the baseball pitcher's knuckle ball, releasing it from a grip in which the finger-tips point down into the ball.

Although cut offers possibilities of association with swing, change of pace and a certain amount of movement off the pitch, the latter is quite limited unless the pitch is highly responsive. Common sense tells us that it is impossible to control a ball and apply violent spin, merely by sliding the fingers down the side of it during delivery. Fast and medium-pace bowlers must recognise that some form of twist, using a proper spinner's grip, is the only way to obtain real deviation off good pitches.

Moving away from "pure" cut we enter an area where some degree of "twist" may be present. The phrase "going with the arm", which is often used to describe one such delivery, has admirably served the cause of all-round puzzlement and prepared many a bowler for the unquestioning acceptance of other equally foggy notions.

"Action break" is another vague term used in the early days to designate this delivery. Fry describes action break as:

> ...the result of spin imparted to the ball by the fingers sweeping across the ball as it leaves them: that is to say it does not come from a twist of the ball activated by the fingers apart from the natural delivery.[7]

A definition such as this, which is no different from our definition of cut, is probably too "pure" to be applicable in practice. A degree of twist in the form of roll or finger-spin of some sort is probably present in most arm-balls.

Bowled by a right-hander, the arm-ball curves from leg to off, and from a left-hander, off to leg. Since the arm naturally swings across the body in each of these respective directions during delivery, we see where the phrase originates. But this sweep of the arm does not guarantee that the ball will curve in the same direction. The right-hand leg-spin bowler swings his hand across the body from right to left, but the ball, which is usually delivered with the axis of spin tilted down at the back to some extent, experiences the Robins Force, and does not go with the arm, but in the reverse direction (fig. 36d).

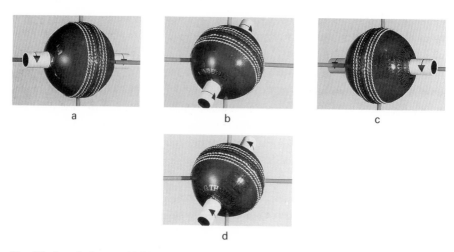

Fig. 36 *Arm-balls;* a and b from the right-hander; c and d from the left-hander; a and c are "pure" swingers with no spin-swerve; b and d will carry spin-swerve only.

The phrase "going with the arm" therefore implies that one or both of the following conditions must be present. One of these for a right-hand bowler is the seam pointing towards the slips (fig 36a) or from a left-hand bowler, to fine-leg (fig. 36c). In other words, nothing more than outswingers or inswingers. The other is a backward-spinning ball with the axis of spin tilted down to the rear on one side, and therefore generating a Robins Force to one side or the other (fig. 36b and d).

Arm-balls are "natural" deliveries only insofar as the hand has a tendency to slide down the right side of the ball, in the case of a right-hand bowler, and the left side in the case of the left-hander. However, the history of cricket tells us that the natural spin, where sharp spin was the aim, was for a right-hander not the off-break but the leg-break.

Bowlers employing arm-balls generally hope to minimise the turn in the reverse direction which may accompany such deliveries. The various degrees of backward rotation (some of which are shown in fig. 36) can be reduced by releasing the ball from fingers splayed out wide on either side of the seam. The technique is the same as that available to faster bowlers and was discussed earlier. Reducing the rotation in this way will generally reduce spin-swerve; therefore any deviation of the arm-ball in the air will derive mainly from swing.

There are two basic ways in which twist rather than cut can be applied to a ball. One is characterised by a release from a grip involving any number of the two to five possible points of contact between the four fingers and the thumb, and the ball. In this case most of the rotation comes from the twisting forearm and upper arm without apparent wrist-hinging or violent change in the position of fingers and thumb relative to each other during release. The other involves obvious wrist-hinging and sharp movement of at least two of the fingers and thumb group relative to each other. A whole spectrum of actions is possible, as the history of spinning reveals.

The interests of good bowling are best served if we resist the temptation to put labels on the two types of twisting described above. Misleading labels are too common in cricket already, and in any case most bowlers who "twist" will probably employ techniques incorporating both of the described methods to varying degrees. The terms "finger-spinners'" and "wrist-spinners" are of no help whatsoever and could be scrapped along with the patently wrong "over-the-wrist" label. The so-called finger-spinners will also rotate the hand while they use their fingers, and the so-called wrist-spinners will use many of the same actions perhaps to a greater degree in most cases. Since the wrist is not a rotating joint but a hinge, the observer watching the so-called wrist-spinner sees wrist movement which really has little to do with spinning but which is a bending and straightening of the hinge, providing mainly forward motion. Fast spinners are not generally described as wrist-spinners, simply because the action of bending and straightening, to the extreme degree shown by slow bowlers, is simply too difficult to carry out quickly enough. In fact, it is quite unnecessary for the faster spinners to indulge in such actions because, for them, the whole complex of finger and arm movements occurs at such a speed that they are able to generate excellent spin with little or no wrist-hinging.

Peebles's description of O'Reilly's leg-break as "rolled" was nothing more nor less than a perceptive way of distinguishing between a wrist-hinger and a non-wrist-hinger. O'Reilly's action was quick enough to provide a more than adequate rotation rate without any other contortions. Peebles' own leg-break at a brisk pace is described as having involved very little bend at the wrist. Alec Bedser, as mentioned earlier, spun his leg-break with twist, not cut.

Another versatile performer, Tom Wass (1873–1953), a genuinely fast bowler who could bowl leg-spin, is described by C. B. Fry as follows:

> He obviously uses his fingers to produce the spin. At present his fast leg-break must be regarded as a curiosity. He turns his hand over as he delivers the ball, somewhat as does the slow leg-break bowler. Bowling at full pace on a good wicket he is sometimes able to impart a genuine finger-spin to the ball, which makes it break from the leg, the width of the wicket: this ball is quite distinct from that which is described as going with the bowler's arm; it is a genuine leg-break.[8]

In spite of Fry's puzzled description of Wass' grip as natural for an off-break, the presence of the first finger on one side and the third finger on the other side, as seen in a photograph of Wass, is none other than the most commonly used grip for leg-spin.

Derek Underwood's protestation *"I am not a cutter"* has also been mentioned earlier. One would hope that his exposure of the profound and widespread misunderstanding of his bowling, which he suffered at the hands of numerous so-called authorities, will go some way towards promoting a more informed appreciation of the bowler's art in future. In his autobiography[9] Underwood says that after two seasons with Kent, in which he bagged a total of 202 wickets (the youngest player to take 100 wickets in a debut season), people began to complain that his bowling style and action were not right. Twelve years and 1,300 wickets later they were still saying it. Such was the criticism, that he was persuaded to try many times to change his action to imitate a classic model.

Because he bowled faster than the classic model, Underwood had difficulty persuading people to regard him as a spinner. It would be difficult to find a more telling demonstration of how some members of the cricket fraternity can lose sight of the rich variety of skills provided by bowlers of the past. Because his attack was not based on flight to lure batsmen down the wicket, he did not regard himself as an "orthodox" spinner, an opinion which prompts me, for this and other reasons, to suggest that the term "orthodox spinner" is meaningless.

Underwood contrasts his freedom from sore and split spinning fingers with the trouble experienced by bowlers who use

> ...violent finger action in order to make the ball turn...I use the word "violent" deliberately because I do give the ball a tweak with my fingers, which is why I say I am not a cutter. At the same time I do employ part of the technique of a cutter by adding to the tweak a dragging motion across the ball as my arm comes over prior to the moment of releasing the ball.[10]

He goes on to describe his bowling as slow to slow-medium left-arm spin. Underwood did not need "violent" finger action; his hand twisted rapidly enough to set the ball rotating at a rate which was at least as great as that of slower action bowlers who were forced to compensate by using an apparently more rapid finger action. I have never read of Bill O'Reilly having finger trouble either.

The fairly narrow range of variations in pace that Underwood employed prompted Mike Brearley to suggest that in Pakistan he should bowl slower to get more turn. Underwood tried this with disappointing results, losing both his turn, his elusive flight and his accuracy. In his account of this, Brearley admitted bewilderment.

> Curiously for so marvellous a spinner, Underwood has always found that he tends to lose so much of his zip when he bowls appreciably slower than usual. His range of pace needs to be small to be most productive.[11]

There is nothing really curious about this at all. My own experience while learning to bowl spin demonstrated vividly during the first few years that the amount of spin was linked to the speed with which my arm came over. It was as if my whole body, from my feet to my fingers, was a machine in which every part worked in a sort of linked precision; slow down one part, such as the arm coming over, and the whole sequence of spinning movements also slowed down, resulting in less spin. With practice I was able to uncouple the spinning movements from the pace-generating movements to some extent in order to be able to bowl a useful range of variations.

The linkage of pace and spin rate must be recognised as an integral part of all spin bowling. Instead of attempting to change Underwood's action, the pundits should have directed their efforts towards providing him and all spinners, fast and slow, with pitches possessing bounce and friction.

REFERENCES

1 E. W. Swanton (ed), *Barclays World of Cricket* (Collins Willow, 1986), p. 218   **2** R. Benaud,

Willow Patterns (Hodder and Stoughton, 1969), p. 173   **3** C. S. Marriott, *The Complete Leg-Break Bowler* (Eyre and Spottiswoode, 1968), p. 46   **4** G. W. Beldam and C. B. Fry, *Great Bowlers and Fielders*, p. 4   **5** ibid., p. 5   **6** ibid., p. 3   **7** ibid., p. 307   **8** ibid., p. 79   **9** D. Underwood, *Beating the Bat* (Stanley Paul, 1975), p. 19   **10** ibid., p. 20   **11** M. Brearley, *The Art of Captaincy* (Hodder and Stoughton, 1985), p. 192

Chapter 15
Coming to grips

THE SEAM PLAYED ONLY A MINOR ROLE in bowling in the period before the First World War. C. J. Kortright (1871–1952), one of the fastest bowlers in the history of the game, interviewed in 1948 said:

> Perhaps one of the greatest differences between modern and old-time bowling lies in the attitude towards the new ball and the method of gripping it. Personally, I didn't worry a great deal about how I held the ball in relation to the seam as long as I got a firm grip on it, and I think most of my contemporaries felt the same. We wanted to be accurate, and to make the ball move a little off the pitch through finger action. For that reason, fast bowlers often roughened a new ball by rubbing it in the dirt, to obtain a good grip. Now bowlers dirty their clothes in efforts to keep the ball shiny, but I feel sure they do not control it so well.[1]

It was not that bowlers were unable to swing the ball in those days, as J. B. King demonstrated with his fast inswingers. Whether the balls they used were made in such a way as to be incapable of swinging as much as today's balls is a question answerable only by finding some century-old new balls and measuring their swing force in a wind tunnel. There is evidence that at least some makes of ball had thinner thread in the stitching than is found on the modern ball. In any case, Kortright and his contemporaries devoted their energies to priming the more enduring weapon of spin at pace.

Why have cricket administrators removed from bowlers the right to improve their grip by rubbing the ball on the ground? When so many factors are stacked up against spin, cricketers should be given the option of doing so. Roughened leather is not only better gripped in the fingers, but is also capable of a better grip on the pitch, a small but nevertheless welcome bonus.

For swing, the grip alone is not in itself sufficient to guarantee success. The various possible positions of the ball at delivery and the consequences of these were set out earlier. The classic coaching book photographs are merely starting points for careful trials to ensure that these angles are maintained after delivery. Depending on the results, the grip is altered to compensate for the distortions introduced by the individual action.

It is not necessary that the ball should actually be seen to swing during these trials. Once the seam is in the right place the bowler can move out into ball-friendly conditions. At least some of the preliminary trials need to be carried out with a reasonably good ball because the fingers sliding down off smooth leather at the moment of delivery will not influence its position to the same degree as when coming off worn leather.

Other skills worth developing in this early stage are the ability to produce a slow seam wobble for experiments with late swing, the whole area of cut and twist, and the skills of change of pace, perhaps involving Spofforth's "small portion" grip mentioned earlier.

Tom Cartwright, a master swing bowler, said:

> The key to all movement of the ball is what you do with your wrist. Above the shoulder it's the only thing I alter each ball. On a wicket which gives some help to bowlers of my type, I reckon to be able to bowl the ball that comes back into the wickets after pitching from outside the off stump at will by pushing the inside part of my wrist through first as I let the ball go while retaining the seam in a vertical position.
>
> If I start bowling and everything doesn't click immediately, I've got eight or nine standard checks I run on my action – rather like a pilot doing a systems test at the end of a runway before taking off. But principally I'm concerned with making sure that my arm is high at the point of delivery and work down the list from there. I can usually do something with the ball either in the air or off the wicket in this country, but swing doesn't get many good players out, in spite of what happened in Massie's Test match at Lord's. That was a rarity.[2]

What better tribute to the attention a bowler gave to that crucial stage in the delivery than R. S. Whitington describing the South African medium-pacer Joe Partridge:

> Often when watching Joe through binoculars I was reminded of a champion rink bowler delivering upside down. Joe released the ball as tenderly and meticulously as any rink bowler, as any trout fisherman casting his fly.[3]

The description of Maurice Tate by John Arlott, also interpreted in the light of the principles we established earlier, shows how brilliantly Tate exploited all the possibilities available to the medium-pacer.

> Bowling into the wind on a heavy seaside morning, he would make the ball dart and move in the air as if bewitched. The inswing and the outswing were there as a matter of course, but, as every man who

batted against him at his best will testify, the ball would sometimes seem to begin to swerve and then straighten again before it struck the ground. Once it pitched, the bound was full of fire and, because Tate was a "long-fingered" bowler, on a green-topped wicket the ball would sometimes strike back in the direction opposite to the swing. That is to say, an outswinger would become, in effect, an off-break off the pitch, or an inswinger a leg-break. Sometimes this happened to his "cutter" because of the tendency of the cut break to swerve; but it could also happen to deliveries which were not "cutters". Tate, of course, like any other swing bowler, could only produce the swing deliberately, the subsequent tricks of the swung ball off the "green 'un" happened, but not within the command of the bowler. When he bowled thus on a green wicket, no batsman in the world was too good to be his victim; the ball pitched and left an ominous black mark on the damp turf where it landed; that was the danger sign. Batsmen, when they saw Tate's mark in the pitch at Hove, resolved to play forward, hold their bats very straight and hope.[*]

The term "long-fingered" fits well with Tate's deceptively fast pace off the pitch. This and everything one reads about him, implies a wonderfully efficient "long lever" between the ball and the wrist-hinge. It means heavy back-spin so that any fraction of the back-spin present as off- or leg-spin will also be accentuated. Arlott, in this otherwise perceptive description, oversteps the bowling crease a little in asserting that swing bowlers only produce swing deliberately. Neither my wind-tunnel results, nor the reported experience of bowlers, provides any support for the existence of such powers.

Does a fast bowler's thumb have any influence apart from supporting from below? It is usual to assume none, but it is possible that the effect of the ball sliding off the thumb, although it occurs before the longer fingers have their effect, does reduce the desired back- and side-spin slightly. Perhaps G. A. Wilson (1877–1962), a leading county fast bowler noted for his ability to curve the ball in the air, had discovered something valuable in his grip which involved the first and second fingers on or alongside the seam as normal, but the thumb well clear of the stitching at the bottom and on the smooth leather. Such a grip would minimise any effect of the thumb in counteracting the back-spin.

Fig. 37 illustrates views (from directly above the bowler's hand) of deliveries used mainly by fast and medium-pace bowlers. Photo *a* represents zero seam angle, with the fingers on the smooth leather; provided that the fingers come straight down off the back of the ball, it will have "pure" back-spin (*see* fig. 2*a*) and will not deviate sideways off a true pitch (although predictable swing, including late swing, is possible). Photo *b* is the same but with the

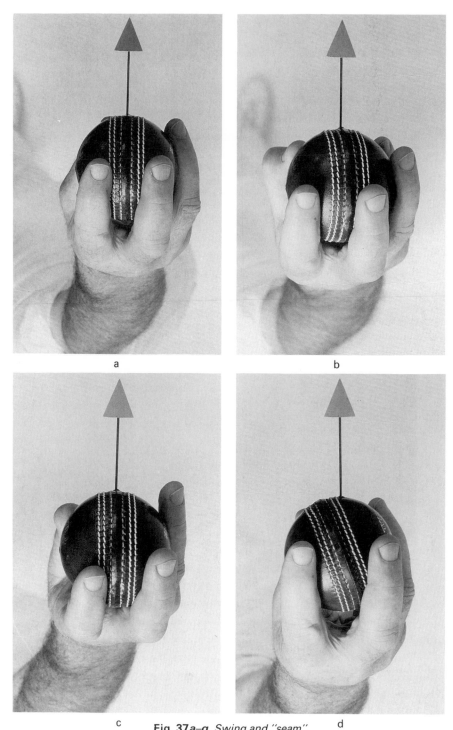

Fig. 37a–g *Swing and "seam".*

e

f

g

second finger on the stitching. Likewise, photo *c* with the first finger on the stitching. In photos *d* and *f* the seam angle is about 30° for the outswinger, with the spin as in fig. 2*d*. Having the first finger on the stitching, *f* will cut back more from the off than *d*. Similarly with photos *e* and *g*: *g* will cut more from the leg than *e* since it has more finger contact, with spin as in fig. 2*c*. The "seamer" – i.e. a ball that deviates off a true pitch – is only possible if the seam is spun at some angle to the line of flight. Other grips, where the fingers lie more across the seam than is the case in the photos, are less likely to produce good, steady, "non-wobbling" seam angles during flight.

Another point worth noting if the fingers are to dominate, is that the more the hand points forwards at release, the earlier the thumb loses contact, and the less its effect in reducing back-spin. This may be another secret of the "long-fingered" fast bowler to add to the obvious advantages of long fingers in providing whip and good contact with the ball during the all important release processes.

Lohmann found when bowling on the matting wickets of South Africa, laid over fine gravel or red dust, that the length was effectively shortened by the back-spun ball gripping the pitch, allowing plenty of time for the shot. This example is a reminder that on the good-gripping spinner's pitch, the faster bowlers must bowl a fuller length.

If back-spin is the aim then the downward moving fingers should be rubbing against the stitching and not the smooth leather, unless it has been worn. If the seam is being held vertical both fingers will contact the seam only if they are close together, in which case the ball leaves a two-finger pushing area which is rather narrow for the best control to be obtained. However, one finger on the stitching and one on the smooth leather has its own unevenness as a pushing force. Spofforth's first and second fingers, which were on top of the ball, were on either side for his swing (which he called swerve), neither of them touching the stitching. If swing alone is the object then this grip is worth trying.

J. B. King, as mentioned earlier, christened his pioneering inswinger "the angler" after the sharp curve or hook near the end of its path. He was careful to point out that it must be used only sparingly among other deliveries. The detailed account he gave of his methods is of great interest alongside our earlier discussion of swing and grips.

> I found a new shiny cricket ball as favourable to a sharp hook but not necessary for it. I found I could hook or angle an old ball as effectively as a new one when conditions were right. My next problem was to examine these conditions, and by trial and error to identify those in my favour.

Some of them were beyond my control – for instance wind and weather. But I could study them and use those which helped most. When I began bowling I liked best a following wind just strong enough to flutter the left corner of my shirt collar. Although later, when I felt completely co-ordinated and physically fit, I could swing the ball with a wind coming from any quarter. I preferred it coming from the batsman's off, and if I could make it to order, I would have a gusty wind sweeping up the gully to the right of second slip.

But still on some days I observed that the ball would swing more than on others; and, being by now convinced that I had in the angler a new and effective ball for occasional use, I began to make a careful study of what in my bodily action produced it.

The fundamental essential I found to be complete relaxation and co-ordination – an absence of any tension in arms, legs, or shoulders. This was necessary because my angler required a whole-souled follow-through of body and arm that would carry me well on down the wicket. When conditions were favourable I had the feeling that I was hurling myself after the ball towards the wicket.

In bowling the hooked or angled curve I found the second essential to be the height of the action and the grip used. I delivered the angler from full height straight above my head, indeed at times from slightly over the left shoulder. I held the ball consistently with the seam just between the first and second fingers, with the thumb opposed. The third finger was just in contact with the ball, and the fourth finger idle. It required only a very slight adjustment of this grip to make the ball go straight without any curve, or to give it enough spin for a slight off-break.

As to the control of the angler, I found it to lie in the wrist and the fingers. A strong yet flexible wrist, and long powerful fingers are desirable in every curve bowler; I found them quite essential for the control of the angler. Indeed the wrist and the first two fingers are the controlling factors in putting this ball where it should be. I felt the ball last, not with the side, but with the tips of the two fingers, and discovered that a delicate control of its flight depended on the final pressure. This finger pressure came at the end of a sharp downward flick of the wrist.[5]

In case the reader should interpret this chapter as an infallible guide to bowling success, let him read of the many sad instances where so-called coaches have interfered with naturally acquired actions. It was only Bill O'Reilly's Irish stubbornness that saved him from one such interference. In his own words:

Arthur Mailey, then approaching the end of his career, was watching my first appearance at the SCG nets in 1926–27, where I bowled for the first time under the gaze of the New South Wales selectors. Himself a selector, Mailey drew me aside to show me the grip he used – fundamentally different from mine – with the ball held in the fingertips of his right hand. He suggested that I should imitate it if I ever hoped to be able to spin a leg-break noticeably. He went so far as to describe my own grip and to draw lines of similarity with the manner in which he himself held a golf club.

This advice appalled me. Here was a man trying to get me to dump all the lessons I had taught myself for nearly ten years: personal lessons which I had learned well enough to find myself in attendance at the nets that afternoon.

Not likely. I thanked Mr Mailey for the great interest he had taken in me but went on to say that I thought it was much too late to be fiddling about with an action which even by that time had become second nature to me.[6]

Among other things, Mailey obviously failed to appreciate that someone going through the complex action of bowling leg-spin at medium-pace, as did O'Reilly, does not need the finger action of a slower bowler in order to achieve the same spin rate.

Another argument against uniformity of grips, and a more fundamental one because it applies to all spinners, arises from the great variety of size and structure of the human hand. In 1927, in one of the rare law changes which assisted rather than hindered the bowler, the size of the Grade I ball was reduced from a circumference which had been between 9in (22.9cm) and 9.5in (24cm) maximum, to 8.813in (22.4cm) and a 9in (22.9cm) maximum. The reduction of 0.187in (4.8mm) seems trivial, but the fact that the smaller ball does feel smaller and more compact in the hand, is a reminder that bowlers with larger hands must also feel the ball differently in their grasp.

Arthur Mailey recognised the value of the smaller ball which was introduced during his active career: "The ball was larger than it is now and consequently more difficult to grip unless you had a hand like a David Nourse or an Australian woodchopper".[7] Ray Illingworth was is in no doubt:

All cricket balls are supposed to be the same size to a fraction of an ounce, but, believe me, they are not! I can tell certain makes with the ball in my hand and my eyes shut. That's how much difference there is in size. In fact, because of this variation in size, it does make my grip vary because I haven't got particularly long fingers.[8]

The 1980 code allows Grade 2–4 balls to be up to 9.063in (23.0cm) in circumference. Two top-grade balls I measured recently had circumferences of 8.86 in (22.5 cm) which means that these manufacturers have added a safety margin of 0.047 in (1.2 mm) to the required minimum size to allow for variation in manufacturing. Bowlers would hope that they could do a little better than that, perhaps 8.83 in (22.4 cm).

Grimmett favoured the larger ball because be claimed that it gave him better variety of flight when thrown into the wind. There would be some slight differences in wind drag and Robins Force with the smaller ball but I doubt whether they would match in significance the major factor of allowing a better grip on the ball in the first place.

The evidence available to us supports the view that the great majority of adult males possess hands capable of performing most of the required spinning actions. David Nourse, a South African all-rounder, was described as having hands bigger than anybody playing cricket, but S. F. Barnes, Mailey, Grimmett, O'Reilly and Laker are said to have had hands which were not abnormally large.[9]

Women's hands are smaller on average and do require a smaller ball. Young bowlers may pose a problem by adopting inefficient grips which suit smaller hands. An example of this would be a leg-break grip employing all four fingers and thumb in an equally dominant role. Most good leg-spinners find that a spinning couple dominated by the first and third fingers is more capable of imparting sharp spin, but such a grip appears to be beyond young hands. It is important therefore that young cricketers use smaller balls.

No bowler should accept the additional burden of a ball swollen beyond normal size. Umpires are required to possess a pair of brass gauges: the ball should be able to pass through one but not the other. Club umpires are unlikely to have them available but will probably have heard of them and be ready to agree to a change of ball.

The question of what size ball is best for cricket should not be regarded as settled. It is clear that a reduction in circumference of only $\frac{1}{10}$ in (2.5 mm) would make spinning just that bit more accessible. In the period 1952–5 a trial was carried out in England under the authority of the ACCC, using a slightly smaller ball with a slightly thicker seam. The final trial took place in twenty-five non-competition matches in 1955. The players were almost totally unenthusiastic, and the idea was dropped.

Whatever the case for a smaller ball, the type of trial that lasts for a period of two or three years for a handful of cricketers is unlikely to be of any use. Unless players are told that the new smaller ball is to be adopted for a period comparable in length with a good proportion of their playing years, they cannot be expected to devote the time needed to become fully accustomed to it and exploit its full potential. Similar considerations apply to other experimental law changes. No one, for example, would seriously expect a short period of trial for a new lbw rule allowing a batsman to be given out to a ball pitching outside the leg stump to lead suddenly to a resurgence in spin bowling, particularly leg-spinning. Nor could players, most of whom have no interest in the art, be expected to show any enthusiasm for the new rule. Yet such a trial was carried out for only one season in New Zealand and Australia in 1980–1. Some experiments in cricket require a long period in which to demonstrate their usefulness or otherwise. It is best that the changes be decided on the basis of sound principles and experience, and then given sufficient number of years in operation to allow both bowlers and batsmen to develop within the new conditions.

Finger length is not the only factor in grip; hand width and finger shape are also important. It is not uncommon for the index finger to be bent around slightly at the top joint in the direction of the second finger. Such a shape is of some value in both off- and leg-spinning as the finger fits better over the ball. Individuals also vary in the size of the various knobs and bumps that are found on finger bones. Here is yet another reason why a particular grip should not be imposed on a bowler. The presence or absence of a particular structure or length of bone may make all the difference to the feel of a ball in the hands without the reason being at all obvious to anyone else.

In addition to these individual characteristics, the ability of bone to respond to the stresses and pressures placed on it means that we influence the structure of our hands to some extent by what we habitually do with them. Frequent pressure on bone will cause thicker cartilage to develop which ultimately becomes bone – bunions on the feet are an example. Spin bowlers can expect this to some degree after years of practice and play. Jim Laker's spinning (index) finger was "swollen and arthritic after years of service"[10], obviously a bunion-like condition rather than thickened skin, because it showed up alarmingly in an X-ray – only bone would do that.[11] Not surprisingly, when Laker taught the young Tony Lock how to really spin the ball he warned him that it would hurt.

Capping the whole pile of difficulties that range against today's spinner is one which is especially tragic in its consequences because it can strike bowlers at the peak of their powers. Finger wear is the problem and there is nothing subtle about it; bowlers may be injured so severely that for days or weeks on end they are simply unable to spin the ball. And it is those bowlers who try hardest to put work on the ball, the very people who would give the game more variety, who suffer most.

The list of bowlers removed from the crease as a result of finger wear during their prime years reads like a *Who's Who* of spin: Wilfred Rhodes (who by standing down because of a sore spinning finger allowed Colin Blythe to make his debut for England), McCool, Benaud, Laker, Gibbs, Pocock and others – a depressingly high toll, especially when most of them have lived in an era when quality spinners were not plentiful. Include all those spinners at

Fig. 38 *Lance Gibbs' lacerated spinning finger.* The best spinners pay too high a price for their efforts.

club level and above who have suffered distressing problems with finger wear and we have a factor of no small significance in today's cricket. We must ask the questions, why does the problem seem to be worse in recent times, and is it avoidable?

Skin is composed of two fundamental layers: an outer layer called the "epidermis" and an inner dense connective tissue called the "dermis". The epidermis contains layers of flattened dead cells derived from the living cells of the underlying layer which steadily move outwards as the epidermis sheds its outer cells. The outer, completely dead part of the epidermis, the horny layer, is normally replenished every two weeks in a mature adult. Its thickness varies in different parts of the body, depending on the amount of pressure applied to the skin. Thickened skin would take longer than two weeks to move through its shedding cycle.

A bowler is subjecting the skin on his fingers both to abrasion, where the surface cells are worn away, and to a tearing action, where the skin is pulled to one side just before and during delivery. Repeated pressure, during weeks of practice, thickens the epidermis which is covered with an intersecting series of delicate grooves to allow stretching and provide friction with other surfaces.

So what goes wrong? In the first place the hand was not designed for bowling; the pressure points are in the wrong places. Not being on the pads of the muscular areas, but mainly on the sides of the finger-tips or joints, the pressure is concentrated unnaturally at these points. Experience tells us that bowlers can build up thicker skin as a protection, but only to a certain extent.

Even when it is toughened by artificial means such as the calamine-boracic acid treatment found useful by Benaud, the problem of splitting and tearing has remained. Other treatment involving softening with oils or greases has not solved the problem either. Naturally, the "strateum corneum" has all the properties needed for normal use, and adheres well to the underlying tissue from which it arises. Thickening can strengthen it, but in spite of all possible precautions, the violent and repeated stress involved in spin bowling can still tear it away from the living tissue below.

The modern ball may well have exacerbated the problem. We appreciate its frequently quite hard and often rather sharp rows of stitching, as at least offering us a glimmer of hope, that as well as being the only thing to grip on an otherwise continually shiny ball, it may also improve slightly the grip on low friction pitches. Whereas in the earlier years the ball wore rough enough to provide a grip over its entire surface, nowadays our grip is frequently confined to the relatively narrow band of stitches for the entire game. Such a concentration of pressure and stress must have contributed to the problem. This factor alone should be enough to encourage the development of a commonsense attitude to the use of skin protection by bowlers. We can and must improve pitches but out-fields friendly to shiny leather are most likely here to stay. We hope the balls will wear more on the better pitches; friction is not possible without wear. A well worn ball brings spin to the fore.

Sharp spinning normally requires two points of intense contact with the ball. For the leg-spinner these are normally the inside of the first finger-tip and the inside of the first joint of the third finger. Only one of these is usually subject to tearing. Over-thick skin or raised jagged edges can be shaved carefully with a razor blade to reduce the chance of tearing at splits. With the long hours of practice that spinners require, finger wear will always be a problem: under the present set-up it is far too frequently an insurmountable one.

So what can be done? Grin and bear it? As Shakespeare put it:

There be some sports are painful
and there labour
Delight in them sets off.[12]

Not much delight if you can't bowl; the matter is too serious to be dismissed.

Back in the early days an enterprising wicket-keeper made a sort of tin thimble to protect two of his fingers. Once into their stride cricketers were not slow in adopting protective devices in the form of leg-pads, gloves, thigh-pads, shin-pads, arm-pads, body-pads, boxes, and helmets, when they needed them. When we consider that wicket-keeping gloves, and helmets, especially the latter when used by close-in fieldsmen, play a direct part in bringing about the demise of the batsman, we may take a different view regarding the more indirect matter of protection for a bowler's fingers. But suggest to fellow cricketers some form of protection for the bleeding knuckle of a spin bowler, and for many of them one may just as well have proposed that Lord's be given over to dog-racing, such is the infamy of the idea.

I was listening to a radio commentary on a Test match from Australia in the 1970s when Dennis Lillee had gone off for treatment to an injury and come back onto the field with sticking plaster on his hand. It must have been his bowling hand because one of the commentators said that there was nothing wrong with Lillee using sticking plaster, but if Ashley Mallett, an off-spinner, had used it he would have been able to generate "fantastic spin". Someone interested in the history of cricket may wish to trace the development of this idea into one of the more powerful myths associated with the game.

I invite the reader to carry out a few simple experiments. Take two cricket balls, one new, the other worn, and using the seam and the smoother portion in turn, rub these surfaces firmly over the skin of one of your fingers. The skin can be moistened slightly if you wish, as you may do to improve the grip when actually bowling. Note the amount of friction. Obtain some sticking plaster; if possible some of each of what are probably three principal types – one with a shiny plastic surface, another with a tightly woven fabric surface, and another with a slightly textured plastic surface. Another type with stretchable rubberised fabric moves too much under pressure and is useless for the proposed purpose. Place a length of an inch or two on your finger and rub the ball over it as before. If one of the fallacies of modern cricket has not taken a body blow in these few minutes I will have been very much mistaken. If there are any significant differences between the grip of a ball on skin covered with sticking plaster as compared with uncovered skin, it is more likely that the result, over the whole range of plasters, is less friction rather than more.

But what if the edge of the plaster is rolled up to expose the sticky part. "You can't expect umpires to go around peering into bowlers' finger-joints all day" – at this point the diehards do us all a service by inviting a more complete exposure of the fallacy underlying the whole idea that sticky fingers help a spin bowler.

Another experiment will readily provide the answer. Put something really sticky, as sticky as sticking plaster, on your bowling fingers. This can be a rubberised glue or some other adhesive. Now attempt to bowl. If you retain any touch and timing at all during the sensitive and intricately programmed operation of releasing the ball, you are better than I am, and I have tried this with a number of different glues. Add to this the problem imposed by the changing stickiness of the grip and the whole idea collapses.

In 1927–8 when J. Newman of Hampshire was coaching in New Zealand, he wore a finger stall in a minor match and was no-balled by the umpire on the grounds that he was employing a means of unfair advantage.[13] The opposing captain should have begged him to keep it on, such is the effect of any covering like that on one's control. Ian Peebles tells us that Walter Robins, a ferocious spinner of the ball, suffered from a raw third finger and used sticking plaster, but adds that it is likely to interfere with a bowler's touch.[14] However, this interference is lessened with practice.

Law 3, Part 7 of the 1980 Code states that "The umpires shall be the sole judges of fair and unfair play". Since the matter presently being discussed is not mentioned directly or indirectly anywhere else in the Code, the question must be open to interpretation by umpires. If a close-in fieldsman, because he is wearing a helmet, can safely creep in an extra two yards to bring about the dismissal of a batsman, that may be classed as an unfair advantage, but I suggest that cricketers think again on the matter of finger protection before automatically accepting misconceived ideas from the past. An informed interpretation on the part of umpires is all that the beleaguered spinner asks for. Since the matter has acquired, in the minds of some cricketers, a significance of unjustifiable proportions, umpires could rightly expect some support for a change of attitude on the part of respected leaders among players and administrators. It is too important to be left to the haphazard solution of mutual agreement between opposing captains.

One suggested law change that would do nothing to help spinners is the lengthening of the pitch by a yard or so. Getting the ball up to the other end while spinning it at the same time places enough stress on the fingers now without adding more. Strong wind, already a serious cause of inaccuracy in slow bowling, would cause even more trouble if the pitch was longer. Quoting extensive figures from English county cricket for the period 1955–84, Robert Letham in an article in *The Cricketer*, entitled "Cricket – more than ever a batsman's game", besides giving weight to many of the points raised in this chapter, dismisses the idea of a longer pitch:

> Hence we are faced with an imbalance in present day cricket in favour of the batsman. To what extreme, it may be asked, have slower over rates and short-pitched fast bowling been perhaps unselfconscious responses to this trend? If, as is advocated by the editor, a lengthened pitch may be required to combat the increasing physical danger occasioned by intimidatory fast bowling, would not such a change irreversibly perpetuate the dominance of the batsman and eliminate the spinner entirely?[15]

Bowlers are familiar with the loss of fine touch in their fingers after stopping a hard-hit shot. How many realise that by fielding at positions where the ball is constantly being relayed back through them to the other bowlers, their hands are subjected to a repeated impact which makes the fingers and palms swell to the detriment of their efficiency as bowlers? For this reason, returns to bowlers should always be a gentle lob from close at hand.

Our discussion of the limitations of human skin under the stress of spin bowling inevitably veers towards artificially-aided adhesion. Although the two subjects strictly speaking are unrelated, they appear to be associated strongly in the minds of many cricketers. The use of resin and other substances has come to be regarded by some, along with finger protection, as unfair play. Again the 1980 Code makes no specific mention of the subject, the sole appearance of chemistry being a ban on the use of artificial substances in polishing the ball – a slight move in favour of the spin bowler, but outweighed by the disadvantage, compared to what was permitted earlier this century, of not being allowed to rub the ball in the dirt to improve grip.

Bowlers who have slipped into their pockets a little of the pale golden powder, the same one that puts music in the violinist's bow and allows the gymnast to grip the bar, are in good company. Arthur Mailey would have no truck with fiddlers of a different sort; rule fiddlers:

> I accepted these standardized rules [referring to various other laws of cricket] because I had come into cricket with them, but when the crazy idea of disallowing the bowler to use resin to allow a better grip of the ball – and a law forbidding the lifting of the seam blew in, I bade good-bye to this form of freedom and became a rebel. Although it was against the law, I must break down and confess that I always carried powdered resin in my pocket and when the umpire wasn't looking, lifted the seam for Jack Gregory and Ted McDonald. And I am as unashamed as a Yorkshireman who appeals for lbw off a ball which pitched two feet outside the leg stump.[16]

Ian Peebles comes down more gently, but still firmly on the side of bowlers:

> There have been innumerable instances of sharp practice in the history of cricket, mostly trivial and usually laughable, to be grouped under the tolerant heading of "gamesmanship". When these have been mech-anical rather than psychological one regrets to say that the bowler has been the more frequent culprit, for, as the prime mover, his opportuni-ties have been the greater. Resin or eucalyptus on a handkerchief, to give more grip, raising the seam, polishing the ball and suchlike, have been hunted down over the years, but the writer has an unconcealed sympathy for such gentle aids, for no petty restrictions are put upon the batsman in the maintenance of his implements.[17]

Because most cricketers regard the whole area of exterior stitching and the leather lips where the main hemispheres abut, as the seam (fig. 39), we must remain in doubt when reading published accounts. As discussed earlier, these could involve the quite legal process of restoring the stitching to its original state, or the illegal interference with the leather lips. This doubt must apply to the story of Brian Statham, the England fast bowler, who was said to have shown his class by being able to "lift the seam" by means of an operation involving only one hand.

Resin is not a sticky substance but it improves grip under pressure. Base-ball pitchers are highly skilled in exploiting the Robins Force by means of a great variety of spins, and also employ a version of seam-induced swing, the knuckle ball. The rules of baseball recognise the need for a good grip on the ball, with the help of resin if necessary so that players can get on with the business of exploiting their skills. In fact, unfair play in baseball includes having so much resin on the pitch that the batter can't see properly through the cloud of powder! The following comments of a leading American baseball coach are highly relevant to cricket:

> The pitcher ought to examine the condition of the baseball in use. When its surface becomes blemished in such a way as to impair the pitcher's ability to work with it effectively, he should request a different ball from the umpire. If, on the other hand, a new ball is too slick, it should be rubbed until the sheen is removed. This duty is assigned to the umpire as a pregame task, but if it has been neglected it can be done by the pitcher or one of his team-mates as long as no foreign substance is applied. A resin bag should always be on hand for the pitcher's use. At any time that his hand becomes slippery or does not supply the desired resistance in releasing the ball, the pitcher should dust his hands by gripping the resin bag and squeezing it several times. Two words of precaution should be added: resin may not be applied directly to the ball, because the rules consider it a foreign substance; and the application of resin should be done judiciously, because an excess of it can cause the fingers to adhere to the ball sufficiently to impair one's control.[18]

a

b

c

Fig. 39 *Seam and stitching: a, b* and *c* are high quality balls. The seam, which bulges only slightly, is seen to run down the dark area in the middle of each photograph. The four rows of stitching vary in thickness among the different balls. Ball *a* is a Kookaburra Turf ball; *b* and *c* are from Alfred Reader. Ball *b* was used for seven years before the thickness of the stitching was called into question and it was replaced by *c*. Ball *c* would appear to be less helpful to spinners and cutters than *a* and *b*.

A spin bowler reacts to a poor hold on the ball by placing it nearer the palm of his hand, the very position that destroys spin. I wonder if the law-makers of the 1920s would have interfered had they known that the ball-polishing out-field era was looming. The time for a return to sanity with regard to resin is long overdue.

A well-worn ball has long ago lost the ability to swing, although there would have remained the potential for spin-swerve. But these sources of deviation are insignificant compared to the highly satisfactory friction which its rough surface would provide both in the spinning fingers and on landing. Such a ball would most likely be rather soft and without much bounce, but today's heavy-batted players would be called on to display all their skill against the big turn from spinners fast and slow.

Would a ball be allowed to wear to that extent today? Assuming that there exists a cricket ground where balls do wear, is it not likely that umpires would intervene long before such a process had gone very far? But we shouldn't blame the umpires for underpinning the sanitised pace-infatuated cricket ethos of today which sends them scampering when a ball gets a little soft or a little out of shape (preventing swing) and which allows them to ban play when the run-ups are a little wet. The cricket world long ago stopped telling them that bowlers of skill can do plenty with a soft, worn or distorted ball, or that they can cut down their run-ups on a wet surface. Not quite all of the cricket world, however: the money-paying public, frequently forced to put up with annoying breaks in play and the most scandalous delays to the start of play, are brought face to face with this modern mollycoddling. Yet their protestations count for nothing in the boardrooms.

As for the lifting of the seam, it is unnecessary if all bowlers exercise their legal right to keep the four rows of stitching clean and unflattened – i.e. in their original state – by frequently running their thumb-nails around all eight sides of the rows. Many cricketers mistake this for lifting the seam.

Cricket may be the only sport in which the ball travelling from the air to the ground is not of even character over its whole surface. The seam, or more correctly the stitching surrounding the seam, covers a major part of the area of the ball. Rubbing the ball on various surfaces shows the great influence of the seam on ball-pitch friction. If the stitching is manufactured to the standard that the bowler deserves, one notices that rubbing across the stitches gives more friction than rubbing in line with them.

Balls vary in several respects of significance to the bowler. The 1980 Code specifies weight and circumference limits but nothing about stitches or thread. Adherence to standards therefore is a matter for agreement at other levels. Manufacturers may or may not adopt some type of standard but whether or not they do, their products and consistency of quality are generally well known to cricketers.

Bowlers should take careful note of the quite wide variation in matters of considerable importance to them. They should seek out balls with the most stitches, the widest area of stitching, the thickest thread and the best bounce. These qualities don't always bring greater cost. Clubs and purchasing organisations can therefore give significant help to bowlers by asking suppliers to provide detailed specifications, and purchasing balls with the required qualities. Stitches must rise abruptly from the surface if they are to serve the bowler: gentle undulations above a sea of lacquer are not good enough. Cricketers throughout the world, hoping for a significant action on the part of ruling bodies to advance the cause of spin, must wonder about the wisdom of banning a Reader ball (fig. 39*b*) with slightly enlarged stitching, a ball which incidentally had been manufactured for seven years. Although it was said to have helped faster bowlers, why was its long-term potential benefit to spinners not recognised? No one told batsmen to go back to using lighter, more manoeuvrable bats.

A simple calculation using a typical good quality ball tells us that the stitching covers 30% of its area, so that if we bowl a ball at random into the pitch, using no particular grip in relation to the seam, it would land on the seam on average about one-third of the time. Not exactly, though. The mark on a ball where it has landed may be $\frac{3}{4}$ in (20 mm) or more in diameter depending on the deformation of the ball and pitch on contact. We may therefore enlarge our figure for the chance that there will be some contact of the stitching with the ground. The extra amount will not be full seam contact, thus illustrating yet another of the fascinating series of properties, aerodynamic and mechanical, the early ball makers unwittingly produced.

In what sense does "seaming" depend on the seam? Is it confined to grip, the grip of fingers on ball, and ball on pitch, or does it involve the ball "falling sideways" off the projecting stitches when it lands, as if we had dropped a box on its edge? The latter explanation, widely held by cricketers, cannot be sustained. New balls are very close to being perfect spheres. Of the dozen or so good quality balls I have measured, there was never more than a 2 mm difference in the two diameters, one from seam to seam, and the other at 90° to it. In the absence of swelling from water or distortion arising from some other influence, we are left with stitching which extends about 1 mm above the surface. There is no chance whatsoever of the ball "moving off the seam" unaided by some action on the part of the bowler. If it "moves" off anything in its path it is an unevenness of grass and soil.

What then are we left with to justify the use of the term "seaming"? We are told that the art of "seaming" requires the bowler to deliver the ball with the seam upright and pointing straight down the pitch. But such a ball landing on an even surface will not deviate sideways at all. Since we know that all "turn", fast or slow, is more productive when the ball lands on the stitching, the term "seaming" is therefore left as an unnecessary reference to a particular aspect of spinning and cutting. In other words "seaming" requires that the bowler pulls his fingers down one side or other of the ball during release.

Kortright didn't worry too much about the seam and I doubt whether many of today's better bowlers are in the habit of exploring the random delivery where both bowler and batsman are uncertain as to how the ball will land.

A similar process of estimating the chance that the ball will land on the stitching must be undergone for all other types of bowling where the intention is to move the ball off the pitch, e.g. off-spin, cutting and the flipper. Here again the video camera or an observer are needed to check on how the ball in flight is rotating relative to the seam.

However, there are a number of situations where the above strategy is deliberately altered, the most obvious being where the bowler has a flutter on the seam-pitch contact lottery and holds the ball "across the seam". The ball rotates in flight and may or may not land on the seam. The chances of a full seam landing are about 20% and at least some seam contact on landing about 30%. The batsman therefore can expect 70 to 80% of those deliveries to skid through off the smooth leather and for the added reason that across-the-seam contact provides the greatest friction of all, the rest to kick a little – but he doesn't know which! For this reason they are an excellent type of delivery for any bowler, especially pace-men, to learn. They will not be as effective on a non-gripping pitch, another example where proper pitch conditions help all bowlers.

Swing is occasionally a disadvantage and must be thwarted deliberately. Whether or not it is accentuated by wind, movement in the air can sometimes defeat all attempts to obtain movement off the pitch. The result is lack of variety. For example, an outswing bowler who brings the ball back off the pitch may find the latter completely losing out to the swing. It would be worth trying deliveries where the ideal seam angle was not consistent throughout flight, and hope for less swing. Again there is a problem with the different feeling of the ball in the fingers, and such changes need to be practised. Where the unwanted movement in the air arises from the Robins Force, the seam angle in the fingers can be changed. The results as shown by my wind-tunnel work are largely unpredictable, but worth a try.

Spin-swerve on an unresponsive pitch may sometimes embarrass the bowler. The Otago right-hand leg-spinner Carl Dickel, bowling almost directly into a strong wind on the Hutt Recreation Ground, could achieve nothing more than a series of slow inswingers. Bowled to a strong leg-side field they needed close watching, but all surprise and variety had been blown away with the papers that scuttled across the grass. The situation vividly demonstrated the reliance of the Robins Force on a strong effective wind speed. Assuming a bowling speed of 40mph and a wind speed of 30mph, the effective wind speed was 70 mph. C. S. Marriott[19] advised against leg-break bowlers bowling into the wind, particularly wind from the direction of third-man.

The flipper strikes back off the pitch, but with a newish ball and into the wind, the seam-towards-slips angle may convert it into an habitual out-swinger. In such a case the seam angle must be changed to an anti-swing wobble. Finally, if we describe grips in terms of the fingers either lying along the seam (or parallel to it), or across the seam, we have two extremes between which lies a whole range of possibilities.

REFERENCES

1 C. J. Kortright, Interview in *Wisden Anthology 1940–63*, p. 987　**2** P. Walker, *Cricket Conversations* (Pelham Books, 1978), p. 69　**3** R. S. Whitington, *Bradman, Benaud and Goddard's Cinderellas* (Bailey Bros and Swinfen, 1964), p. 145　**4** K. Gregory, *In Celebration of Cricket* (Hart-Davis, Magibbon, 1978), p. 155　**5** J. A. Lester (ed), *A Century of Philadelphia Cricket* (University of Pennsylvania Press, 1951), p. 167　**6** W. J. O'Reilly, *Tiger: 60 Years of Cricket* (Collins, 1985), p. 45　**7** A. Mailey, *10 for 66 And All That* (Phoenix Sports Books, 1958), p. 113　**8** R. Illingworth, *Spinner's Wicket* (Stanley Paul, 1969), p. 62　**9** I. Peebles, *Bowler's Turn* (Souvenir Press, 1960), p. 142　**10** M. Williams, *Double Century*, from an article by John Woodcock (Collins Willow, 1985), p. 525　**11** I. Peebles, *Bowler's Turn*, p. 142　**12** W. Shakespeare, *The Tempest*, Act 3　**13** G. Broadribb, *Next Man In* (Putnam, 1952), p. 74　**14** I. Peebles, *Bowler's Turn*, p. 142　**15** R. Letham, "Cricket – More Than Ever a Batsman's Game", *The Cricketer*, December 1985, p. 31　**16** A. Mailey, *10 for 66 And All That*, p. 113　**17** I. Peebles, *Bowler's Turn*, p. 142　**18** L. Watts, *The Fine Art of Baseball* (Prentice-Hall, 1975), p. 58　**19** C. S. Marriott, *The Complete Leg-Break Bowler*, p. 76

Chapter 16
The flipper

GOOD SPIN BOWLING IS A THING OF DECEIT AND TRICKERY and good batsmen take pains to learn as much as they can about it, long before the ball is on
its way. Naturally, spin bowlers must be secretive, or at least reticent, con-
cerning the more subtle and perhaps newly-developed aspects of their craft.

Norman O'Neill tells the story[1] that when preparing for a Test in Brisbane
in 1958, Peter May described Richie Benaud as a good steady bowler not
likely to present any particular difficulties. After allowing two leg-breaks to
pass harmlessly on the off, May, sincerely believing his own advice, padded
up to the third and was out lbw for four. Writing twenty-seven years later
May described this delivery as a googly.[2] Benaud's intensive two year (or
more?) course in learning and developing what was for him an entirely new
type of delivery, had obviously been kept discreetly "within the family".
Benaud's delivery was not a googly but a flipper.

Even now, more than thirty years later, I am prepared to lay a tidy bet that
not one cricketer or cricket watcher in ten thousand understands what a
flipper really is. Not that there are plenty, including media commentators,
who think they know.

My own contact with the flipper dates from the time I began to look
around for a more reliable accompaniment to the leg-break than the too often
wayward and muscle-tearing googly. What I found was a vignette of
incomprehension without equal in the literature of cricket. Clarrie Grimmett
would have regarded such confusion as a highly satisfactory state of affairs as
he turned to walk back to his mark.

Probably Grimmett himself was the principal instigator of this confusion,
in spite of giving an account of the delivery and its variations when he wrote
his book[3] in 1948, twelve years after his last Test. In an earlier book published in 1932[4], he outlined a number of spinning techniques employing the
thumb, but did not propose them all as serious contenders for a place in the
bowling repertoire. Although its emphasis is puzzling in parts, and the after-
math even more puzzling, one cannot accuse Grimmett of withholding the
directions needed by those seeking to imitate him. I had read the 1948 book
many years earlier, but because I did not get out and try every delivery that
he described, I failed to distinguish the useful from the merely possible.

Grimmett was telling us that in the transition from under-arm to over-arm bowling, we had unnecessarily discarded a valuable means of spinning the ball using the thumb. In his own words:

> In most of my experiments I bowled under-arm with a tennis ball and afterward adapted the principle to over-arm.
>
> I was impressed about this time by a very fine under-arm bowler named Simpson-Hayward, who toured New Zealand with an English team. He could spin a ball more than any bowler I had seen at the time [see fig. 4c]. How could such vicious spin be applied under-arm, I wondered. Surely some different principal of spinning must be involved.
>
> If I had asked Mr Hayward, perhaps I would have evolved my Mystery Ball sooner. But as it was, I went on experimenting and eventually realised that much more spin could be applied by holding the ball between the thumb and the second finger. The problem was, however, to adapt this to over-arm bowling.
>
> I put in hours of practice and experiment at this, and it was only after much hard work that I was satisfied and decided to use it in matches. The reason why I waited so long before trying it in a match was that pride in my bowling wouldn't let me bowl a ball that didn't fit into the main scheme of my methods. This conception of bowling, too, caused me to use the pruning knife from time to time; so that when I had perfected this new kind of spin, I practically discarded the old googly. I used it only on very rare occasions, usually when I was opposed by a left-handed batsman. I realised that the new delivery had great possibilities. And it was sound in principle to concentrate on my leg-break and straight ball, since the fewer other balls I bowled the less risk I ran of losing control.[5]

Grimmett was fifteen years old when he saw Simpson-Hayward in Wellington in 1907, old enough to have gone to the Public Library in the city and read that remarkable book *Great Bowlers and Fielders* by George Beldam and C. B. Fry, published in 1906 and discussed in earlier chapters. In this fascinating collection of photographs and detailed analysis of the methods of the bowlers of that time, one stands out (fig. 40a and b). Walter Mead (1868–1954) "A medium-pace bowler of the highest class, full of life, very accurate in length, rather deceptive in flight and able to break the ball both from leg and from off" is shown holding the ball in:

> ...a very curious grip for his off-break; the ball sits in a kind of cup made with the thumb and second finger [both under the ball] and the first finger is hooped around over the top of the ball; the first finger

aided by a quick twist of the wrist, manages to put a great amount of spin on the ball.[6]

Although it is highly probable that the young Grimmett, intensely interested in bowling, would have read Beldam and Fry (the same copy in fact that eighty years later the Wellington Public Library staff retrieved for me from their basement), it is unlikely that the technique of one medium-pace bowler out of the sixty-seven bowlers of all types depicted, would have stood out. The spotlight was on the googly artists, Bosanquet and Schwarz, who occupy forty pages of the four hundred devoted to bowlers.

Mead was not only one of the best slow-medium bowlers of his day, but, from the clear evidence in that book, should now be regarded as a fine exponent of thumb-spin, a missing link between under-armers like Simpson-Hayward and the Australian flipper merchants. He is described in a recent biographical work as "generally off-breaking but sometimes sending down a leg-break or googly to good effect".[7] H. S. Altham also credits Mead with having bowled the googly inadvertently, before Bosanquet.[8] This must now be reinterpreted, and the evidence from photographs and comments is that he bowled the flipper: Altham was by no means the only one who was confused by it.

W. G. Grace, as if his monumental batting was not enough, enters the picture as yet another missing link with his slightly above the shoulder round-arm delivery. Not only has he a claim to being a pioneer of the top-spun leg-break with his hand turning anti-clockwise, but with Fry's description that he "could put drag spin on it by turning his hand the reverse way and cutting under the ball"[9] enters the lineage of the exponents of the modern flipper (fig. 40d). Fry admired W. G.'s bowling greatly: "[It] looks a great deal simpler than it is. A spectator watching from the side of the ground can easily see the length of the ball, but the batsman is often deceived by the flight".[10] We will see later that this inability of the batsman to judge the length accurately arises from the subtle difference in the influence of back-spin as opposed to top-spin.

The grip Grimmett refers to, and which is shown in a photograph (fig. 40c) in his book, is identical with Mead's except that his first and second fingers are much closer together than Mead's. The thumb is bent under the ball which rests on the upper edge of the thumb along the area between the joint and the thumb-nail. The other half of the grip involves the end joints of the first three fingers. Precisely which of these fingers, if any, dominates is a matter for personal experimentation. The second may dominate to some extent, but all three may well be important in working together. Now with a flick resembling the action used in playing marbles, or flicking a ball of paper

a   b

c

Fig. 40 *Pioneering spinning grips employing the thumb. Photo a: Walter Mead, pioneer of the flipper.* The ball sits in a cup made by the thumb and second finger, while the first finger is curled around the top of the ball. During release, as seen in this view, his first finger would move to the left, while his thumb would straighten out to the right to deliver an off-break. (Photo from G. W. Beldam and C. B. Fry's *Great Bowlers and Fielders.*) *Photo b: Mead's grip for the leg-break.* The thumb is now away from the palm. The first finger – ready to flick to the right in this view – and the third finger – ready to straighten out to the left – deliver the spinning power. The first-and-third-finger spinning couple is the classic grip for this deadly ball. (Photo from Beldam and Fry.) *Photo c: Grimmett's grip for the flipper,* similar to Mead's but with the ball resting on the *third* finger and thumb. The photo (from *Grimmett on Cricket*) is the batsman's view just before the thumb snaps out to the right to impart off-spin. The spin appears as a "pure", square off-spin, but the modern flipper also carries a good deal of back-spin.

Fig. 40d *W. G. Grace kept them guessing.* Is the hand rotating clockwise or anticlockwise? Here it looks like a topspun leg-break but he could also turn the hand under the ball and bowl a flipper-type delivery. (Photo from Beldam and Fry.)

from the hand, quite good spin is obtainable. This is the basic spin for a related family of deliveries.

The following is an adapted account of Grimmett's description of the deliveries possible with this grip (fig. 41, pp. 118–9).

1. With the hand held in front of the body, the back of the hand facing the batsman and the fingers pointing to the left and somewhat back towards the bowler, the spin is from leg to off.

2. Reverse the hand so that the back of it is facing the bowler. The result is off-spin.

3. Point the hand and arm towards the batsman with the palm facing left and slightly upwards. The spin is now top-spin. Grimmett calls it "over-spin". It will carry straight on after pitching.

4. Quoting Grimmett's exact words: "Reverse again the position of the hand so that it is on your right side, with the fingers pointing to the right and the back of the hand facing the batsman".[11] This time the ball has back-spin and slows up when it hits the pitch.

5. Later in the book Grimmett adds another, in which the hand, held out to the right of the body, is turned further over than in 4 so that the back of the hand faces the batsman as for the googly. The result of the thumb flicking out underneath is a leg-break or the "wrong wrong-un" as he describes it. It looks like a wrong-un but is actually a leg-break!

6. In yet another part of the book he reveals his Mystery Ball (fig. 42, page 120), again employing the same grip, but applying more spin than when bowling his ordinary leg-break. I find this hard to believe. He states that he was only interested in balls that "made pace off the pitch" except as an occasional variation. For twelve years he practised it, summer and winter, gradually increasing his length. As he spun it:

> the hand had to be pointed across to the left towards cover, the wrist had to be bent and the ball allowed to leave over the top of the hand, the back of which was facing the batsman. However, the real problem was to propel the ball and at the same time to synchronise the spinning of it with the moment of release. The hand had to be in exactly the right position, because even the slightest variation caused the ball to leave the pitch slowly . . . This proved to be a very successful ball being much harder to detect than the ordinary googly because I did not have to drop my left shoulder to bowl it. Its plain merit however was its pace off the pitch.
>
> By varying the hand position slightly at the moment of release I could bowl several different balls but they were slow off the pitch and I hardly ever used them.[12]

For the reader who sees these six deliveries as opening up a new era in spin, a word of caution. Grimmett himself nowhere says he regarded all as worthy of development. We must see at least some of them as nothing more than the academic hypotheses of Clarrie wearing his gown as "Professor of All Possible Spins".

We can dismiss number one as an extremely awkward method of bowling a leg-break, and not to be taken seriously. The same goes for number five, which is another impractical method for the leg-break and lacking the partial top-spin component which gives the orthodox leg-break its life. Nor does it possess back-spin which, as we shall see later, also confers an advantage.

Delivery two, the thumb-knuckle off-break, is worthy of attention, but if delivered as "pure" off-break, it is another ball which possesses neither the top-spin nor the back-spin component.

Delivery three, a top-spinner, and delivery six, the Mystery Ball (a top-spinning off-break), are really minor variants of the same ball. I wonder very much about this ball. Writing in another publication Grimmett says: "I always remember my first try-out against an experienced player after I had mastered the ball that goes straight through with over-spin."[13]

No one, as far as I am aware, bowls this ball. If they do, then it must resemble the weapon of science fiction, that having destroyed its victim, self-destructs to obliterate all trace of itself. I invite readers to try it with a cricket ball after having examined the photograph (fig. 42) reproduced from Grimmett's 1948 book.

The arm is stretched out in front of the body, the hand no higher than his cap, the first and second fingers around the front of the ball with the thumb out of sight, presumably cocked behind it. I am reminded of nothing so much as the story of J. M. Barrie of whom it was said that he bowled so slow that if the delivery was not to his satisfaction he had the time to reach out and snatch it back.

I have tried the Mystery Ball for a few hours, an insultingly short time I suppose, in view of the years he worked on it. My results were either "pure" off-spin or off-spin of the back-spinning variety, with no trace of the top-spin which Grimmett states is the essence of the ball.

The main problem is that the motivating forward force appears to depend heavily on the thumb during the final part of the delivery, and that the thumb is incapable of supplying the pace or zip at the angle required. Grimmett states that the "wrist had to be bent" but in the photograph the wrist is perfectly straight. Perhaps it was bent in some direction (down?) before the final instant. If you hear a clicking noise sometimes, it is probably Clarrie making doubly sure we remain confused down here. I think I now understand why one writer wrote of him:

> He produced a book on how to take wickets, but only told us how he
> took them himself... Besides, you might as well have read Dan Leno
> on the art of making faces, or the wind on the art of blowing.[14]

Delivery four however is in a class of its own. With the addition of an element
of off-spin from delivery two, it is the modern flipper, Grimmett's most
significant discovery (or rather re-discovery). In demonstrating the use of
the thumb in over-arm spin, and it must be added that this is not necessarily
restricted to slow bowling, he re-discovered a delivery potentially more
useful than the over-rated googly.

I had floundered around the literature on the flipper for a few years,
finding it incoherent and useless. Grimmett's book, read thirty years previously, meant nothing to me in this vital area. The director of coaching for
New Zealand, Martin Horton, could not help me. As a last resort, in 1982, I
wrote to Richie Benaud who obliged with a clear and simple reply as follows.

> The "flipper" was a ball that came out from underneath the hand. If
> you hold your arm erect with the back of the hand pointing towards
> the sky and turn your hand anti-clockwise, that would be a leg-break –
> but if you think in terms of the ball being held in the fingers and then
> "flipped" out upwards and, in effect, clockwise, that is the "flipper". It
> actually comes from underneath the hand rather than from over the
> top of it. The result for the batsman is something like a skidding
> off-cutter and the palm of the hand will end up facing the batsman.[15]

Fig. 41(2) would appear to illustrate this delivery fairly accurately.

We now have practical descriptions of two deliveries, one from Grimmett,
a top-spinning off-break delivered over the top of the hand, the other from
Benaud, a back-spinning off-break delivered from under the hand. The first,
meeting Grimmett's requirement (so he thought) of pace off the pitch, the
product of twelve years' work and described by him as "a very successful
ball", appears to have been universally rejected by bowlers: the second,
apparently rejected by Grimmett because he (wrongly) regarded it as being
slowed when it hit the pitch, has been embraced by perhaps the majority of
the best leg-spinners of the second half of the twentieth century.

Since most writers regard these two deliveries as being identical, it is not
surprising that when discussing the Grimmett–Pepper–Dooland–Benaud
genealogy they seem suddenly bereft of the ability to use words precisely.
The examples that follow are not quoted in order to ridicule the authors of
some interesting and instructive books, but to illustrate the problem the
flipper has caused. Discussion on the matter should also prove useful in
removing the widespread ignorance of the more general topic of the relation
between spin, flight, bounce and pace off the pitch.

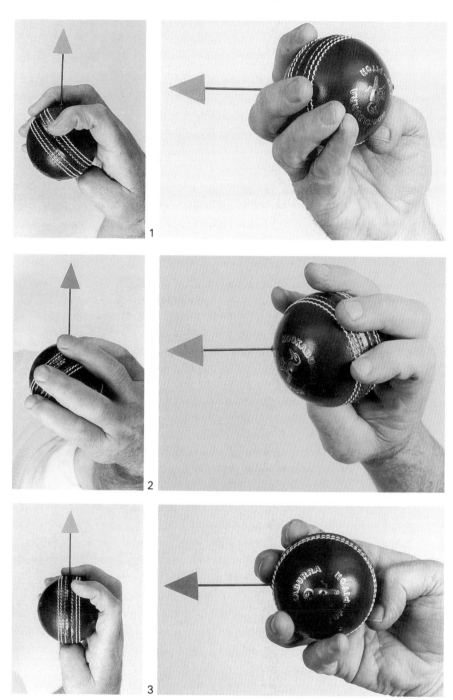

Fig. 41 *Modern reconstructions of Grimmett's six thumb-generated spins, including his "Mystery Ball"* (*6*). Some of the photos may not appear to fit Grimmett's description exactly since, for clarity, they are shown at a more advanced stage of the release process.

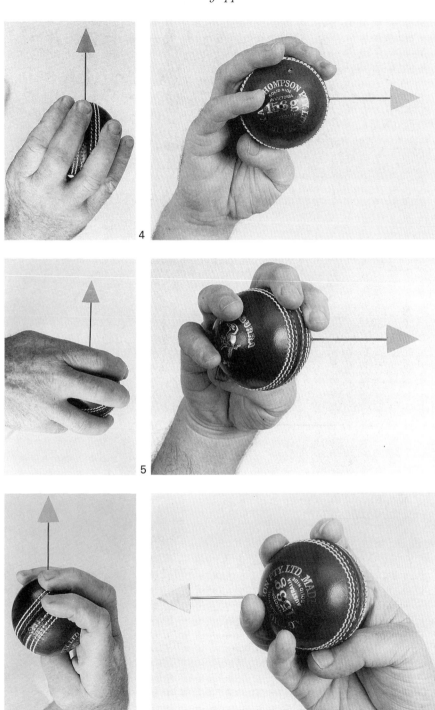

Fig. 42 *The following description accompanied the above photograph in Grimmett on Cricket:* "The 'Mystery Ball' is about to be released. The spin is applied at that moment. Note the position of the hand, with the thumb on the opposite side moved upwards to give forward-spin."

Ray Illingworth leads off into the confusion with: "The ball which goes straight on – at uneven height – is called the top-spinner or flipper: the one which goes the other way is the googly or Bosie."[16]

Vic Marks, taking a wiser course, opts out completely: "The action should resemble a leg-break but the ball is squeezed out of the hand in a variety of individually-devised ways".[17]

Bruce Dooland, who with Ces Pepper first brought the flipper into post-Second World War cricket and used it with notable success, gives an interesting account of it, but in using the highly misleading term "top-spinner" has lent his considerable authority to a widespread misconception of its real nature. His account which includes the role of the thumb, an omission from Benaud's reply to my enquiry, is as follows.

> There is another type of delivery at the call of a wrist-spinner, one that should only be tried and persevered with after control has been learned and you have mastered the stock deliveries.
>
> This ball took me at least five years of constant practice before I attempted to use it in a match. It is very effective when bowled properly, combining the bosie and skidding top-spinner, together with a rather flat trajectory, floating it further up to the batsman than any other delivery.
>
> It has been called the "flipper" as the ball is flipped by the thumb and second finger, much the same as clicking these fingers together, imparting an off-spin, which turns backwards to the line of flight. The great advantage of this delivery is that although acting like a bosie-top-spinner, unlike the bosie the ball comes from the front of the hand like a leg-break, and is harder to detect than a googly. Once again as in all deliveries by a wrist-spinner, the wrist plays a very important part, and must be snapped out straight.
>
> The present Australian captain, Benaud, learned this ball in Nottingham in 1956, and I believe that it took him quite a number of years to master it. To the best of my knowledge he is the only bowler using it today in first class cricket.
>
> From this it can be seen that the "flipper" is a post-graduate delivery, and concentration for the younger wrist-spinner should be on the normal leg-break and googly.[18]

Dooland passed the knowledge of the flipper on to Benaud at Nottingham during the 1956 Australian tour of England, but C. S. Marriott in his book *The Complete Leg-Break Bowler* wrongly understood it to be the googly.[19]

No one would be much the wiser after reading Jack Fingleton's account of Grimmett's ball " ... known as the flipper because of the click of the fingers as he released the ball. He bowled it with a leg-break action and the ball making pace from the pitch would come in from the off".[20]

Ray Robinson is equally vague in describing Benaud as:

> Commanding respect with length leg-breaks, he set batsmen up for his top-spinner. Pushed lower through the air his flipper usually caused them to play back and be trapped by its quicker nip. If pitches allowed enough grip for his wrong 'un he posted a leg-slip as well as a slip.[21]

An early revision of *The Dictionary of Cricket* by Michael Rundell must be in order:

> flipper, a relatively slow ball that behaves somewhat like a top-spinner and is produced by a particularly convoluted variety of wrist-spin. It is typically produced by gripping the ball mainly with the tips of the first and third fingers and squeezing or flipping it out so that it emerges from the back or the side of the hand with an extra helping of top-spin on it. If successfully executed it will hurry through without deviation, gaining pace as it pitches and keeping low. The flipper has been described as "the most arcane and esoteric ball in cricket" (Scyld Berry, *Observer* 11 March 1984) and its invention is usually attributed to Clarrie Grimmett; more recent exponents include Richie Benaud and Abdul Qadir.[22]

At least Scyld Berry found a couple of good adjectives to describe the confusion. Bruce Dooland, who could bowl the flipper at "a Bedser-like pace" might not be too happy with the "relatively slow" label. In fact, if a general speed tag is to be applied to the flipper it is "relatively quick".

In a description where exhilaration compensates in some degree for scarcity of solid information, Patrick Murphy, writing of Dooland in *The Spinner's Turn*, says:

> In addition to the traditional leg-spinner's gifts, Dooland had another deadly delivery under his command: the flipper. He spun that from out of the tips of his fingers and it zipped through from off to leg at speed. It is quicker than the googly and Dooland caught out countless batsman with it: they would shape up for the pull, only to see it hustle through, bowl them off the inside edge or trap them lbw. "Roley" Jenkins, no stranger to the arts and crafts of leg-spin says: "How Bruce did that was beyond me. He bowled it at a different pace from the googly with no change in action and it would come off the pitch like an Alec Bedser delivery." Doug Insole remembers: "Bruce used to get me out as a pastime. To me, his flipper was indistinguishable from his googly. As far as I was concerned, he had seven or eight different types

of delivery and I was on the edge of my seat all the time. He didn't bowl loose balls like Doug Wright, either. He was the best bowler I've ever faced, an artist".[23]

Murphy describes flipper exponent Intikhab Alam as "regularly undoing younger players" and quotes the Northamptonshire wicket-keeper George Sharp describing another Pakistani spinner, Mushtaq, rather vaguely: "He'd bowl flippers and googlies and roll them over – they'd play back and be trapped in front by the flipper or they'd try to off drive and be bowled through the gate by his googly".[24]

Batsmen would find Tom Graveney's stark description of Benaud's flipper upsetting: "It skidded on to you. If it caught you on the back foot it nailed you before you could do anything else".[25]

What ball Ian Peebles is describing in the entry on Grimmett in a recent reference work is anybody's guess:

His googly was a more modest affair, clearly discernible and used mostly for tactical purposes. His top-spinner was, on the other hand, a wicket-taking weapon, delivered rather faster and tending to dip late in its flight.[26]

Grimmett says he had discarded the orthodox googly to all intents and purposes for the most successful years of his career.

The Lord's Taverners Cricket Clinic, in the caption to a photo of Benaud bowling, fell at the last hurdle:

Benaud's repertoire included the leg-break, googly, top-spinner (the ball which gains pace off the wicket but doesn't turn), and the "flipper" – flipped out of the hand from underneath the wrist and in effect an off-spinning top-spinner.[27]

An old mate of Benaud's, Norman O'Neill, gave an account stronger on adulation than information:

Most people have heard of Richie's "flipper". This ball is extremely difficult to bowl. It is released with a quicker trajectory from the tips of the fingers and hurries straight on. It has taken him a long time to develop the action. But his determination was so great that he worked for years to perfect it. Many bowlers would have given up but not Benaud. If he makes his mind up to do something he usually does it, no matter how long it takes. His hard work has been worthwhile as I have seen many top-class batsmen left standing when he has bowled this ball. He must get immense satisfaction out of seeing his "flipper" hit the stumps, as batsmen set themselves to pull what they think is a long hop and are deceived from pace. His great patience and determination have certainly paid off.[28]

John Arlott writing in *In Celebration of Cricket* is non-committal:

> Grimmett's basic strategy, when he was fighting rearguard actions on Australian pitches, was to harp away on a restraining length constantly varying his flight and pace until he snared the batsmen into playing back to his favourite flipper, which skidded through to rap their padded shins in front of the stumps. One-fifth of Grimmett's victims in Tests against England were leg-before-wicket, and on Australian turf the proportion rose to more than one-third.[29]

John Gleeson, himself a versatile bowler and experimenter, leaves us in the dark with "...flipper, a bosey or wrong 'un which hastens off the pitch with top-spin".[30]

Brian Close describes the results accurately without detailing methods:

> Richie Benaud and Ces Pepper were great exponents of the flipper. It is bowled with a slightly lower arm action and quicker on a lower trajectory, making the batsman expect a long hop. After committing himself to the pull, he finds the ball rushes on off the wicket, catching him half-way through this intended stroke.[31]

Likewise, Trevor Bailey: "Personally I found his [Benaud's] 'flipper' his most difficult delivery. He concealed it with a great skill, and made it hurry off the pitch in such a way that the batsman would still be completing the stroke when rapped on the pads".[32]

Although many of these accounts are not without interest, they share a number of features arising not only from ignorance but also from carelessness. The word "top-spin" as used unambiguously for many years in sports such as golf, tennis, table tennis and cricket, means the reverse of back-spin. C. B. Fry, eighty years ago, left the reader in no doubt with "over-spin" and "check-spin" but this has not prevented Peter Philpott from giving us the "back-spinning top-spinner"[33] nor an Australian Cricket Board coaching book from stating "this top-spinner and the over-spinner are completely different"[34]!

The term "googly" means an off-break with a particular origin but "wrong 'un" in the hands of some cricket writers can apparently mean anything different from normal, whatever that might be. Used this way, "wrong 'un" declares an ignorance which bowlers encourage.

The quotation describing Grimmett's flipper was deliberately included with those describing the deliveries of others, for the purpose of suggesting to the reader that Grimmett's flipper may not have been any different, coming through quickly and low, always threatening an lbw. The question now arises as to whether, in spite of his own writings, Grimmett's flipper was not the Mystery Ball at all, but was in fact Mead's ball, arrived at independently or not, and passed on to Pepper, Dooland, Benaud and the others.

Benaud has written about the flipper in several publications. Coming from one of the masters of the delivery his words would be expected to be gospel. But alas, even here, "the cloud of unknowing" obscures the view at times. In other words, Benaud was a true son of the cagey Grimmett in this aspect of the art as well. When he wrote *Richie Benaud's Way of Cricket*[35] in 1961 his harvest, long in the ripening, was beginning to come in and more awaited the gathering during the next two years. Here was a ball, unknown to most modern readers and players, and the story of its first apparent use in Test cricket after the Second World War.

The journalist in him would not allow a good story to go begging. But it was not the time to write a coaching manual for the batsman facing up at the other end. The result is two pages of cricket history, bearing the threat of trouble in store for batsmen, and quite unencumbered by useful details such as the grip, the under-hand delivery and the type of spin given to the ball. "I recall adding to my variety after a chat with Bruce Dooland during the 1956 tour". Surely this must be one of the more casual descriptions of the priming of one of the big guns in cricket history. Benaud continues:

> There was a lot of talk in 1956 of how Bruce took wickets with his "flipper". This was a delivery that was spun out of the tips of the fingers and hustled in off the pitch from off to leg at great pace. He explained the grip and then I went through the motions. The first few I tried either slipped straight through as full tosses, or dropped halfway down the pitch. I kept at it however and when I eventually landed one or two I was delighted to see how they fizzed through.[36]

Then follows an account of the airing of the flipper on the South African tour of 1957–8.

> The pitch was slow and my normal leg-break and wrong 'un lacked penetration. Clive Van Ryneveld was batting against me and I thought: "I'll try the flipper". It dropped short, Clive stepped back to square-cut and the ball nipped back off the pitch and bowled him. It had worked like a charm. That success has encouraged me to use the flipper ever since, but not too liberally. It does not always take a wicket, of course: in fact it often gets hit for four. But I'm glad to have it as a trump card to be used in times of trouble.[37]

The flipper also brought Benaud success on the Pakistan tour of 1959.

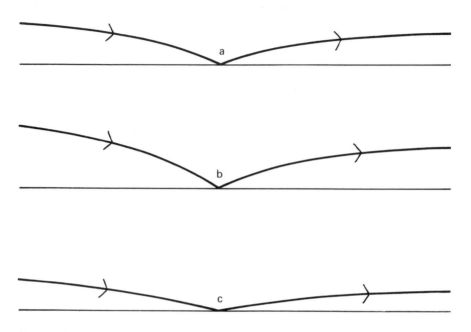

Fig. 43 *Angle of arrival of ball on to pitch as it affects bounce: a* normal delivery; *b* delivery arriving more steeply due to top-spin and therefore bouncing off more steeply; *c* low-angle arrival and bounce caused by back-spin during flight which gives no grip or kick on landing.

Later, writing in 1984[38], he was more forthcoming about vital details.

The relation between spin, flight, bounce and pace off the wicket is commonly misunderstood. The basic rule is the simple one, probably learned at school, describing the reflection of a ray of light from a mirror: the ray reflects off the mirror at the same angle as it arrives. Grimmett illustrates this by describing the two ways of throwing a flat stone into water; a high dropping flight, when it will sink immediately, and a low skimming flight when it will bounce off the surface.[39] In general terms, that is how a cricket ball behaves. Fig. 43a can therefore be regarded as illustrating the path of a simple delivery carrying no spin.

Consider a ball carrying at least a major proportion of top-spin. The Robins Force arising from that spin will push the ball downwards in flight and the bowler compensates for this by tossing it higher. We saw from the wind-tunnel results that the Robins Force is greater if the wind speed is greater; slow bowlers bowling into the wind must therefore toss the ball even higher; the topspun ball, whether bowled into the wind or not, lands at a steeper angle (fig. 43b) and therefore has less forward momentum than the ball in fig. 43c.

Bill O'Reilly, writing Grimmett's obituary, said of him: "He seldom bowled the 'wrong 'un' because he preferred not to toss the ball high".[40] Grimmett liked the ball to come off the wicket quickly, and since the "wrong 'un" (googly) carried a fair amount of top-spin, it suffered from the loss of forward momentum described above, an effect accentuated by the fact that he generally bowled upwind.

Although a spinning ball coming down steeply on to the wicket will grip more than a ball coming through at a lower angle, the pitch, these days normally slow, will not give the bowler a return for his efforts because the energy of the dipping ball will have been dissipated in the turf. The steeply dipping ball is quite innocuous therefore if it is not followed by sharp upward movement off the pitch. Bounce could force the batsman into a more awkward series of actions which may end in him giving a catch. Good bounce is therefore critical to any form of upwind bowling involving an element of top-spin whether it arises from the top-spinning leg-spinner, "pure" top-spin or the top-spinning googly.

Grimmett (possibly), and some notable leg-spinners who came after him, faced this problem and adopted a novel solution – the flipper. Because the flipper carries a predominantly backward direction of spin, i.e. the bottom of the ball spinning fowards, the Robins Force acts upwards against the force of gravity, thus flattening to some extent the normal downward-curving trajectory. The contrast in flight resulting from the difference between upward and downward Robins Force is one of the surprises of the flipper when bowled after a series of balls carrying top-spin of one sort or another. This feature, frequently commented on by batsmen, recalls Fry's description of Mead's deliveries as "rather deceptive in flight". Arriving at a flatter angle it therefore comes off the wicket at a flatter angle (fig. 43c). This means good forward momentum with little bounce; just the ball to scuttle through and cause havoc.

A more subtle aspect of this flight is that because it approaches flatter through the air, the batsman is more likely to misjudge the length by thinking that it must drop down and land short like a normal topspun delivery. He will therefore go back to wait for it only to find it further up than expected as well as coming in with a certain amount of off-break.

Why did Grimmet think that all backspun deliveries come off slowly, and how does the idea of pace off the pitch fit in with all this? The two questions can be answered together.

In the present discussion, pace off the pitch is of most significance when the bowler can make it change from one delivery to another.

Although Grimmett used the analogy of the stone skimming through the bounce when thrown flat across water, he does not seem to have connected this with the type of flight shown by a ball carrying back-spin. This flight almost invariably overrides any slight slowing down caused by the bite and kick that sometimes result when a backspun ball lands, particularly on gripless pitches. Grimmett was right insofar as a ball landing with top-spin will come off the wicket faster than a ball coming in at the same angle with back-spin, but the essential point is that topspun and backspun deliveries seldom do land at the same angle, because the Robins Force gives them a different flight, especially against the wind.

Pace off the pitch, in this discussion, depends on how much of the total energy given to the ball by the bowler goes into forward movement on landing, and how much goes into upward movement. The flipper has pace off the pitch because a high proportion of its energy ends up as forward momentum. It is worth noting that the kick occasionally expected from the flipper has been reported as "variable bounce". Such a kick, and in fact the grip the flipper must get on the ground to show any off-break, will depend on how much friction is felt on impact, a matter which was discussed earlier.

It is not my intention to conclude this little saga by agreeing with those authors who shake their heads and warn us off the flipper as a most difficult delivery to learn. Rather, I would prefer to look at the known facts and compare the flipper with other deliveries in the repertoire.

Since the whole essence of the flipper is concerned with variation, contrast and surprise, one would normally advocate its use as an accompaniment for the leg-break. However, a lateral-thinking medium-pacer may see it as worth a trial as a new type of off-break to accompany other deliveries such as swing, or a ball that turns from leg to off. In this connection I should mention that with a little practice I found it possible to deliver the flipper with the seam pointing towards the slips, and remaining in that position during flight, i.e. as in fig. 32b for the outswinging off-break. Bowled after a series of in-swerving leg-breaks, this ball will surprise batsmen, even if it doesn't turn back greatly. But a slowish outswinger is probably not the intended result and the bowler may choose to nullify the swing which tends to counteract the off-break. If unwanted swing does occur the ball must be delivered with enough quick wobble in the seam to negate it.

When exploring the off-break capabilities of the flipper it is useful to remember that by bringing the palm of the hand up and around a little to face the off, more off-break can be obtained. However, this will partly reduce the low-skidding back-spin component of the off-break which is the whole basis of the flipper's unusual flight and bounce. Such an action may also make the flipper easier to distinguish from the leg-break. Mead's off-break, discussed earlier, was in fact the flipper. Fry's description of its behaviour along with the previously discussed grip, matches the modern flipper perfectly:

The batsman cannot easily get to the pitch of the ball to drive and yet has very little time to watch the ball from the pitch if he plays back. Some bowlers who command a good off-break on sticky wickets are fairly easy to hit with a certain amount of pull in the stroke, but Mead's bowling comes off the pitch in a way that baulks the success of the pulled drive.[41]

Used in conjunction with the leg-break, both at medium pace, Mead was a most effective bowler. Compare this account with Alan Border's description of Trevor Hohn's delivery in the fourth Test of the 1989 Australian tour of England. Hohns had bowled a long-hop in the previous over:

Next over "Cracker" produced the "flipper". This pitches half-way down too but it doesn't sit up and say "Hit me!" It just looks like a long-hop. In fact what it does is skid through fast and lowish. Gower went back to belt it over mid-wicket but his bat was hardly even into the downswing when the ball rapped him on the pads. Out leg before...[42]

The photographs (fig. 44) show the essential features of the flipper delivery.

If we are to find the proper place for the flipper in the repertoire of spin, we must face the fact immediately that its most famous exponents adopted the flipper because they were dissatisfied with the googly, which by its nature, at any pace, is normally a more flighted delivery. Bill O'Reilly overcame this problem by using his height to deliver the googly in a more downward direction than that available to bowlers of lesser height, and also by bowling downwind. Bosanquet's legacy, which I will discuss in Chapter 21, is something of a mixed blessing, to say the least, and I would suggest that bowlers give serious thought to taking up the flipper as an alternative.

Grimmett's twelve years are probably more interesting now as myth than as a practical guide to learning time. O'Reilly says that Grimmett used the flipper to good effect in his record-breaking last season before the Second World War.[43] Fry does not single out Mead's ball as causing any unusual learning problem. If we ignore the influence of Ring we must assume that Benaud took no more than two years to bring it right into first class cricket. This would be a remarkable feat for the student of any sort of delivery, but he was no ordinary student! However, Dooland, as mentioned earlier, says Benaud "took quite a number of years" learning it. Dooland's own apprenticeship was at least five years of constant practice.

Benaud tells us, in a tribute to Ken Barrington, that Ken picked up the flipper quite quickly, and was bowling it well after a couple of years.[44] Trevor Hohns is quoted as saying that he had worked on it for six years. My own experience, involving only spasmodic periods at it, has seen a steady improvement over about seven years and I might add that I am well past the colt stage. Until one hears of failures, more serious and widespread than the disasters frequently associated with the googly, there is no reason to believe that bowlers will experience any unusual problems with the flipper. The advantages of a ball which comes through quicker and lower, especially on a slow pitch, are obvious. The future of this rivalry of the wrong 'uns should be full of interest, and as long as cricket writers keep using the term "wrong 'un", and misunderstanding the flipper, the confusion that bowlers thrive on will continue to flourish.

Benaud mentions shoulder trouble which forced him to give up bowling the flipper on the 1961 Australian tour of England, but none of the other

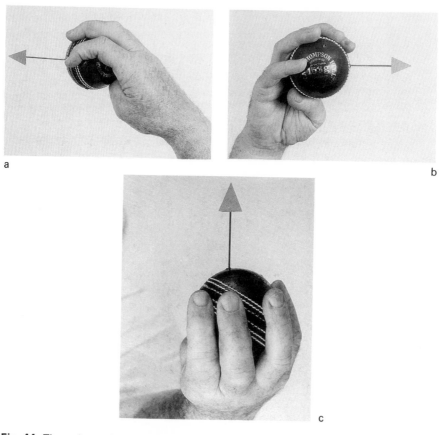

Fig. 44 *Three views of the flipper just prior to release,* when the thumb flicks out, moving the bottom of the ball towards point: *a* from the bowler's side; *b* from the leg side; *c* from above the hand. The thumb bent under the ball is visible only in *b*. The first three fingers above the ball move down backwards behind it during release. Most of the force on top may come from the second finger which is in line with the arrow in *c*, but individual actions will vary.

exponents appear to have reported such problems. One suspects that Benaud's problem arose not from the flipper but from the more general effects of years of intense practice and play. Leg-break bowling alone can cause problems, but he also bowled the googly, which is notorious in this regard. My own experience is that the flipper causes less strain on the bowling muscles than does the leg-break.

Benaud's comments on disguising the grip contain valuable advice:

> Bruce Dooland used to have a long run when he played in Australia, but when he came to England he cut it down, and concentrated on disguising his hand before he released the ball so that the batsman couldn't see what was happening, whether the ball was coming out of the top of the hand or the bottom. The batsman could see that something was going on but couldn't pick it out clearly. This was one of the reasons why I chopped my own run-up down to six paces.[45]

These bowlers appear to have improved on Mead in this respect since Fry observes:

> It is easy to detect whether he is bowling the off- or the leg-break because when he is going to use the latter he changes the ball in his hand at the last moment and arranges his grip with very obvious care. Needless to say the batsman, although he knows what is coming, is not thereby relieved of all difficulty.[46]

As for pace, it could be said that there are two general strategies to choose from: one, like Dooland's where the ball rips through much faster than the previous deliveries at a lively medium pace, or the other, where the pace as picked up early in the flight by a good batsman is indistinguishable from the rest. In the latter case it is the subsequent behaviour of the ball that causes the batsman trouble. Since this ball must also be of a reasonable pace, the strategy requires that the accompanying balls (such as leg-breaks) must also not be very slow. Careful practice, with the help of an observer or a video camera, can help the bowler to keep as many of these actions as possible indistinguishable when bowling the flipper among other deliveries.

Fig. 44 shows a grip for the flipper. The seam rests on the thumb and the fingers lie on the other side of the ball. The action should not be difficult for anyone familiar with the off-break. In my early experiments I sought to use the second finger as the only spinning force opposing the thumb. Later, when I engaged all the first three fingers in the process, having them spaced and roughly opposite to the thumb, I achieved better control. As the arm is raised, the compression in this grip is increased to be released as the thumb flicks out straight, probably in the direction of third-man, and the three fingers rip down to the leg side behind the ball. There should be a comfortable feeling of control. The pace should be no greater than accuracy will allow, and the hand should twist as sharply as possible during release. The arm should be high and the wrist bent to the same position as for the leg-break with plenty of body behind it in the follow through.

The flipper is at least a hundred years old, but through neglect and misunderstanding its true value has remained hidden. The time is ripe for bowlers to rediscover it.

REFERENCES

1 N. O'Neill, *Ins and Outs* (Pelham Books, 1964), p. 214 2 P. May, *A Game Enjoyed* (Stanley Paul, 1985), p. 160 3 C. V. Grimmett, *Grimmett on Cricket*, p. 42 4 C. V. Grimmett, *Tricking the Batsman* (R. M. Osborne, 1932), p. 59 5 C. V. Grimmett, *Grimmett on Cricket*, p. 40–3 6 G. W. Beldam and C. B. Fry, *Great Bowlers and Fielders*, p. 234 7 C. Martin-Jenkins, *The Complete Who's Who of Test Cricketers* (Orbis Publishing, 1983), p. 104 8 H. S. Altham and E. W. Swanton, *A History of Cricket*, p. 214 9 G. W. Beldam and C. B. Fry, *Great Bowlers and Fielders*, p. 338 10 ibid., p. 338 11 C. V. Grimmett, *Tricking the Batsman*, p. 59 12 C. V. Grimmett, *Grimmett on Cricket.*, p. 42 13 J. Pollard (ed), *Six and Out* (Jack Pollard Publishing, 1980), p. 214 14 R. C. Robertson-Glasgow (Alan Ross, ed), *Crusoe on Cricket* (The Pavilion Library, 1966), p. 171. Dan Leno (1860–1904) was the greatest comedian in the history of music hall. He was able to convulse his audience with a look 15 R. Benaud, letter, 1982 16 R. Illingworth, *The Young Cricketer* (Stanley Paul, 1972), p. 65 17 V. Marks, *The Test and County Cricket Board Guide to Better Cricket*, p. 102 18 J. Pollard (ed), *Cricket – The Australian Way* (Landsdowne Press, 1961), p. 110 19 C. S. Marriott, *The Complete Leg-Break Bowler*, p. 62 20 J. Fingleton, *Fingleton on Cricket* (Collins, 1972), p. 167 21 R. Robinson, *On Top Down Under* (Cassell, 1975), p. 248 22 M Rundell, *A Dictionary of Cricket* (George Allen and Unwin, 1985), p. 89 23 P. Murphy, *The Spinner's Turn*, p. 59 24 ibid., p. 163 25 T. Graveney, *Cricket Over Forty* (Pelham Books, 1970), p. 147 26 E. W. Swanton (ed), *Barclays World of Cricket*, p. 478 27 A. Gover (ed), *The Lord's Taveners Cricket Clinic* (Graham Tarrant, 1986), p. 75 28 N. O'Neill, *Ins and Outs*, p. 216 29 K. Gregory, *In Celebration of Cricket*, p. 160 30 J. Pollard (ed), *Cricket – The Australian Way*, p. 122 31 D. B. Close, *Close on Cricket* (Stanley Paul, 1986), p. 56 32 T. E. Bailey, *The Greatest of My Time* (Eyre and Spottiswoode, 1968), p. 188 33 P. Philpott, *How To Play Cricket* (Jack Pollard Publishing, 1973), p. 58 34 Australian Cricket Board, *Skills and Tactics* (Landsdowne Press, 1982), p. 84 35 R. Benaud, *Richie Benaud's Way of Cricket* (Hodder and Stoughton, 1969), p. 57 36 ibid., p. 57 37 ibid., p. 57 38 R. Benaud, *Willow Patterns*, p. 182–3 39 C. V. Grimmett, *Tricking the Batsman*, p. 34 40 W. J. O'Reilly, *Wisden Anthology 1963–82*, p. 924 41 G. W. Beldam and C. B. Fry, *Great Bowlers and Fielders*, p. 232 42 A. Border, *Ashes Glory* (Swan Publishing, 1989), p. 101 43 W. J. O'Reilly, *Wisden Anthology 1963–1982*, p. 924 44 B. Scovell, *Ken Barrington – A Tribute* (Harrop, 1982), p. 79 45 ibid., p. 79 46 G. W. Beldam and C. B. Fry, *Great Bowlers and Fielders*, p. 232

Chapter 17

S. F. Barnes: leg-spin, off-spin, swerve and pace

THE NAME SYDNEY FRANCES BARNES no longer appears in the coaching books. Coaches could be forgiven if, like the worshippers of old, they were in dread of even uttering the name of the awesome deity. Is a bowler who could curve the ball both ways in the air and break it both ways off the pitch, all at more than medium pace, too remote a model for mere mortals? His 189 wickets in 27 Tests at an average of 16.43 certainly inspire awe.

Why do so few of today's bowlers try to imitate him? I suggest that our thinking today takes us past him, leaving him mounted as some sort of museum piece. Explain this attitude and you explain a good deal of twentieth century cricket: preoccupied with swing and cut. Barnes didn't merely swing and cut, he swerved and spun. He was satisfied with nothing less than spinning and swerving in both directions. He upsets our preconceptions of what fast bowlers do and what slow bowlers do. Standing astride the boundary between the two he tells us that there is no boundary.

Barnes lived a long and active life, during which he wrote a little and talked freely about his bowling. As a result we are able to piece together a picture of his development and methods. There will only be one S. F. Barnes, but why should bowlers born a century after him not aim to use those same methods, adapted to their own powers?

Fry's description, although vague in parts and written during the middle years of Barnes' Test career, paints a picture of a great bowler:

> In the matter of pace he may be regarded either as a fast or a fast-medium bowler. He certainly bowled faster some days than others; and on his fastest day was certainly distinctly fast.
>
> He obtained his pace from a peculiarly loose, long, circular swing; he did not put much body weight behind the ball and, unlike most bowlers of his pace, he obtained very little power from the bend of his back. The life of his bowling came from the liveliness of his swing. At the same time he had a remarkable power of hand, and worked the ball with his fingers at the moment of delivery in a way which is very uncommon with bowlers of more than medium pace. He is usually regarded as being able to break from leg as well as from the off, his leg-break being similar to that of a slow bowler. But his leg-break was

not really quite of this kind. He had a natural power of bowling a ball which swung from leg to the off after pitching, and he increased this cross swing by finger work so that it became something more than merely "going with the arm" and yet was not genuine break. In any case it was a very difficult ball to play.

When he was bowling well he kept a very accurate length on the off stump, and made the ball go first one way and then the other without betraying any difference in his delivery. As his bowling came very quickly from the pitch he was troublesome to the very best batsmen. To get his best results he required a wicket with a bit of life in it.[1]

Modern coaches intent on getting young fast and medium-pace bowlers to bend their backs, perhaps excessively, could learn something from the above account: unlike many of today's bowlers, Barnes remained untroubled by spinal injuries throughout his long career.

He began as a fast bowler, playing an occasional county game without much success. In later years he commented that fast-medium is the ideal pace on which to build a range of variations of spin and pace, adding that: "It is much easier for a fast bowler to become a slow or medium-paced bowler than for a slow bowler to become a fast bowler".[2] He might also have said that since faster bowlers vary in their actions, not all are necessarily destined to make the transition with equal ease. Barnes himself, relying more than many on arm action, is a case in point. Tall at 6 ft 1 in (1.85 m), but by today's standards not unusually so, he was noted for his high, smooth, flowing action. Building on this foundation, he turned to spin. In three hours of coaching he learned how to bowl an off-break, but having decided that it was the ball going away off the pitch that would cause batsmen most trouble, he set out to teach himself the leg-break.

His grip for the leg-break (fig. 46a) was identical with that of most slower bowlers. The first and third fingers did the work, with the ball held out on the first joint of these, along with the second finger and thumb for support. But there was no slowing down; his leg-break was perhaps faster than any seen before, and his accuracy unrelenting. With his new-found skill, he took more than a hundred wickets in his first season for Lancashire in 1902, at a tidy average. Obviously he didn't feel the need to use his off-break, since *Wisden* that year said that he needed to cultivate one. Nor did it hold back his rocketing career. A. C. MacLaren, the previous year, invited him straight from the Lancashire League to join the English team to Australia for the 1901–2 tour. When the off-break became an integral part of his attack it was, like Barnes himself, something out of the ordinary.

Before that comment appeared in *Wisden* Barnes had encountered M. A. Noble in Australia, and learned from him about the ball which swerved from leg to off, then broke back into the wicket. Noble, right-hand medium pace, and George Hirst, a left-hander faster than Noble, pioneered the curved ball derived from baseball, that strikes back in the reverse direction off the pitch. In acquiring this knowledge, Noble and Hirst demonstrated the principle that for every ball bowled by a left- or right-handed bowler there is a corresponding exact mirror image available to the bowler of opposite hand. Hirst bowled the ball that *curved in* to the right-hander before *turning away* off the pitch; Noble bowled the ball that *swerved away* to the off before *turning back* off the pitch. As we would expect, Hirst was most effective when bowling into a head wind which had the additional effect of making the ball swerve late in flight. But all the exponents of swerve have experienced its unreliability, and Barnes was no exception. "It would simply drift in late, driving all the way" he said, dismissing such an innocuous parabola. "When you were bowling it well, it would go [straight] and then dip in".[3]

How did Barnes and Noble bowl this ball, and why was Barnes' leg-break famous, particularly for curving to leg before effecting its more obvious destructive purpose? A bowler, who in eleven overs can take five wickets for six runs to remove the cream of Australia's batting, as Barnes did in Melbourne in 1911, must have something special that we could learn about.

Accurate fast-medium to medium-pace leg-breaks were special enough on their own, but when we look at Barnes' hand, high above his head at the point of delivery, we can't help noticing how different it is from the numerous leg-spin bowlers photographed since then. Many writers have attested to this individuality. As if in royal command the wrist is straight or as in some photographs of Barnes, bent back, and the palm faces the batsman or a point above the batsman. No horizontal crooking or inward curling of the wrist here, but a rapid rotation of the forward-facing hand as if unscrewing something anti-clockwise from an imaginary ceiling above him, while at the same time imparting a violent leg-break flick with powerful fingers. Now we see that there was more to Barnes' high action than achieving height and bounce, important though these are.

The action described here is potentially capable of imparting "pure" side-spin which would give, by means of the Robins Force, nothing more than swerve from off to leg as well as being likely to land on the smooth part of the ball most of the time. But, like most of the situations in bowling, Barnes' ball was a mixture of spins, in this case mainly side-spin and leg-spin. Improving on the analogy, we now say that he wasn't unscrewing something from the ceiling *immediately* above, but from a surface above, yet somewhat in front of him. For the out-curving off-break we may repeat the analogy exactly, except that in this case the hand is screwing clockwise rather than unscrewing. His grip for this ball differed from the leg-break grip in the position of

Fig. 45 *S. F. Barnes:* four views of the great bowler; the hand bent back at the wrist to produce devastating spin-swerve; the powerful first-and-third-finger spinning couple, ready to impart off-spin with away-swerve, or leg-spin with in-swerve. See fig. 46 for a modern reconstruction of all these deliveries.

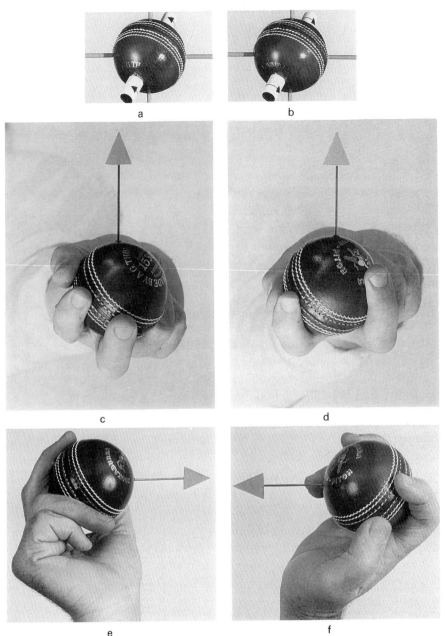

Fig. 46 *The two principal Barnes balls: a,* in-swerving leg-break, the stock ball of the great left-hander George Hirst, the mirror image of M. A. Noble; *b,* out-swerving off-break, learned from Noble. Balls *c* and *d* are viewed not from behind as in *a* but from above. Likewise, *d* is the top view of the Barnes-type off-break. Balls *e* and *f* are side views of the Barnes-type leg-break and off-break respectively; in *e* the third finger generates most of the spin, whilst in *f* it is the first finger. Note the hand bent back, the essential feature of the Barnes deliveries.

the index finger which now lay more along the seam than across it. As with all off-spinners the index finger generated most of the spin.

Another notable characteristic of Barnes was his ability to conceal his intentions from the batsman. Without needing to resort to the googly, he solved the problem of making the leg-break and off-break indistinguishable in a number of ways. "I want to drive home that the whole run-up action and follow through should be the same", he said. "The arm should stay at the same height and come over in the same way."[4] The hand action described earlier maintains the deception by avoiding the typical leg-spinner's coil and uncoil which is frequently not difficult to distinguish from the usual high, forward-facing hand of the off-spinner. What little indication the batsmen had of the direction of spin took place at such a rapid rate as to increase their difficulties even further. Because of the high proportion of side-spin generated by his action, the amount of top-spin would be less, in proportion to the leg-spin, than that bowled by the other bowlers. However, some top-spin must have been present, since P. F. Warner wrote of the deceptive dip of the leg-break:

> On first going in to bat one is apt to think, judging by the flight of the ball, that this leg-break will pitch off the leg stump, while, as a matter of fact, eight times out of ten, it will pitch on the wicket. This is probably due to his bowling from the end of the crease.[5] [Barnes said in later years that he did not use the width of the crease, but simply concentrated on a good foothold.]

Barnes said he attacked the stroke rather than the stumps: "At the start of an innings, when the wicket was absolutely true, I always used to bowl outside the off stick so that when the ball did dip there was a chance of hitting the wickets. It was also a good ball against left-handers".[6]

His field for the famous performance in Melbourne in 1911 had only three men on the leg side: short square-leg, mid-on and fine-leg. He was meticulous in setting his field. Captains found him difficult to handle and openly critical of their methods. Captains nowadays, so many of whom have had little or no experience of handling spin bowlers, may be fortunate that Barnes is not still around.

For C. S. Marriott as a boy in 1912, the sight was overwhelming:

> Never again have I seen such bowling: I sat there deaf and blind to everything except the miracle unfolding before my eyes, memorizing every move, my fingers itching for the feel of the seam. Without the slightest change of action he bowled every conceivable variation of pace from fast-medium to slow, making the ball hang in the air, and dip and leap like a devil from the pitch.[7]

Marriott, spurred by this experience, later became a star leg-spinner himself and he too, at a slower pace than Barnes, based his attack on the leg-break and the off-break, having abandoned the googly, but nevertheless very satisfactorily solving the problem of concealing his intentions from the batsman.

We give The Master the last word, taken from a letter he wrote to Jack Fingleton. Comparing himself with swing bowlers he said:

> I thought I was at a disadvantage in having to spin the ball when I could see bowlers doing the same by simply placing the ball in their hand and letting go; but I soon learned that the advantage was with me because by spinning the ball, if the wicket would take spin, the ball would come back against the swing... I may say I did not bowl a ball but that I had to spin, and that is, to my way of thinking, the reason for what success I attained.[8]

REFERENCES

1 G. W. Beldam and C. B. Fry, *Great Bowlers and Fielders*, p. 195   **2** L. Duckworth, *S. F. Barnes – Master Bowler* (The Cricketer-Hutchinson, 1979), p. 21   **3** ibid p. 21   **4** Coaching notes written by Barnes in 1948, edited by L. Duckworth and published in *The Cricketer*, March 1978, p. 25   **5** L. Duckworth, *S. F. Barnes – Master Bowler*, p. 21   **6** Coaching notes   **7** C. S. Marriott, *The Complete Leg-Break Bowler*, p. 25   **8** A. Ross (ed), *The Cricketer's Companion* (Hutchinson, 1979), p. 256

Chapter 18

Choosing weapons

DO COACHES FOLLOW TRENDS OR LEAD THEM? Following may not lead to anything out of the ordinary, and leading may stifle the extraordinary. Top players may inspire, but, as coaches, be limited by being able to pass on only what they themselves do. Whether or not coaches give their pupils the knowledge, drill and inspiration to move out freely beyond coaching, they are all swimming in a sea of widely held and agreed ideas and assumptions that make up the cricket culture of their age. The bowling paradigm, like a giant ocean tanker that takes miles to turn around, has an overwhelming momentum. Years of experimentation and development must precede the flowering of a good bowler, even at club level. If changes are to come about it is up to players themselves, as individuals, to think afresh and break out of the conformist mould.

No one would question the idea that spinning the ball in two directions is better than spinning it in one. This concept, a corner-stone of cricket thinking, is proving, in the way we have used it, to be somewhat less solid than is good for us because it leaves out five vital words, "all other things being equal".

To begin with, discussion on two-way spin would be more enlightening if greater attention was paid to spin-swerve, which usually acts in a direction opposite to that which the ball turns off the pitch. On a pitch not offering much grip, an off-break, carrying a sufficient amount of side-spin, will swerve away to the off and carry on in that direction after landing. Similarly a leg-break may swerve in and carry on inwards. From one type of delivery the off-break bowler may achieve an off-spinner if it grips, or a ball that goes the other way if it doesn't. The leg-spin bowler in the same way can achieve what is effectively an off-break on such an unresponsive pitch. Where friction on the pitch is variable, or where the amount of spin is varied deliberately, such a bowler, capable of using the wind and a certain amount of minor variation including top-spin, can be very effective without having mastered the art of spinning the ball both ways. Dick Tyldesley (1898–1943) needed only the leg-break and top-spinner. He played seven Tests for England and helped Lancashire dominate county cricket in the late 1920s. He gained many lbw decisions with his top-spinner.

Young bowlers, at least in the early school years, will normally bowl at a gentle, uncomplicated medium pace, learning the rudiments of run-up, delivery and length. We will assume also that they possess the spark to go and explore the limits of their ability. What then are the influences that govern their choice? If their heroes are seen too frequently in the one-day game, our young bowlers might look in vain for inspiration. But let us hope that they, and bowlers of more mature years, who, like many before them, have decided to develop, can find plenty to interest them in the vast literature on the game.

Coaching books should be treated warily. We looked critically at some commonly held ideas earlier. Why should a young bowler be warned against learning to swing the ball both ways right from the start? There is no evidence, as far as I am aware, that being grooved first into swinging in one direction offers any advantage. Spin at pace is usually described as "cut", whereas cut is frequently only one element in the action. Spin, by faster bowlers, using finger and hand movements resembling those of slow bowlers, is played down as something of an oddity, extremely difficult and accessible only to a few. As a result, the genuine spinner's grip, say for a fast leg-break as used by Wass, Barnes and Bedser, is unlikely to receive a mention. As for advice on the mechanics of obtaining spin-swerve, cricketers at best are usually left to interpret an unexplained photograph or two.

Why do coaching books often play down the idea that a bowler could or should learn to bowl both off-breaks and leg-breaks? Before Mount Everest was climbed there was another barrier ranging behind the gaping crevasses – the unstable ice, the inhuman severities of wind, cold and lack of oxygen: this was the psychological barrier. No one had done it; could it really be done? About 300 people have now climbed Everest; the dangers remain, quite a number die in the attempt, but still they go, confident in a good chance of success. The removal of the psychological barrier means nothing to cricket coaches. Perversely, they are inclined to erect the barrier after the breakthrough.

The off-break/leg-break twin peak was well trodden by the first years of this century. Barnes was by no means the only fast or medium-pacer of that type in those years. At least half-a-dozen others were in the highest class, including Hugh Trumble (1867–1938), Australia's great medium-pacer. One is tempted to describe A. G. Steel (1858–1914) as the Sir Edmund Hillary of slow off- and leg-break bowling and in a sense he was; but when he took his 788 first class wickets at 14.80, and his 29 Test wickets at 20.86, he may not have had to suffer the psychological barrier of modern discouragement against such an undertaking.

Some not so modern discouragement came from W. G. Grace who, in 1907, warned against the dangers to accuracy of bowling both off-breaks and leg-breaks and the physical dangers of bowling leg-breaks and googlies. We can be thankful that all who came after him did not regard the off-break/leg-break twin peaks as off limits, otherwise we would not have had the likes of C. L. Townsend, C. S. Marriott, T. B. Mitchell, S. Ramadhin and K. J. O'Keeffe.

From the time B. J. T. Bosanquet bowled a ball that bounced four times at Lord's in 1900, and had an unfortunate named Coe stumped from it, we have had available to us three methods of bringing the ball back off the pitch from the off – the off-break, the flipper and the googly.

Derek Underwood based his brilliant career on spinning in one direction, from the leg, but he offers an incentive to bowlers to learn to spin both ways:

> My line has always been to push the ball in the direction of the leg stump against the right-handed batsmen, tucking them up and forcing them to play on the leg side. But today more and more batsmen are standing outside their leg stump and are still able to hit through the offside.[1]

A young bowler developing both types of spin may not use both in serious games for many years. Nevertheless, the sooner he embarks on the long process of perfecting both, the better. Assuming that our bowler decides to spin both ways, he is faced with the decision on which of the four off-break techniques to adopt as an accompaniment to the leg-break. A bowler cannot avoid a certain amount of trial and error but, in the initial stages at least, it would be wasteful of time and effort not to draw on the experience of other cricketers, provided that this experience is reported objectively. Scientists are not condemned to repeat all the experiments of their predecessors before they attempt to launch out from existing boundaries.

"Orthodox" is not much of an adjective to apply to a bowler who puts every fibre of his being into each delivery; the term tends to drain its subject of individuality. It implies a rather mean little package, lacking flair and imagination. We could well do without the word in the language of cricket. Off-spinners and left-handers probably suffer most from it.

Is off-spin really as easy to bowl as many imagine? The fact that the fingers of a right-hand bowler tend naturally to come down slightly on the right-hand side of the ball at the moment of release might give this impression, but has it got much to do with sharp attacking spin? I would call the natural delivery a "slider" because the fingers do nothing more than that. Such is the reason why off-spinners are regarded as steady and accurate; many don't do anything much with the ball, good or bad. As for good, sharp off-spin, it is not "natural" at all and not in the slightest degree more or less difficult to bowl than the leg-break. Lance Gibbs didn't rip the skin from the inside of the second joint of his right index finger by bowling sliders.

On the evidence presented in Chapter 16, candidate number two, the flipper, also has a strong claim as the accompaniment to the leg-break. There is no reason to believe that it presents any unusual difficulty in learning or in execution. As for the googly, Bosanquet shook them alright: the cricket world still vibrates. Purple prose flows freely at its mention. Media commentators see googlies where there are none. Every time a top-spinner, or a leg-break that fails to grip, or one that swerves or angles inwards, hits the pads, the magic word cascades forth. So potent are the mystical properties of the ball that for many the possibility of a cool assessment doesn't exist. Yet the construction of a profit and loss account for the googly is not too difficult; plenty of information is available.

C. S. Marriott, one of the leading spinners in England between the wars, who like many others suffered from "googly disease" (in his case a torn muscle in the elbow), found the off-break to be a very adequate choice to go with his leg-break and top-spinner. He writes:

> Which of these forms of off-break the bowler uses is immaterial provided it is absolutely first-rate of its kind. This includes the skill to conceal it from the batsman and in the case of the googly, the physical ability to bowl it without strain. It is true that the googly has some advantage on a fast wicket because of its extra pace and lift from the pitch, but a bowler using the off-break, who possesses a top-spinner as well, need not worry as I proved for myself by experience. For me the top-spinner and the off-break did everything that the googly could have done.[2]

Marriott didn't know about the flipper, but it was to the flipper that Richie Benaud turned when shoulder problems associated with the googly threatened to end his cricket career. Irreversible damage had already been done, but the fact that for the last five or six years of his career, in spite of his shoulder trouble, he found the flipper not merely an adequate substitute for the googly, but superior to it, is cricket history.

We now begin to see that when it comes to choosing which technique to use in making the ball go the other way off the pitch, "other things" are by no means equal. Yet writers of coaching books, following a well-worn path, offer the off-break (possibly with a few variations) as one set of possibilities, and the leg-break, top-spinner and googly as another, not forgetting to include the old nonsense about leg-breaks being difficult, inaccurate and likely to be expensive. Depending on one's point of view, such advice is either highly complimentary to leg-spinners or quite irresponsible; highly complimentary in the sense that whereas the off-spin bowler is entrusted with the relatively

modest task of mastering spin in only one direction, along with a few associated tricks which don't cause exceptional difficulties, the leg-spinner is
assumed to be capable of producing spin in two directions; irresponsible
because one of these deliveries, the googly, has caused many, including some
of its best practitioners, to question its worth and abandon it in favour of an
alternative.

REFERENCES

1 D. Underwood, *Beating the Bat*, p. 29
2 C. S. Marriott, *The Complete Leg-Break Bowler*, p. 73

Chapter 19
Off-spin

OFF-SPIN BOWLING OF SLOW TO SLOW-MEDIUM PACE can look vulnerable under pressure; more so than leg-spin. A murderous batting onslaught is one of the highlights of the game, so they say; clapping by bowlers is optional. But it is a truism that the ball coming in to the bat often seems to be helping itself on its way to the boundary from the time it lands. R. C. Robertson-Glasgow puts it bluntly:

> Now the off-spinner is a good prop, but a remarkably poor stick: a sudden off-spinner inserted in a series of swinging deliveries will sometimes find the batsman unready, but the habit of bowling off-spinners regularly, on all types of wicket as practised and advised so much by many school professionals of the recent past, is a drudgery that neither "makes the action fine" nor leads to success. It may worry an average amateur player; but, to a first class professional or amateur, it is a prolific source of run-getting, even of amusement. Correct back-players have little or no difficulty with it: after a few such balls the amount of the spin on a good-length ball is easily gauged; and if over-pitched ever so little the off-spinner is the heaven-sent ball for a big hit, a four or a six over mid-on or mid-wicket's head.[1]

The modern off-spin bowler is frequently aided by a helmetted close-in fieldsman crouching at the bat-edge. The stalemated long series of low-scoring and wicketless overs that frequently accompany such tactics demonstrate that even the best off-spinners are achieving little in the way of effective variation. The choice of weapons for effective variation lies generally between two groups: firstly, off-spin, out-swerve and/or outswing, and top-spin; secondly, off-spin and leg-spin, with swerve or swing as desired. It is assumed that the basic ball is the off-break in both cases, and that this ball can be spun sharply and bowled accurately over a range of paces. It is not necessary that this range be very great: subtle variations are the stock-in-trade; thunderbolts or donkey drops may be useful if strictly rationed. Out-swerve resulting from spin, or the outswinger resulting from seam angle, are probably easier to master than the top-spinner.

Members of the family of off-spins are shown in fig. 47. Group *a–c* spins on a level axis while group *d–f* has this axis tilted back, in this case 30° towards the bowler. The latter group represents the more common type of delivery, carrying side-spin as well as off-spin, and will swerve out before turning in. More tilt gives more swerve. A pronounced tilt will prevent the seam from being under the ball to grip when it lands, resulting in less turn, a deadly variation to get the edge of the bat, hopefully held waiting for the inward turn. It is worth examining the mark on the ball after a delivery to check the contact. The technique for increasing the amount of tilt has been introduced when discussing S. F. Barnes and is discussed in more detail in the section on leg-spin.

It is characteristic of the off-spinner's action that at least a small degree of back-spin is much more common than for a leg-spinner. The off-cutter, pure or with twist, almost always carries some back-spin.

The most common grip for the off-spinner has the seam pointing behind square-leg at about 45° to the line of the wicket. But this is not to say that the normal off-break delivery in the air has this degree of forward-spin. The first finger, which does most of the work, lies across the seam, and, depending on the length of the fingers, may be hooked around so that the first joint lies partly along the seam. The second finger is also on the seam but spread out wide, away from the first, and it is probably good that a certain amount of tension is felt between the two. The third finger is tucked away under the ball more or less opposing the pressure of the first finger. The thumb steadies the grip and the little finger plays no part. A less common variation of this grip

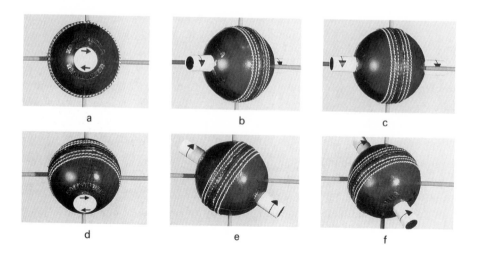

Fig. 47 *Family of deliveries for the off-spinner: a* is "pure" off-spin; *b* and *c* spin on horizontal axes at various angles to the line of flight; *d, e* and *f* all have axes tilted backwards; *b* and *c* will *swing* away before turning back; *d, e* and *f* will *swerve* away before turning back.

uses finger separations identical to the above, but has the seam pointing more or less towards slip and the first finger running along its left-hand edge. A rare but effective grip was that used by the Australian Bruce Yardley who spun the ball with his second finger instead of the index finger. Such a grip requires that the major splitting of the fingers is between the second and the third. Whatever the grip, a good, sharp clockwise twist of the hand must be made during release.

As bowled by the off-spin bowler, the top-spinner requires that the palm of the hand be turned more to face the off and the first finger rolled over the top of the ball, in the direction of the batsman, during release. Like all topspun balls it will dip in flight, pulled down by the Robins Force. To prevent it from dropping short, it must therefore be flighted a little higher, depending on its effective wind speed. When bowling directly into a strong wind where the Robins Force will be at its greatest, plenty of allowance must be made. Because there is less feeling of the hand being behind this delivery than there is with a leg-spin bowler's top-spinner, it is probably much more difficult to bowl than the latter. However, its variation in flight and the resulting higher bounce on hard pitches makes it worth the effort. Reading published accounts of off-spinners' top-spin, one wonders whether they achieved as much top-spin as they believed. I suspect that such deliveries carried a significant element of side-spin and simply drifted away. Since that ball may

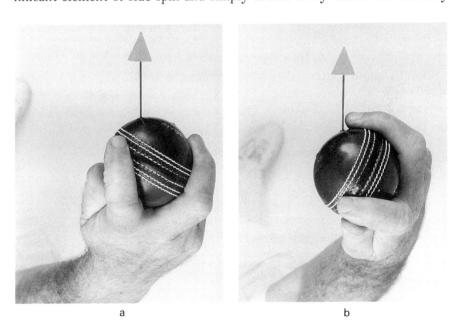

a   b

Fig. 48 *The off-break delivery as seen from above the bowler's hand; a* carries a certain amount of back-spin as in fig. 47*b,* whilst *b* carries a good deal of top-spin as in fig. 47*e.*

often land on the smooth leather, inward turn off the pitch is also lessened.

The out-swerve is delivered by keeping the palm up facing the batsman and bringing the hand around the "equator" of the ball on the right during delivery. A degree of round-arm action is found helpful by some bowlers wishing to accentuate the out-swerve. The feeling here, and it is nothing more than a feeling, is that the hand is sliding underneath the ball. If swing is chosen, the normal outswing bowler's action is used with the seam pointing somewhat wide of the slips. Obviously, swing is only possible if the condition of the ball allows it.

The demands faced by a good off-spinner are evident in the following remarks about Fred Titmus by his wicket-keeper John Murray:

> Even when Fred was an established Test player, I'd get him in the nets and tell him what he was doing wrong. If he was bowling badly, he was being cut to the boundary; his arm would get a little lower and I'd do my sergeant-major bit and remind him of the basics. For a slow bowler, it's important to realise that the margin of error is just a few inches. To bowl at middle-and-off from 22 yards takes hard work and great skill and I'd point out to Fred that off-breaks on leg stump was a case of bad bowling.[2]

The second group – off-spin and leg-spin – is, as we saw earlier, a proven winner. Adding the off-spinner's top-spinner to this combination would not seem to be worth it. Even if the leg-spinner's attempted top-spinner often turns out to be a slight leg-break, there are plenty of balls that simply fail to bite and end up effectively as top-spinners.

Disguising the difference between the off- and leg-break is the secret of success here. The hand, usually bent inwards towards the forearm as the arm swings up, signals the leg-break loud and clear. C. S. Marriott, who solved the problem, has this to say:

> The leg-break bowler must conceal his off-break until his arm is coming over at the top of the delivery, when his hand is moving at its fastest. This is done by still crooking up his wrist as he runs up, to make it look like the leg-break, and only allowing it to straighten as his arm swings over. If he finds this a little awkward at first, he will soon get used to it. The gain is more than worth the trouble.[3]

Sonny Ramadhin shone brightly among the stars of the twin skills of off- and leg-break bowling. His 158 Test wickets at 28.98 runs each attest to superb concealment. When English batsmen finally began to interpret the signs, one of which was the higher flight of his leg-break, it is said that he was poorly handled by his captain and over-bowled: a warning that batsmen do learn, and that for a bowler there is no such thing as invincibility.

On which line should the off-spinner bowl? The answer must depend very much on whether or not a leg-break is likely to arrive at any time. If it is, then we have yet another reason for taking John Murray's advice to Fred Titmus seriously – bowl nothing outside off; then there is no let-up for the batsmen. The various problems posed for the batsman who is not sure which way the ball will move off the pitch are obvious enough, but what if he can tell which way it will go?

There has probably never been a bowler who at some time in his career has not been worked out by a batsman. Even S. F. Barnes was worked out, by the South African batsman Herbert Taylor who said he looked at a spot a yard above the bowler's head as his arm came over. Such a diagnosis can be based on the whole range of signs from bells ringing and lights flashing to differences so subtle as to produce nothing more than a vague feeling of "something different". No matter at what part of this range of uncertainty the batsman is operating, the necessity for constant vigilance puts the bowler at an advantage. At the very least it upsets the routine, in the same way that a change of bowler may break a partnership. At best the bowler will dominate completely. Even if a few batsmen in a team work a bowler out, there will always be some who don't. Other factors which may change by the minute, the hour or the match can affect the degree of doubt: whether or not the batsman has previously faced that bowler, and if so how often; the light and background as it affects the view of the bowler's hand; whether or not players have been briefed about the opposing bowlers. Even clothing may have an influence: Ramadhin bowling with his shirt sleeve buttoned up to the wrist must have made it just that bit more difficult for the batsman to see which way the forearm was turning to generate spin. Tom Graveney tells of having difficulty with Ramadhin only when the background was bad or the sun directly behind the bowler;[*] dark skin may have added to the difficulty. Whatever means of disguise are adopted, the universal rule is that the quicker the movements, the more difficult it is for the batsman to read them.

Without the leg-spinner, there is still plenty to try: different batsmen, different lines, consistency, variations used sparingly. A batsman eager to sweep from the leg stump may fall lbw to the out-swerve which unexpectedly lands on middle. If the swerve is good and the break not so good, attack through the off side can be accented by posting a gully and short-cover. Conversely, if the break is good the leg-side field can be strengthened.

Where, through his own ability, alone or with the help of the pitch, the bowler obtains sharp turn, there is less demand for subtlety: the ball is pushed through accurately and the rewards will come. Where, through lack of real ability or because of a frictionless pitch, little deviation is obtained, we arrive at the classical dilemma which all bowlers will have faced: bowl faster and flatter, and in doing so reduce even further the chance of deception; or keep flighting the ball and "buy" a wicket. The choice depends on whether the state of the game allows buying or demands stealing. Putting on one's sweater may be called for, assuming that such an option has not been removed already by the artificial demands of limited-over bowling.

Body action for spinners gets a good deal of attention from coaches. Since many of the best bowlers in the history of cricket have had unusual actions and have resisted attempts to change them, caution is called for. When M. A. Noble delivered his famous out-swerving off-break, C. B. Fry noted that he achieved the early release from a bent-back hand, which is essential for the side-spin on this ball, by going down "rather low" over a partially-collapsed left leg. Modern coaches, obsessed with the high, straight-braced left side as the essential basis of right-hand bowling, would have soon nipped that one in the bud!

Rather than starting from some uniform, mass-produced set of actions on which a bowler is advised to build a range of variations, we would run less risk of stifling unorthodox talent if we let the process work in the reverse order. This entails allowing the bowler complete freedom in developing his repertoire from the fingers, hand and arm and then, if necessary, paying attention to other factors (if these have not sorted themselves out in the meantime). Careful experimentation, where the bowler is alert to every result of his actions, is the essence of such development.

REFERENCES

1 Earl of Lonsdale and E. Parker (eds), *The Game of Cricket*, (The Lonsdale Library, 1930), p. 79   2 P. Murphy, *The Spinner's Turn*, p. 166   3 C. S. Marriott, *The Complete Leg-Break Bowler*, p. 73   4 T. Graveney, *Cricket Over Forty*, p. 155

Chapter 20
Leg-spin

LIKE THE GIANT PANDAS carted around the world's zoos and stared at by millions, leg-spin bowlers, also an endangered species, attract attention which is inversely proportional to their numbers. Selectors, normally hard-headed members of the cricket establishment, can suddenly become irresponsible gamblers at the sight of a right-hand bowler turning the ball from the leg. Such a madness, which exists at all levels of the game, has, on a grand scale, resulted in leg-spin babes (*from their mother's womb untimely ripp'd*) being sent on major tours, with less than notable results. New Zealanders Bill Bell (South Africa, 1952–3) and Graham Vivian (India, Pakistan and England, 1965), and the Australian, John Watkins (West Indies, 1973) are examples. We applaud the tacit recognition of an effective bowling skill, but just as the pandas need a friendly natural environment in which to thrive, so do leg-spinners need a cricket world where they are no longer oddities, but a natural part of the game.

The first used method of spinning the ball, as described in the earliest recorded accounts of the under-arm game, was from the leg to the off, the finger and hand movements being no different from those required for the over-arm leg-break bowled today. The rotation is anti-clockwise whether it is below the shoulder, level with it or above it. Off-spin came later. Neither history nor the structure and function of the arm and hand support the contention that leg-spin is less natural than off-spin.

There were a few good leg-spinners bowling in the late nineteenth century and plenty in the first half of the twentieth. We know that for various reasons conditions are now less favourable to spin than they once were, but where did we get the idea that leg-spin poses, for bowlers, difficulties which are found nowhere else in the game?

If leg-spin was inherently more difficult than other types of spin we would not have seen it proliferate everywhere cricket has been played. Australia, on the basis of its population, must have been the greatest producer. In the first half of the twentieth century nearly every leading cricket team throughout the world contained a right-hand leg-spinner; two in a team was not uncommon. Even these days, a considerable number of club cricketers can bowl leg-spin in the nets; but why not in games as well? What do we do to them?

My first suggestion is that we should stop regarding them as charming curiosities, the last of the dodos. We can then go quietly about the task of encouraging them, restoring friction and bounce to pitches, mitigating the bad effects of the limited-over game, and allowing bowlers to regain the right to take measures to prevent crippling skin injury and keep an adequate grip on the ball.

As discussed earlier, another unnecessary difficulty placed in the path of leg-spinners is the almost automatic assumption, on the part of the cricket world, that they should choose the googly as their main variation. The number taking this path who have maintained consistency and a freedom from injury is disappointingly small throughout this century: the number who have failed to master the combination is by no means small.

Why do writers of coaching books, after discussing off-spin and topping it off by indicating the valuable accompaniment available in the form of the arm-ball, then ignore the corresponding ball when discussing leg-spin, and move straight on to the googly? I refer to the ball delivered with side-spin to make it swerve in to the bat.

Of all the barriers placed in the way of the leg-spinner there is one which will be more difficult to remove than any of the others. I refer to the spendthrift label, the conviction that the leg-spinner is expensive by nature. Repeating a familiar phrase, Richie Benaud ensures survival of the image when he says: "The over-the-wrist spinner distributes his gifts like a millionaire".[1]

Benaud was obviously too modest to admit his own miserliness. Come to think of it, who exactly were these generous bowlers? Are we expected to believe that selectors have been including leg-spinners in teams for the last hundred years knowing full well that they were almost certain to be expensive to the embarrassing degree suggested by much modern comment? The bowling analyses we read in the history books simply don't support the notion. Even Arthur Mailey, the archetypal millionaire, who on occasion could be expensive compared to other top bowlers, took his Test wickets at 33.91 apiece, only 7.7 runs more than Maurice Tate, 7 more than Wilfred Rhodes and 5.5 runs more than Harold Larwood, all of whom bowled under more or less the same conditions. More than this, like many leg-spinners he took his wickets quickly enough to give his teams the priceless gift of time, without which victory is impossible in true cricket. I don't think he was chosen from among the bountiful crop of good leg-spinners in Australia at the time so that Neville Cardus could wax lyrical on the delights of the summer game.

C. S. Marriott spoke from personal experience:

The truth is, that if a leg-break bowler has learned his art in the right way and, by hard practice, has achieved real control of length, there is no reason whatever why he should be any less accurate or any more of a gamble than say a Titmus, an Illingworth, an Allen, a Cartwright or a Shackleton. What is more, he should be able to maintain that accuracy for fifty overs in a day's cricket, or right through an innings, in any conditions or situation.[2]

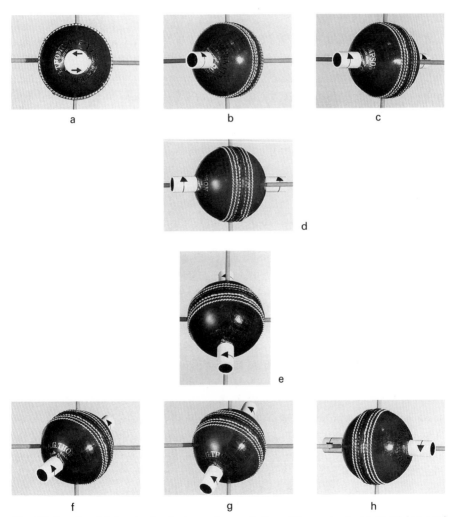

Fig. 49 *Family of deliveries for the leg-spinner: a* is "pure" leg-spin; *b* and *c* both leg- and top-spin; *d* almost "pure" top-spin with a little leg-spin; *e* leg-spin on a backward tilted axis, giving in-swerve; *f, g* and *h* all leg-spin, top-spin and in-swerve; *i* the only back-spinning leg-spinner and the only inswinger in the group – the fast or medium-pace cutter will be of this type. All will turn away off the pitch. Deliveries *b, c* and *d* will *swing away* before turning; *e, f, g* and *h* will *swerve in;* delivery *i* will *swing in* before turning.

The leg-break bowler must earn his place like every other bowler. There may be periods in a game when tactics demand that runs be given away for some reason or other, but unless he has complete control over his stock ball, he has no claim to a place at the bowling crease. Many leg-spinners have achieved this goal; they could defend or attack and they were neither odd nor extravagant.

The family of leg-spinning balls (fig. 49) can be looked at in the same way as for off-spin. Any ball landing with the contact point moving more or less from left to right is a leg-spinner. The possibilities range from a nearly pure top-spinner (*d*) to a nearly pure back-spinner (*i*), both with level axes of spin. Tilt this axis back and we get another series (*e, f, g, h*). Tilt it much more than that and there is less chance of the ball landing on the stitching to obtain a grip on the pitch, although the in-swerve is increased. In this case it will carry on in to the batsman instead of turning back to the off. As for the off-spinner, it is worth checking the landing mark on the ball. Balls carrying top-spin are the typical products of finger movement and hand rotation; those carrying back-spin are the typical products of the fingers being dragged down the back of the ball and slightly to the left side of it. We saw earlier that it is often incorrect to place fast leg-spinners in the back-spinning (cutting) group. Any bowler who does not apply a twisting force to both sides of the ball is a pure cutter and will impart some degree of back-spin.

Tilting back the axis of spin to increase the amount of swerve either way as developed by S. F. Barnes, G. H. Hirst and others was discussed earlier. The analogy of screwing or unscrewing something on the ceiling above and somewhat ahead of the high delivery arm was used. Both for the out-curving modified off-break and the in-curving modified leg-break, the palm of the hand must be more or less facing the batsman during the finger-spinning and hand-rotating delivery. This is awkward to achieve merely by bending the hand back at the wrist, but if the ball is released slightly earlier than normal there is more chance of the hand being at the right angle. However, unless some adjustment is made this will always be a slower and flightier delivery which may not be intended. The adjustment is to get the body ahead of the arm and release the ball slightly behind the body without loss of pace. Wrist flexibility for this delivery can be improved by means of an exercise where the bowling hand is pushed backwards using the other hand.

In Chapter 15 I discussed the in-swerving leg-break which failed to grip and became a slow inswinger. This quite common situation, especially when bowling against the wind, requires that the line of attack is moved from middle-and-leg to the off stump or just outside off. Most deliveries will be played as inswingers but one may grip occasionally and take the outside edge of the bat.

Leg-spin

The pure top-spinner is a most useful ball and methods of accentuating the top-spin component of the leg-break demand experimentation with a ball carrying a white painted seam. First an experiment in the opposite direction, a "square" or "pure" leg-break. Bowl a leg-break with a fairly round-arm action and with the fingers pointing towards the batsman at the instant of release. This ball should turn a good deal; but it may not carry much top-spin and therefore may not come very quickly off the pitch.

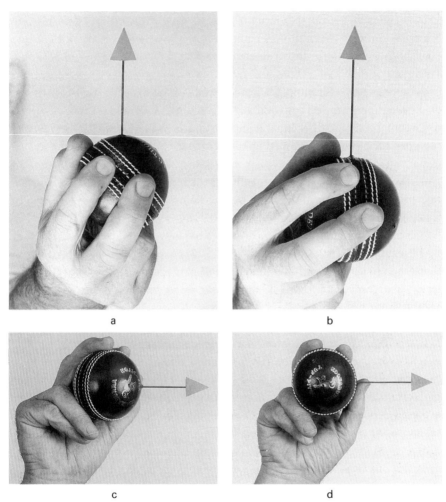

a   b

c   d

Fig. 50 *Delivering the leg-break and the top-spinner: a and c are the leg-break as seen from the top and side respectively; b and d are the top-spinner viewed from the top and side. The thumb is merely helping to support the ball, while the principal spinning force is felt between the first and third fingers, the latter being bent partly out of sight and also placed on the stitching. The different angles of the hand to the line of flight can be seen in a and b. For the top-spinner, the hand follows more over the top of the ball in the direction of the arrow than it does for the leg-break, where it moves out to the left.*

The top-spinner is a different ball in a number of ways. The less the arm swings across the line and the more it swings up over and straight down the line, the better. The hand should be bent down at the wrist more than for the leg-spinner. It is better for some bowlers that the ball be held out in the finger-tips, although with most hand sizes this is not possible. Since the cross-the-line phase of the swing is the last part of the action, it helps to release the ball a little early. Needless to say, it must be thrown a little higher to allow for the downward force of the top-spin, especially against the wind. It is worth trying a more square-chested action for the top-spinner. The idea here is to imitate the action of some inswing bowlers who, by not rotating their bodies around to the off side, ensure that their arms can swing through straight.

A useful set of variations for leg-spinners involves bringing the arm over at different heights. With practice it is not difficult to bowl anywhere in the arc, from round-arm to high over the head. Whilst the high delivery is obviously the best for generating bounce, and whilst the ball coming steeply down on the pitch will generally grip more, a surprising result from the round-arm leg-break is that the ball will turn more generally. This is simply because the direction of the spin on the ball as described above is "purer" leg-spin, i.e. more like the ball illustrated in fig. 49b than in d. Furthermore, a ball coming from a different angle upsets the batsman's rhythm a little as he prepares for the stroke.

Hold a cricket ball with the tips of the fingers and thumb arranged more or less equally spaced around it and facing away from you. Now try a few combinations for turning it anti-clockwise. We would be unwise to condemn any particular grip, otherwise we fall into the trap that Bill O'Reilly escaped. If sharp spin is generated, what more is required? (Remember that an apparent lack of sharpness, when demonstrated with the stationary arm – for example an action that some may class as a roll – may in fact produce a perfectly adequate rate of spin as part of a quick delivery action.) We all have our views on grips however, and there is plenty to be thought about when we look at what bowlers have been up to.

Using all five is cumbersome. The little finger in such a combination is merely a passenger; but given a course of strengthening exercises along the usually recommended lines of spinning tennis or other soft balls, it could possibly be used even as the back or bottom half of a spinning pair, the other half of which is the first or second finger. Doubtless this has been tried, but it illustrates the limitation imposed by the shortness of the little finger. Since each of the pair must spring in different directions to spin the ball, the short finger is incapable of the long and rapid movement which accompanies good leverage. The thumb and little finger or thumb and third finger as spinning pairs are also possible, but their impracticality for the average hand illustrates an important principle in this area: the necessity of proceeding from a state of compression on the ball, this compression being suddenly released as spin. The pairs mentioned are rather too far apart to generate such a force.

While the little finger can probably be dismissed, even from a supportive role, not so the thumb. The thumb is one of a notable spinning pair in what has been named the "Iverson grip", after Jack Iverson (1915–1973). It has also been called the "Iverson-Gleeson grip"[3] (since that used by Johnny Gleeson is virtually identical), but could properly be renamed the "Armstrong grip". Warwick Armstrong (1879–1947), Australian captain and all-rounder, used the three-point grip of thumb, first finger and second finger, fifty years before Jack Iverson. Photographed by Beldam, the second finger is bent under the ball, although not quite as tightly into the palm as with Iverson or Gleeson. Fry's comment appears to give Armstrong clear priority in this particular invention: "An uncommon grip for a leg-break bowler. Apparently the second finger, curled under the ball against the seam, is the one that takes the purchase when the hand is turned".[4] Armstrong's bowling was noted more for its accuracy than sharp spin. He didn't bowl the googly but got many of his wickets lbw with top-spinners, or leg-breaks which failed to grip.

Where Armstrong, Iverson, and Gleeson differ, however, is in the variations they used to accompany the leg-break. Armstrong didn't bring the ball back from the off but Iverson did, by letting the ball go when the back of this hand was facing the batsman. By this means he converted anti-clockwise spin to clockwise. Gleeson also bowled this ball, but added a normal off-break to his repertoire, thus having two types of off-break to add to his leg-break.

Related to the Armstrong grip, but placing more work on the first finger, was the grip used by "Tich" Freeman (1888–1965) who had comparatively small hands. He bunched his second, third and little fingers under the ball and gripped it between his first and second fingers and thumb. He took 2,776 first class wickets at 18.42 runs each.

We now leave the thumb in a minor supportive role and focus on the first three fingers. Photographs showing the ball resting within these three and the thumb fail to convey their relative importance. Whilst many leg-spinners appear to use all four, it is the first and third which possess the length, leverage and strength for explosive compression and release. The third finger is under the ball and bent in towards the palm as far as is comfortable, with the first finger opposite and stretched out across the seam. The second will also be across the seam, helping to steady the whole grip. Abdul Qadir uses a version of this grip, unusual in that the first finger is not straight across the seam on top of the ball but hooked a little towards the thumb.

Without wishing to discourage experimentation, I conclude this account of grips by pointing out that the majority of top-class bowlers – fast, medium and slow – who used the leg-break as their stock ball or as a variation, employed the first-and-third-finger grip (fig. 50). The pressure points for this grip – the inside of the end section of the first finger and the inside of the first knuckle of the third – vary in the relative amount of wear and tear they suffer. Sometimes, for no apparent reason, one appears to take over some of the punishment being inflicted on the other. But wherever it is felt, this damage is a sign that the bowler is well on the way towards real spin.

Fig. 51 *a–d* *Warwick Armstrong and Jack Iverson,* pioneers of the thumb-and-second-finger spinning couple. Photo *a (above)* shows Armstrong's grip which allows the second finger to snap up and the thumb to snap down, producing leg-spin.

Fig. 51 b *Armstrong's delivery stride* for the leg-spinner.

Fig. 51 c *Iverson's grip*, with the second finger closer to the palm than in Armstrong's.

Fig. 51 d *Iverson's release –* his best ball was an off-spinner which he is seen delivering here, with the grip as in *c* and with the back of his hand facing the batsman.

The first-and-third-finger grip, with the thumb and second finger in support, is also likely to be the best bet for fast and medium-pace bowlers. Skin wear is unlikely to be a problem; at that pace there is simply insufficient time for the fingers to generate the high compression and release of slow bowlers, nor, as we mentioned earlier, is it necessary. A quicker bowler beginning to practise this leg-break need only roll the fingers and hand around a little on release, maintaining control, and gradually building up a tighter spinning action. Few batsmen will find a ball turning at this pace easy to score from, even when it is somewhat inaccurate.

We encountered the fast and medium-pace leg-break earlier in connection with swerve and swing. Less well-known than Barnes and Bedser is a bowler who greatly impressed the Australian batsman C. G. Macartney in 1921, who wrote:

> South Africa that season had in J. M. Blanckenburg a bowler who should have been a world's champion. He was a medium-paced right-hand bowler, who spun the ball both ways, but was not a googly bowler. His deception in delivery was perfect, and all he had to do was to bowl to hit the wicket during the first few minutes. This, he did not do for some unknown reason, and therefore lost his opportunity.
>
> I have never batted against a bowler who was so difficult to "find" for the first few overs as Blanckenburg and I know of no more peculiar feeling than to be opposed to such deliveries. I can only compare it to a soldier out in the open when an aeroplane was dropping bombs at night, wondering where the next one is going to land.[5]

Like the great batsman he was, Macartney was being perfectly honest in admitting to no more than a temporary embarrassment, but Blanckenburg's figures of 60 wickets in 18 Tests at 30.28 runs each proves that for many of his opponents, the embarrassment was more than temporary.

Both the development and the maintenance of leg-spinning skills and in fact all bowling skills depend to a large extent on solitary practice with a box of balls and the willingness to think hard about every delivery. An unexpected bonus from such dedication, even for experienced bowlers, is the way it can allow them to forget that the batsman is there at all. Such was the advice given by Richie Benaud to help leg-spinner Bob Holland cope with bowling to Ian Botham: "Imagine that there is no batsman at the other end – pick out your spot and bowl line and length".[6]

Solitary practice of another sort is required to develop the ability to rehearse in the mind. Just as a top athlete prepares for a big race by mentally working through every detail, so must a bowler be able to bowl an entire over in the same way. The feel of the ball in his hand; the run-in; the delivery; the range of variations – all can and must be felt, in the mind.

Many a page has been written arguing the matter of whether a bowler should learn spin first, or line and length. Why should we focus on this particular division of skills when every single delivery requires the co-ordination of dozens of muscles from the toes to the finger-tips? Every time we bowl we should hope for a satisfactory outcome in all respects. If we accept that one or more of these is less worthy of our attention at any particular time, we are not only wasting time but in danger of wrongly grooving certain movements while we attend to others. Specifically, a leg-spin bowler should experiment with spin over a range of different speeds. The limits will become apparent soon enough. No bowler will persist with hopeless inaccuracy for very long. He will reduce the amount of spin action or pace or both, in order to arrive at a combination offering at least a glimmer of consistency, even though acceptable results may be some years away. At the beginning of the process it may involve nothing more than spinning a tennis ball against a wall.

Assuming that the bowler has a range of speeds to choose from in deciding on his particular path to stardom, we can advise him to look in two directions: firstly, back through a century of spin; secondly, at the realities of cricket as played today. Fortunately, the answer from both is the same: bowl leg-spin as fast as possible, or if adopting a relatively slow pace, opt for a low trajectory. Most of the reasoning for this verdict will already be obvious to the reader. Few of the successful leg-spinners of the past have bowled high and slow. From the time of Barnes and the pacey leg-spinners of the early years of the century, through Grimmett, O'Reilly, Wright, Ramadhin, S. P. Gupte, Dooland and Benaud, the most successful have made it extremely difficult, even for the most agile batsmen, to move out safely to the pitch of the ball.

Grimmett and O'Reilly paraded their contrasting methods throughout the most successful bowling partnership in the history of cricket. Grimmett – short in stature, delivering from no more than about head height, not quick, upwind, with a low, constantly modulated flight, probing with leg-breaks, seeking to drive the batsman back to be trapped in front by what may have been the flipper or sometimes the top-spinner. O'Reilly – tall enough to bounce a near medium-pace leg-break, downwind, drawing the batsman forwards to what was sometimes a googly, a little slower than expected, aimed like the leg-break at the middle and leg stump, and giving the close-in leg-side catch.

Today's leg-spinners, seeking to follow the example of some famous bowler from the past, must be selective in what they adopt. The first lesson to be learned is that although famous bowlers themselves were influenced and inspired by seeing or reading about other great figures, they were, in the end, unique. Spin in particular helps make a bowler unique; too many medium-pace bowlers look as if they came off a production line.

Coaching books usually advise slow leg-break bowlers to bowl into the wind; such advice is questionable. The normal left-hand spinner and the off-spinner are unlikely to be able to bowl to advantage against the wind because they don't employ top-spin to any great extent. In Chapter 16 we discussed how any ball carrying top-spin, including the leg-spinner, the top-spinner or the googly, will dip so sharply against a wind as to suffer a loss of forward momentum which is exacerbated by landing on a pitch lacking pace and bounce. A ball landing even slightly short of a length is simply waiting to be hit. Even moderate breezes can bring about this undesirable state of affairs. Slow bowlers would like to have the wind as their ally, utilising all the extra subtlety that it can offer, including a magnification of the Robins Force. Unfortunately, this assistance must be forgone on many occasions. If wickets were fast they could bowl effectively against the wind more often than at present. A gentle breeze can be helpful but a strong wind, as well as causing the problem of loss of pace, can also cause loss of turn by accentuating the in-swerve. This may happen with the wind direction any-where from the wicket-keeper to cover-point. A wind from the leg side will oppose the in-swerve, but any wind that aids pace is helpful to the leg-spinner on a slow wicket.

An attractive combination is the variation of the influence of wind, pitch and leg-spin from ball to ball. One ball may swerve in and not grip suffici-ently to turn away (the commentator's googly), another may not swerve but turn away, and another may swerve in *and* turn away.

A few years ago a New Zealand television commentator complained that the tactic of a leg-spinner bowling around the wicket to a right-handed batsman and landing the ball in foot marks "is coming to be regarded as contrary to the spirit of the game", adding that it prevents the batsman from scoring to about three-quarters of the ground. None of this is true, but it reminds the leg-spin bowler of one of the most adventurous directions he can take. Risks and rewards are its hallmark: batsmen and bowler can find them-selves fighting on a cliff-edge, disaster beckoning either protagonist. For the bowler the task is to land a full length leg-break on a line just outside the batsman's legs, preferably in foot marks. A short ball outside the leg stump will usually be expensive. For the batsman the task is to avoid being bowled behind his legs, getting a top edge from an attempted sweep shot or an off-side edge from any other forcing shot on the leg side. On a wicket with some bounce there is also a chance of the forward defensive stroke popping up a catch to slip or gully.

Richie Benaud bowled leg-spin around the wicket to snatch victory for Australia at Old Trafford in 1963 against an England side needing 254 and coasting to victory at 150 for 2. He took 6 for 70 and England were all out for 201. Whilst I have never heard of any Englishman complaining that this historic use of the around-the-wicket leg-break was contrary to the spirit of the game, a number have pointed to the inadequate technique of Peter May and others in playing such bowling.

But it is not all easy pickings, as Abdul Qadir discovered at Hyderabad during the 1977–8 season. Boycott (100) and Brearley (74), who took England to a draw at 186 for 1, had worked hard on the problem during the rest day of the Test, using Ken Barrington to bowl his leg-breaks to them in the nets from around the wicket.

Leg-spinners may be a little amused to read that wide leg-side bowling of leg-breaks was employed by Armstrong in some of his Tests for Australia against England in 1905 and also in 1921, as a purely defensive measure. In one of these Tests his analysis read 52–24–67–1 and merited the comment that it "shows what dull stalemate play such tactics can produce".[7] Armstrong could bowl accurately at a fairly brisk pace and must have been difficult to get away without risk, but the modern restriction on the number of fieldsmen behind the wicket on the leg side, along with numerous other discouragements, have now helped swing the balance against the bowler.

Before Armstrong, another Australian, W. H. Cooper (1849–1939), instituted leg-break leg theory on the 1884 Australian tour of England. He was said to be able to subdue even the best batsman with only two fieldsmen on the off side. W. G. Grace and L. C. Braund (1875–1955) also used leg-spin outside leg successfully. We are inclined to forget that the famous googly with which Hollies ended Bradman's last innings was delivered around the wicket. Its effectiveness may well have derived as much from its unusual angle as from any other factor. Even with modern field restriction, the challenging technique of bowling around the wicket is well worth the attention of leg-spin bowlers today.

Bowling leg-spin to left-handed batsmen often elicits the comment that it is not very effective. The basic ball is now a top-spinning off-break. Accurately pitched by a right-hand off-break bowler bowling to a right-handed batsman, it would most likely attract admiration. From the leg-spin bowler to the left-handed batsman it is no less a delivery. Bowled over the wicket and pitched on or just outside the off stump, it comes off hard pitches quickly and causes a hurried shot.

Another generally unrecognised but most effective variant of such bowling is the ball pushed through a little more quickly, delivered over the wicket and wide on the crease, with the arm as high up over the head as possible. It carries as much top-spin as possible as opposed to leg-spin and is pitched well up towards the bat and a little wider to the off than normal. All of these features, particularly the angle of delivery across the pitch, give this ball a good chance of beating the bat on the outside. But bowling around the wicket to a left-hander shuts out this form of attack and can make life difficult for the bowler unless there is some compensation available from foot marks.

Pitching on the leg stump to a left-hander won't help the cause at all. Delivery towards the off can be aided by a more angled run-up and by more body twist around to the right as the bowling arm goes back before coming over.

"Spin and spin hard" should be the motto: even on unresponsive pitches, spin is always likely to do something in the air and may do the unexpected off the ground.

REFERENCES

1 R. Benaud, *Willow Patterns*, p. 174   2 C. S. Marriott, *The Complete Leg-Break Bowler*, p. 132   3 P. Philpott, *Cricket Fundamentals* (Batsford, 1982), p. 88   4 G. W. Beldam and C. B. Fry, *Great Bowlers and Fielders*, p. 326   5 C. G. Macartney, *My Cricketing Days*, p. 134   6 F. Keating, *High, Wide and Handsome – Ian Botham* (Collins Willow, 1986), p. 120   7 G. Broadribb, *Next Man In*, p. 82

Chapter 21
Variations

NOVELTY BRINGS REWARDS TO BOWLERS, but batsmen can develop resistance and thrive again. Bowlers have recognised the value of depriving batsmen of the opportunity of learning to cope with their tricks. John Emburey played with Graham Gooch in the same team in South Africa and bowled to him a good deal to help him sort out his problems; now, to protect himself, Emburey refuses to bowl to Gooch in the nets. Grimmett, likewise, refused to bowl to Australia's best batsmen in the nets. The batsman who most relished facing Gleeson was his wicket-keeper for Australia, Rod Marsh.

S. F. Barnes had only two full seasons of county cricket, playing the rest of his career in the northern leagues. As well as avoiding the danger of burn-out from too much cricket, he certainly ensured that the top cricketers of the day did not become familiar with his bowling.

Novelty wreaked havoc when the tall and powerful Bosanquet wheeled over his contorted arm to deliver what looked like a leg-break, but was really on off-break. Bosanquet (1877–1936) recalls the first time it was ever bowled against the Australians: "... at Lord's, late one evening in 1902 – when I had two overs and saw two very puzzled Australians return to the pavilion. It rained all next day and not one of them tumbled to the fact that it was not an accident".[1]

Arthur Shrewsbury, one of England's best batsmen, complained about Bosanquet's bowling saying that "it wasn't fair". The great A. C. MacLaren exclaimed in 1907: "If this sort of bowling becomes general, I'm packing my bag for good and aye, and what's more – goodbye to all style and attractiveness in batting."[2]

R. E. Foster, England's captain, bludgeoned by the onslaught of the South Africans who boasted no fewer than four googly bowlers in their 1907 team, wrote:

> Personally, I think it will deteriorate batting. For this new kind of bowling is a very great invention, and it is possible it may completely alter cricket, and no one who has not played against it can realise the difference it makes to a batsman and his shots. It must again be reiterated that this type of bowling is practically in its infancy, and if

persevered with – as it surely will be – must improve and become more difficult to deal with. Now a batsman when he goes in may receive a ball which either breaks from the off, perhaps from the leg, or again may come straight through very quickly. If he survives half-a-dozen overs he ought to be getting set, but such bowling never allows the batsman to get really set, because he can never make or go for his accustomed shots.[3]

– a batsman's point of view. But the learning was already under way and Foster's team in fact won the series of three three-day Tests with one win and two draws. What a sight it must have been to see that quartet operating on the bouncy South African pitches the previous year, when South Africa beat England 4–1. The subsequent history of the googly, while not bearing out Foster's fears, has been fascinating in ways he did not foresee.

Fingers wrapped around a ball smaller than a cricket ball are free to spin it in any direction. Jack Iverson, in Port Moresby during the Second World War, discovered his unusual method with a table tennis ball. Bosanquet says he discovered the googly while playing a game where two people sat in chairs on opposite sides of a table and bounced a tennis ball across it, each trying to deceive the other with spin. This was "somewhere about 1897" he wrote[4], but his brother, in a letter to *The Times* in 1936, talks about flicking a tennis ball across the uncovered slate of a billiard table about 1892.[5] Years of practice with a solid rubber ball followed, involving his cousin Louise retrieving tennis balls in the garden for hours on end.

Spinning was only an amusing sideline when Bosanquet played for Oxford University from 1898 to 1900. Although he was a useful medium to fast bowler and a good bat, his "star turn" (as he called it) was to bowl to famous batsmen who were enticed to the nets at Oxford during the lunch intervals:

> I was brought up to bowl him two or three leg-breaks. These were followed by an "off-break" with more or less the same action. If this pitched in the right place it probably hit him on the knee, everyone shrieked with laughter, and I was led away.[6]

Progress was slow as Bosanquet gradually dropped his fast bowling. He accumulated a good deal of experience in captaining private teams to America in 1901 and to the West Indies in 1901–2. In 1902–3 he toured Australia and New Zealand with Lord Hawke's team with no great success but one delivery worth remembering.

The mystique surrounding the googly, enriched by journalists, victims, bowlers themselves, and nurtured on frequently erroneous observation, may have reached unjustifiable proportions. But there are two well authenticated deliveries at least which deserve a place in the history books, and which in fact may have contributed substantially to that image. One of these is the ball with which Hollies dismissed Bradman in his last Test innings, at the Oval in 1948, for a duck. The other was forty-six years earlier when Bosanquet delivered the first googly to be seen on the Sydney Cricket Ground, and kept an appointment in history with Victor Trumper, clean bowled, third ball.

At home in 1903, still with more promise than achievement, Bosanquet took 63 wickets for 21 runs apiece, using leg-breaks and the occasional googly. This gained him a place in the MCC team to Australia where, with novelty value at its maximum and on fast bouncy pitches, he played a major part in England's win in the series.

Bosanquet took pains to conceal his methods and always tried to convey the impression that the dismissal was caused by something other than his trickery. In a county game in 1904 he is reported in *Wisden* as bowling a "wretched length" to collect 10 Yorkshire wickets for 248. In another report *Wisden* claimed "The home side indeed were quite demoralised by Bosanquet who although making the ball turn, bowled in the first innings in very erratic fashion"; he took 14 wickets for 190 in that game. Surveying the season at its end, *Wisden* saw Bosanquet in a different light: "The best man in the event . . . a match-winner . . . unequalled in any county".[7] *Wisden* can be forgiven for having difficulty understanding the new species; such a hot-and-cold attitude has been characteristic of the way cricket has treated googly bowlers ever since.

During his active cricketing days Bosanquet seems to have confided in only one person, his close friend, the South African R. O. Schwarz[8] (1875–1918). As if to emphasise the value of his own coaching, Bosanquet took 9 for 107 in one innings for MCC against the touring South African team in 1904, of which Schwarz was a member. The game, the first of the tour, was washed out, but two games later Schwarz showed what a good student he was by taking 5 wickets for 27 runs and ended the tour with 68 wickets at 18.26 runs apiece.

South Africa's 4–1 series win over England in 1905–6 marks the summit of googly history, along with the 1907 tour of England, when they showed that they were still a force on pitches less lively than South African matting. R. E. Foster has left us an account of the bowling of the famous quartet – Schwarz, A. E. E. Vogler (1876–1946), G. A. Faulkner (1881–1930) and G. C. White (1882–1918) – in which he describes them as coming off the pitch at an extraordinarily fast pace in spite of seeming to be comparatively slow through the air and not very deceptive in flight. They were all in fact closer to medium or slow-medium pace than to slow. Although Foster was one of the three or four really great batsmen of the early 1900s, he had to learn to cope with a quickish off-break of a new type, one that carried heavy top-spin. Later batsmen familiar with the left-hand chinaman would be less surprised by this delivery. It appeared to be slow because it needed to be thrown a little higher to allow for the downward push from the top-spin. The loose balls that came along were hard to hit because of the speed with which they came off the bouncy pitches; six men frequently placed on the leg side made the big hit risky.

Vogler was the finest of the four, concealing his grip well during the run-up and possessing very deceptive variations of pace. He often started with fast-medium off-spin with out-swerve or outswing; then, with the shine off the ball, he bowled slow-medium leg-breaks, with the googly introduced perhaps once every two overs. His leg-break turned from 2 or 3 inches up to 18 inches; the googly spun rarely more than 3 or 4 inches, often coming straight through as a top-spinner. A dangerous ball of his was a slow yorker which seemed "more to quiver than swing in the air". Who knows what witch's brew of varying Robins force and swing, each possibly changing in dominance during flight, this ball represented? C. S. Marriott also records that the leg-break:

> ... sometimes performs an amazing kink about three-quarters of the way along its flight; I have generally heard this called "corkscrew", which is near enough, but not strictly true because there is no circular motion. What actually happens is that the ball suddenly swings very sharply and swiftly in the air three or four inches to right and left, and then goes straight on. I have often done it, but never knew when it would happen nor what caused it. The bowler can usually see it himself, although I have noticed that it shows up more plainly in a certain light. One of the finest examples I can remember was when A. E. Relf was coaching. Although then getting on in years, he was still bowling that beautiful leg-break at medium pace; quite often his leg-break performed this astonishing kink in its flight from side to side. Once or twice I even saw a bit of real evidence for calling it the corkscrew, when it occurred so late that the ball had already begun to dip: the first short swing was to leg, which meant that it began by moving in a semicircle, and although the quick return-swing was horizontal, the illusion of a genuine corkscrew movement was apparent enough. I asked him about it afterwards: he said he had always done it, but could offer no explanation beyond the blend of leg- and top-spin on the ball.[9]

(The famous Mailey full tosses that dismissed Jack Hobbs twice in Test matches, at Melbourne in 1925 and the Oval in 1926, came out of the same aerodynamic box of tricks. Later Mailey said of one of them that it was not a full toss but a high one that dipped suddenly.)

Faulkner bowled the leg-break and googly at slow-medium pace with great control and fierce spin, concealing the googly well. White was similar but spun the ball less. Schwarz was the odd one because he had the googly but not the leg-break. Foster thought that he should have been scored off more than he was. Batsmen didn't need to worry about possible spin in the other direction; he was purely a top-spinning off-break bowler with a googly action. Too many batsmen tried to hit him. Foster's advice was to play him off the pitch for two's and three's rather than going for the big hit. Many tried the latter and made his figures compare well with the others.

The averages in 1907 were: Schwarz 137 wickets at 11.79; White 56 at 14.73; Vogler 119 at 15.62; Faulkner 64 at 15.82. Schwarz required 31 balls for each wicket, the others 30. In the 1909–10 series, played in South Africa, Vogler took 36 wickets and Faulkner 29 in beating England, while Schwarz and White were not selected. Vogler, Schwarz and Faulkner toured Australia with the South Africans in 1910–11, but met with little success. Vogler had taken to the bottle, and batsmen were learning about googlies. For the 1912 Triangular Tournament in England Vogler did not go, Faulkner had partly lost the knack, and Schwarz had lost it completely. The great quartet had finished.

The origin of the name googly is about as clear as the googly itself was to its early victims. "Googler" is a word known to have been used in 1898–9 to describe some unspecified type of bowling in England, before Bosanquet. The Australians called the new ball the "bosey", and to the South Africans it was the "wrong 'un".

"Googly" and "wrong 'un" gave way to "bosey" after the First World War. No English googly bowler was a world force after that time, in spite of the excellent records of Freeman, Wright, Hollies and others at home. H. V. Hordern (1884–1938) led the way for the Australians in the pre-war period, giving the South Africans a taste of their own medicine in a 4–1 series win in 1910–11. He took a long run and bowled accurate googlies and leg-breaks with a high action at medium pace. In the following season, also in Australia, he took 32 wickets for 24.37 against England. Returning to full-time dentistry, Hordern retired from top cricket after two seasons, never having toured England with an Australian team. Brilliant bowler though he was, relatively brief exposure at the top level must preclude any claim of greatness for him.

Coming after Hordern were two, and I think it is correct to say the only two, right-hand googly bowlers who pass the test of being successful with the googly and who maintained success at a reasonable level throughout the whole cricket world over a number of years. These were Mailey and O'Reilly. The Indian leg-break and googly bowler S. P. Gupte, with his 149 Test wickets at 29.55 in 36 Tests, pushes for a place alongside Grimmett and O'Reilly. Grimmett's 216 wickets at 24.21 in 37 Tests is undoubtedly better and, unlike Gupte, he was a force in England. Comparisons such as these are difficult however, because by the time Gupte appeared on the scene, conditions in England had already become unfavourable for spin. At the same time the cricket world had expanded to include the West Indies, India and Pakistan, in all of which he was very successful.

Grimmett tells us that he virtually abandoned the googly during his career, since it didn't fit in with his bowling plan. Herb Collins told him during the 1926 tour of England not to bowl any more googlies on the tour, although he could bowl them quite accurately. Grimmett thought Collins feared that he would lose the leg-break. The subsequent development of Grimmett's bowling, and the way in which he was able to maintain a low trajectory and off-break without the googly, has been discussed earlier. Although he says he used the googly very rarely, and then mainly against left-handers, anyone who knows the difficulty of pulling out a delivery like that for a rare occasion only would be surprised to find Grimmett – of all people, with his exacting standards of accuracy – taking such a risk, especially when he already possessed an accurate substitute, probably the flipper.

Ring and McCool bowled googlies, but through no fault of their own were denied the chance to walk the larger stage. Dooland, who also had limited exposure in international cricket, could bowl the googly, but it was his masterpiece, the flipper, that took him to the heights. Benaud crippled himself with long hours practising googlies and leg-breaks and more than once in a less than brilliant early bowling career was on the point of giving up before bravely and successfully adopting the flipper.

Arthur Mailey moulded the leg-break, top-spinner and googly, all at a higher altitude than that of his famous googly predecessors, into a match-winning combination. He dominated the world of spin in the 1920s and with the possible exception of S. P. Gupte, no bowler of the slow googly has matched him since that time. Ian Peebles admired a fellow leg-spinner with the following description:

> The enormous spin was the product of an ideal leg-break bowler's action. Mailey ran a few springy paces at an angle to the wicket, curled his wrist up in the region of his hip-pocket, and flipped the ball out with nicely co-ordinated movement of arm, wrist and fingers. He was a dangerous bowler in the air as well as off the pitch, for the fast-revolving ball dropped steeply at the end of its flight. The batsman who made any misjudgment of length was in poor case to combat the sharp break in either direction. Mailey played twenty-one times for Australia and took 99 wickets. That they cost 33 runs apiece is neither

here nor there. In 1920–21 he took 36 wickets in the series, an Australian record.[10]

Mailey's brand of all-or-nothing cricket, his humour and wonderfully refreshing approach, reached the public not only through his deeds on the field, but also through his pen as a cartoonist and writer. Anyone interested in an expert's account of the hey-day of spin and in a warm and human attitude to the game of cricket should read his book *10 for 66 And All That*[11], the title being his figures for one innings against Gloucestershire in 1921. Such was his faith in his methods that as his career developed to Test-match level, he gave the ball more air than he had done earlier.

O'Reilly bowled with aggression, pace, spin and accuracy of length and direction, during twenty years for New South Wales and twenty-seven Tests. Others before him had spun the leg-break further and bowled it faster; others had bowled the googly at speed. When he came on the scene the googly had long since lost its novelty value against top batsmen, but in O'Reilly's hands the combination was indeed formidable. Only on pitches made dead and gripless by being doped with cow dung was he defeated, as at the Oval in 1938. Coaches presuming a right to change a bowler's action should note O'Reilly's ungainly run-up and delivery, "all flailing arms and suggestion of a stoop", and ponder its effectiveness.

As for a bowler's attitude to his craft, O'Reilly recommends a version of the martial arts mentality, in an article he wrote for his club report:

> You can never become a good attacking bowler if you do not develop a bowling "temperament". A happy-go-lucky, good-natured and carefree outlook is of no use whatever to an ambitious and competent bowler. He must be prepared to boil up inwardly on the slightest provocation, and opportunities are so common that there is no need to cite even one.
>
> Conceal that desirable temperament from the public, but reveal it in all its force and fury to your opponent, the batsman.[12]

Adding to the batsman's discomfort, he was better at concealing his googly than his temperament. In another account written in his old age, he revealed details of his technique and strategy:

> With my bowling, my cardinal rule was that I always had my eyes glued on the spot where I was going to pitch the ball. I wasn't a slow leg-spinner, I bowled medium pace. The leg-spinner was my stock ball, but I bowled the wrong 'un more frequently than any other leg spinner I've seen. It was nothing for me to bowl it three times in an eight ball over: I had complete confidence in my ability to bowl a wrong 'un to length and direction, and I could really get it to bounce,

so I used it as a variation of flight and bounce as well as spin.

When I started I used to bowl the orthodox off-break, but I gave that up because it interfered with my rhythm, but my straight faster ball got me a lot of wickets – I even had a bouncer of sorts.[13]

Although for obvious reasons we are not likely to be furnished with such information by bowlers operating today, the prying video camera provides a substitute of sorts, although the limitation of frames per second in most cameras may leave the action blurred at critical points. The players' information network, and most of all, experience out in the middle, must remain the batsman's principal defence.

The question of how to "pick" it, or whether in fact it can be "picked" at all, is virtually the province of the googly and nothing else in the entire art of spin bowling. When were cricketers last drawn into an intense speculation on whether it was possible to pick an arm-ball or a top-spinner from an off-break? "How I picked it", or the rather more brief "Why I didn't" accounts are compulsory autobiographical material.

A. A. Thomson tells of the attitude of a seasoned veteran Arthur Shrewsbury, whom W. G. Grace considered the next best batsman in England to himself:

"If this kind of bowler," said Shrewsbury, "pitches a ball outside my off stump, I expect it to break in from the off and I'm ready to play it that way. If it breaks the other way I leave it alone. But if it pitches on my legs or between my legs and the wicket, I expect it to break in from leg; if it does, I play it, if it doesn't, I leave it alone. And what's more," added Arthur shrewdly, "I bide my time, because I never saw one of those chaps who didn't bowl one or two bad balls in an over, and I'd get a four off those..."[14]

Bosanquet, always inclined to be wayward in length, gave up county cricket in 1905, and his career as an effective bowler ceased at that time. He had good days but his length was described as generally "irregular" and his claim to fame must be more as pioneer than polished practitioner. Defending the googly against the accusations of the type made by R. E. Foster, he wrote in 1925: "But, after all, what is the googly? It is merely a ball with an ordinary break produced by an extraordinary method. It is not difficult to detect, and, once detected, there is no reason why it should not be treated as an ordinary break-back!"

Bowlers wishing to try this "extraordinary method" may find the following description useful. The hand must hinge in at the wrist at delivery much earlier than for the leg-break. The back of the hand faces the batsman and there is a feeling that the ball is being flipped out over the top of the little finger. As the bowling arm comes up the wrist should not stiffen, while the hand rolls over to bring the palm facing upwards. Dipping the left shoulder earlier than for the leg-break, and perhaps turning more to face the batsman, make this difficult delivery a little more feasible.

Unless the whole action is completed at a height close to that of the leg-break, the difference is likely to become obvious to many batsmen. A variation of the googly action, which may make it more difficult to detect, is to point the hand more to the rear than down to the side as it comes over high. This may well be the secret of its more successful exponents.

Whereas the final stage of the leg-break action involves the fingers flicking over the ball in a direction somewhere between the slips and extra-cover, the googly action involves the fingers flicking over towards a point between fine-leg and mid-wicket. All else failing, most batsmen go on the back foot and read the ball off the pitch, or make sure they get out to it and smother the spin.

The caution required of the batsman in sensing and combatting the added danger gives the bowler an advantage, especially when there is no guarantee that the ball will actually grip and turn as expected. This danger applies every time a batsman "reads" a bowler, fast or slow. The really successful googly bowlers possessed the flexibility to carry out these actions quickly and easily and with a minimum of strain.

Every possible give-away sign has been spotted by batsmen at some time or other: the run-up, the grip, a little finger sticking out, the lower hand, the higher flight, the way the ball spins in the air. Their conspicuousness may depend on the rapidity of the finger action, the clarity of the light and the type of background.

Abdul Qadir, a bowler of great interest to the cricketing world, spins his googly with a quick enough action to make it difficult to detect from his hand; but his impressive attacking qualities are too often unaccompanied by the necessary consistency and patience.

The Somerset batsman Harold Gimblett, who was having trouble playing leg-breaks and googlies, asked Walter Hammond for advice. The reply he received follows.

Hammond gave me a long stare. "Forget 'em Harold. Ignore 'em".

"That's all very well for you," I said. "You can play them with your eyes shut. It's something I haven't learned to do."

"First of all, clear your mind of this nonsense about them turning one way or the other. Just play every ball on its merit, where it pitches."

Hammond was not an easy man to talk to. But he was very helpful to me. He explained that if the ball was a half-volley I should aim for somewhere between mid-on and mid-off, that arc. If it was a leg-spinner, the shot would go past mid-on.

"There's one golden rule," he said. "Normally to play back, you're supposed to get into a position where you are absolutely right behind the ball. But not with these boys. They can catch you with a top-spinner or one that hurries off the wicket. You've got to give yourself a bit of room. Go forward and backwards on the leg stump. If it's slightly short, you can play back and, outside the off stump, you have all the arc in the world, square to cover-point and beyond, to hit it where you like as hard as you like. If it comes into you [the googly] you've still got plenty of time and room to play wide of mid-on for 2, 3 or 4."

I couldn't wait for leg-spinners after that.[16]

Writing of googly bowling in 1907, W. G. Grace, said:

With my long experience I have rather a suspicion that it will never become universal ... My reason for this is that the bowling of googlies well – and there is nothing easier to score from when they are bowled badly – is a much greater physical strain than is any other kind of bowling. The bowling of leg-breaks is a greater strain on arm and body than the bowling of off-breaks. I have heard many a bowler who had a good off-break lament the day when he learned to bowl leg-breaks. Now the genuine googly requires even more effort of a peculiar kind than does the leg-break. In my opinion, a bowler cannot last who has any trouble over his delivery. The longest-lived bowlers are those whose action is the reverse of troublesome.[17]

Grace was right; a significant number of googly bowlers have suffered serious problems of one sort or another. R. O. Schwarz lost the ability to bowl the leg-break. Ian Peebles (1908–1980), the great hope of English spin in the 1930s, severely damaged his shoulder bowling leg-breaks and googlies; after only four Test series he was forced to withdraw and ended his career bowling off-breaks. Likewise, J. H. Cameron, a West Indian, found the strain of bowling leg-breaks and googlies too much during the 1939 tour of England and settled for off-breaks. Garfield Sobers' spinning career ended in 1966 when his shoulder went as a result of bowling the googly; an injury that never completely healed. Richie Benaud developed chronic fibrositis during his Test career. Benaud, like Peebles, had been prepared to devote the great amount of time to practice that is demanded of a bowler attempting to tame the googly. R. S. Whitington described the pain:

Benaud had withdrawn from the Lord's Test owing to his very painful, fibrositic bowling shoulder. Watching Richie don and remove his sweater during that cold summer was as excruciating as two hours with a dentist. I watched the expression on his face through binoculars once, and once was enough. Few noticed how Richie always faced away from those on the field when he donned and removed that sweater.

He could hardly have suffered a less favourable preparation for the ordeal he knew he must undergo on that last day at Manchester. He had to eliminate the googly from his scheme of things as his shoulder could not allow him to deliver it.[18]

Problems like these have afflicted googly bowlers at all levels of cricket. If the extra stress its contortions place on the muscles doesn't cause actual injury, the danger of permanent stretching remains: in this case the effect may be just as serious because the leg-break is lost through insufficient tension remaining in the muscles.

Apart from causing injury and loss of the leg-break, the googly among all the possible deliveries in cricket is the one most likely to be punished. It may not necessarily be the most inaccurate, although the awkwardness of its release makes it likely to be so. It is the combination of this basic inaccuracy, with a slower speed, and inward turn, that makes it more vulnerable than most other bowling.

Bob Holland, a successful Australian Test leg-spinner in recent years, said in a television interview that he didn't bowl his googly in international cricket because it wasn't one of his good balls and he hadn't full control of it. The reply from the interviewer encapsulated perfectly the widespread ignorance of the googly and displayed a lack of appreciation of the honest, considered and successful strategy that had just been revealed to him, by saying: "I think you should bowl a few wrong 'uns just to make the batsman think", adding the advice that Holland should work on that ball at the nets!

History tells us that Mailey and O'Reilly were unique in their own different ways. If better bowlers of their type should ever appear, such an event will be just as freakish as they were themselves. Because the googly is such a poor ally, it is harmful to the re-emergence of spin bowling to regard either of them as practical models for young bowlers to imitate.

It is easy to knock the record of the googly for six, as did Alan Fairfax, an Australian Test batsman of the 1930s:

This type of delivery attracts more attention than it deserves because it is a freak which few can bowl. Anyway, it is used much less frequently than newspaper writers would have us believe. It is my firm belief that the overrated googly is the ruination of many potential leg-break bowlers.[19]

When spin regains a significant place in the game, new generations of bowlers will rise to the challenge of the googly and cricket will be all the richer for it. If they do, then a little gentle cynicism is called for, along with R. C. Robertson-Glasgow, who penetrates the world of at least one googly bowler and perhaps of nearly all of them:

> They are always going to do the trick. They feed on hope, die by murder, and are born again. Reasons, evasions, and open lies live around these googlies. It is the wrong end, the wrong slope, or too cold. Some day all will be warm and right. But I don't think so. Never the time and the place and the googly all together.[20]

REFERENCES

1 *The Wisden Book of Obituaries 1892–1985* (Queen Anne Press, 1986), p. 93 **2** C. H. B. Pridham, *The Charm of Cricket – Past and Present* (Herbert Jenkins Ltd,) 1949), p. 130 **3** ibid., p. 131 **4** *The Wisden Book of Obituaries 1892–1985*, p. 93 **5** Letter to *The Times* by Bosanquet's brother Nicholas, October 14, 1936 **6** E. Parker, *A History of Cricket*, The Lonsdale Library, Vol. 30, p. 119 **7** ibid., p. 119 **8** Letter to *The Times* **9** C. S. Marriott, *The Complete Leg-Break Bowler*, p. 146 **10** E. W. Stanton (ed). *Barclays World of Cricket*, p. 209 **11** A. Mailey, *10 for 66 And All That* (Phoenix Sports Books, 1958) **12** J. Pollard (ed), *Cricket – The Australian Way*, p. 151 **13** W. J. O'Reilly, *The Bradman Era* (Collins Willow, 1984), p. 102 **14** A. Ross (ed), *The Cricketer's Companion*, p. 275 **15** *The Wisden Book of Obituaries 1892–1985*, p. 93 **16** D. Foot, *Harold Gimblett, Tormented Genius of Cricket* (Heinemann, 1982), p. 85 **17** E. Parker, *A History of Cricket*, p. 120 **18** R. S. Whitington, *Bradman, Benaud and Goddard's Cinderellas*, (1964) p. 20 **19** A. Fairfax, *The Science of Cricket* (1953) **20** R. C. Robertson-Glasgow, *More Cricket Prints* (Werner Laurie, 1948), p. 137

Chapter 22

Left-hand bowling

RIGHT-HANDED CRICKETERS, both batsmen and bowlers, outnumber their left-handed counterparts by about four to one. Untangling the reasons for the handedness of the human race has kept a great number of people busy for many years. Somewhere in the background of it all we must accommodate the fact that the right side of the brain carries out some functions not carried out by the left, and vice versa; but I doubt that this explains why we are so lopsided in our attitude to left-hand bowling.

If ever a bowler was the victim of stereotyped thinking along the most unimaginative lines possible it is the left-arm spinner. For some reason we have come to regard a bowler who wheels up a gently spinning ball, which will drift a little in the air if the wind is in the right direction, and may very occasionally turn on landing, as indispensable to the attack (if that is the appropriate word) of every cricket team. A simpering off-break action that would be eminently unremarkable from a right-hander, is elevated to a sublime level.

Colin Blythe and Tony Lock were left-hand spinners in the very best sense. They spun the ball with an action which if transferred to the mirror hand would rank with that of the most notable off-spinners. Unfortunately they were not the models for the droves of left-arm, so-called spinners whose principal function it seems is to bowl inexpensively enough to impress a certain type of captain, take up so much time that victory is out of the question, regard wicket-taking as something for others, and ultimately play batsmen into form. The sight of one such delivery actually turning is a noteworthy event at any level.

If any logic does exist within this gentle occupation, it is most likely to be found in the emphasis which is placed on flight. Fortunately, right-arm leg-spinners operating from the same side of the wicket and actually succeeding in their appointed task of turning the ball away from the bat, are not allowed to base their career on such a narrow foundation. The delicate finger pressure required would at least guarantee a minimum of lost skin.

Everything discussed earlier in connection with the off-break and its accompanying variations can be applied to the left-hander. The implication in this set of deliveries is that the stock ball is the leg-break, the ball which will cause the right-hand batsman the most embarrassment.

Wilfred Rhodes (1877–1973) was a spinner of high class, a slow left-hander who, as well as scoring nearly 40,000 runs in 37 seasons, took, 4,187 wickets. He was one of the most successful bowlers ever, a master craftsman of curving flight, subtle variations and spin. Some details of his methods as passed on by Hedley Verity and C. B. Fry are included in the biography by A. A. Thomson. First Verity:

> ...the left foot behind the bowling crease, the right foot out on the off side. Then, just before the left arm comes out to deliver the ball, the batsman catches a glimpse of the bowler's right shoulder-blade.
>
> The ball is spun on a line from mid-on to third man. On delivery, the wrist turns and the knuckles go up and out from the hand, the ball being spun from the first finger.
>
> The momentum of run-up, through arm, shoulder, body, and turn of wrist, goes into the action, the bowler following through automatically, up and over his front foot.
>
> In such an action there is both ease and power, and the curving flight, with the ball travelling upwards from his fingers, takes the spin better than any straight flight.[1]

and Fry:

> How does the batsman see Wilfred Rhodes? Hostile meaning behind a boyish face, ruddy and frank; a few such easy steps and a lovely swing of the left arm, and the ball is doing odd things at the other end: it is pitching where you do not like it, you have played forward when you do not want to – you have let fly when you know you ought not; the ball has nipped away from you so quickly; it has come straight when you expected a break; there is discomfort.[2]

(Verity's observation that the ball was "spun" on a line from mid-on to third-man refers to the direction of the hand twisting across behind it.)

Tony Lock based his career on the conviction that left-hand spinners should be attacking bowlers, able to turn the ball on most pitches. Even Rhodes and Verity were frequently stock bowlers rather than wicket-takers. But Lock bowled at a brisk slow-medium pace, seldom using the chinaman and almost never the googly. His leg-break and associated variations brought the rewards he sought, and in his time he was the most dangerous attacking left-arm spinner in the game. In 49 Tests he took 174 wickets at 25.58 each.

I discussed Derek Underwood's spinning action earlier. What more damning commentary could be made on modern cricket than that of his team mate Chris Cowdrey[3] when he expressed the widely held view that Underwood was: "...a freak talent... no other modern cricketer has successfully bowled medium-pace spinners"? Since Underwood described himself as "slow to slow-medium"* we must question at least part of that statement. Nevertheless, the sad isolation of Underwood was there for all to see; like trees gradually killed off by acid rain, the line of great slow-medium spinners of earlier years was virtually down to one survivor. On his retirement Underwood complained bitterly about the bounceless pitches on which he was forced to bowl. Earlier he pointed out the drastic reduction in the use of spin in one-day games.

At the beginning of his county career Underwood grappled with the problem facing all left-handers, that of bowling around or over the wicket. Over the wicket he found it necessary to pitch just outside the leg stump in order to hit the wickets, allowing for the angle of delivery. To the slow left-hander this may sound far-fetched; but it must be remembered that a good length for a faster bowler like Underwood is somewhat shorter, and that the shorter it pitches the wider is the straight path missing the off stump. The problem is even more acute for medium and fast left-handers. However, a left-hander basing his attack on the off-break would need to bowl over the wicket. Underwood's ball that swerved and possibly swung from off to leg also caused him problems, it tending to carry on down the leg side and remove any chance of an lbw decision. He also found it difficult to avoid running on to the pitch; running across in front of the umpire standing back would have required a drastic change in his entire bowling action because of the completely new angles involved. Wisely making his own decision in the face of advice to the contrary from some highly-regarded cricketers, he settled for bowling at his normal pace, around the wicket with the umpire standing up. He pitched between wicket and wicket or just outside off and the in-swerver was always likely to get an lbw.

Underwood revealed the basis of a memorable career in these words:

> I rely on subtle variations of pace for my wicket-taking ability, allied to bowling a tight line and length, just as any other spinner would do on a good wicket, the difference being that my stock ball is faster than their's. If the conditions help the ball turn more sharply, then I consider that a bonus. Again just as any spinner would do.
>
> Length and line coupled with the ability to disguise a slower delivery have always been my main assets ever since my school days... More often than not this was sufficient to take wickets at schoolboy level and even at village green level. Moving up a class to play club cricket for Beckenham made me realise I had to do a little extra.
>
> That was the time I added a great variety to my bowling. It was at this stage that Kent began playing a part in my development and

Claude Lewis, a left-arm spinner himself, influenced these variations when he told me, "For every wicket on which you play there is a pace to bowl."

My stock delivery then was fairly flat and from that I developed a quicker ball, a slower ball, another one slightly slower still, giving it more air, and so on. My bowling remains basically the same today. The one great difference being that I have now become better at adapting my style to different wickets and at exploiting wickets which really give me encouragement.[5]

We have been discussing the left-hander's leg-break, delivered with the same action as a right-hander's off-break. When we move on to its opposite number, the left-hand action mirroring the right-hander's leg-break, we come to something of a cul-de-sac in the development of left-hand bowling.

Used by the left-hander, the right-hander's range of techniques for the leg-break will deliver a range of off-breaks. But we seem to have gone out of our way to make left-handers wishing to bring the ball back in from the off feel odd. We adopted a curious name – the "chinaman" – and to add to the confusion, sometimes wrongly apply it to the left-hander's googly, which of course is a leg-break to a right-hand batsman. The name is thought to have been coined by an English batsman during the 1930 MCC tour of the West Indies. After being bowled by an off-break from Ellis Achong, a Trinidadian of Chinese extraction, he uttered the remark, "Fancy being bowled by a Chinaman".

Perhaps it is their relatively small numbers which attracts this sort of treatment. Unless we encourage such left-hand bowling a significant proportion of cricketers will not be testing their potential skills to the fullest extent. Research indicating that about one-quarter of all young children have no preference for a particular hand, raises the possibility that the game could be enriched by more young cricketers being encouraged into left-handedness. Even mature cricketers are known to have changed over, and there are some who could bowl with both hands.

Fast, medium and slow, left-handers have always been valued members of many bowling attacks. For their stock ball they all bring their hand down to the left of the ball during release and, depending on the axis of spin, obtain varying degrees of inswing, in-swerve and leg-break. A few can also swing the ball away from the right-hander by drawing the hand down on the right side of the ball and using an action which mirrors that of a right-hand inswing bowler.

Fry's analysis[6] treats only a few left-handers but there is one, S. Hargreave (1876–1929) of Warwickshire, a slow-medium bowler whose methods point to a deficiency in our modern approach. Hargreave was noted for his accuracy, his ability to vary pace and length, and his effectiveness on all types of wicket, fast and slow. After describing Hargreave's ability to bowl a leg-break at full pace using "finger-spin", Fry describes his slower ball, which "drops shorter than expected and nips along quickly". The ball "is a very good one which is liable to beat the batsmen not only off the pitch, but in its flight". The accompanying photo shows the first-and-third-finger grip, the mirror image of the one found to be most effective for right-hand leg-break bowlers. Fry's caption under the photo reads: "The ball is held apparently for the off-break. But this bowler does not break from the off in using this grip unless he turns his hand at the moment of delivery so as to put on intentional finger-spin". Hargreave's ball was therefore a chinaman of slow-medium pace.

An interesting feature of the above account is the apparent acceptance that the first-and-third-finger grip is normal for the left-hander's off-break. This is exactly what we would expect as a natural technique if left-handers reflected the method of right-handers. In other words, medium-pace left-handers of a century ago were rotating their forearms, turning their hands and working their fingers as right-hand leg-break bowlers have been ever since. Whether they hinged their wrists is immaterial because, as we saw earlier, finger movement and hand rotation at speed give ample spin.

But why the slow-medium pace off-break, carrying (like its leg-break mirror image) a good deal of top-spin – the very ball that modern right-hand off-break bowlers strive for as an invaluable variation – should be adopted so rarely is difficult to understand.

Cricketers clever enough to see the great worth of such a ball can do no better than study the highly effective methods of Ernest Toshack who played for Australia just after the Second World War. The war and the fact that he lived in the Bush combined to make his debut late and his Test career short, but in twelve Tests he took 47 wickets at 21.04 runs each. His pace was medium to slow-medium and he bowled his stock delivery from over the wicket, spinning the ball from off to leg. He could curve the ball either way in the air and occasionally spun one from leg to off. His faster ball was exceptionally good and he had remarkable accuracy. Toshack was therefore in a direct line of descent from Hargreave half a century earlier. It is said that he practised every morning at five o'clock in the nets across the road from his home in Sydney, bowling to a single stump to improve his accuracy.

Certain left-hand spinners, slower than Hargreave and Toshack, form a truly amazing group. Not content with the uncommon enough though not exceptionally difficult skill of being able to bowl the left-hander's off-break, they also adopted the googly. The South African C. B. Llewellyn (1876–1964) has been credited with being "The Bosanquet of the Left". After him the better-known exponents were the Australians Fleetwood–Smith (1910–1971), Jack Walsh (1912–1980), George Tribe, Johnny Martin and David Sincock; Johnny Wardle (1923–1985) and Dennis Compton being the only Englishmen.

Following our critical analysis of the right-hander's googly, with all its problems, it would be surprising if the mirror images appeared any different. Fleetwood-Smith was a right-hander who changed to left near the end of his school days, following a broken arm. His stock ball, at a pace above slow, was the off-break which spun at an exceptional rate; the leg-break was the googly. For Victoria he took 295 wickets at 24.40 runs each, with some amazing performances. Sometimes he was unplayable, but in Tests his erratic form meant that he was not a match winner in the Mailey mould. He played ten Tests, taking 42 wickets at 37.38 runs each.

Walsh went to England in 1936 at the age of 23 and remained there for the rest of his cricket career as a prodigious spinner and a batsman. His 1,127 first class wickets cost 24.25 each. Tribe had three Tests for Australia against England in 1946–7, beating the bat often enough but not having the success needed to remain in the side. Like Walsh he enjoyed a long and successful career after moving to England.

Martin is remembered more as an enthusiastic cricketer and an aggressive batsman than as a bowler. Although he took 3 wickets in 4 balls in his Test debut against the West Indies in 1960–1, he never repeated that success and in 8 Tests took only 17 wickets at the high cost of 48.94 runs each. Sincock, once described as Australia's most exciting wicket-taker, whilst bowling some unplayable deliveries, was also erratic and failed to hold his place after three Tests in which his 8 wickets cost 51.25 runs each. Wardle's bowling career reflects the problems facing anyone who sets out to master every type of spin known at that time to a left-hander. J. M. Kilburn said of Wardle: "Spin sometimes took precedence over the need for basic accuracies and on occasions he neglected opportunities presented by the circumstances".[7] In 28 Tests he took 102 wickets at 20.39, not a great number per Test, but economical enough.

This tiny band of pioneers attracted plenty of interest, including that of selectors willing to give them a role. They enriched the game and deserve the gratitude of cricket lovers everywhere. But like most of the disciples of Bosanquet, the China men had feet of clay: none reached the height of a Mailey or an O'Reilly, and on the evidence available to us they would have been well advised to seek something other than the left-hand googly as a ball to accompany their left-hand off-break.

If there is to be a future for the left-hand off-break bowler we must find a way out of the impasse described by A. G. Moyes:

A left-handed "bosey" bowler runs counter to nature, in that his normal delivery is an off-break, and the leg-break, which should be his normal turn, is the surprise. He suffers because the greater proportion of batsmen play right-hand, and thus his usual delivery is an off-break to them. The result is that he must use over-many "boseys" if he wants big results. The right-hand "bosey" bowler is rarely at his best against the left-hand batsman, and the same applies to the left-hand bowler and right-hand opponent. That is why it never surprises me if they fail against the men who are tops in the batting art. Fleetwood-Smith was often a demon against ordinary first-class batsmen, but when he met the Hammonds, Huttons, and Comptons he mostly seemed to have left his trident in the dressing-room ... He had some good days, but not proportionate to his natural ability. Taking it on the average, I don't think that the left-hand "bosey" bowler can ever be a consistent menace in the highest circles, simply because nature is against him.[8]

First we will ignore the googly (a leg-break) and, concentrating on the off-break, consider whether the left-hander's off-break is the same as, or better or worse than, the right-hander's off-break. If both types of bowler were operating from behind a screen, would "Johnny" Moyes be able to distinguish one from the other? The answer would depend largely on whether they were bowling against an appreciable wind or not, whether or not they used a low trajectory, and how fast they were bowling. Into a wind of even moderate force, the top-spinning off-break from the left-hander would need to be thrown up higher because it would dip quicker. It would also lose more forward momentum on a slow bounceless pitch than would the right-hander's off-break. Such a delivery dropping even slightly short is easily forced away on the leg side. Bowling with the wind there is no problem.

Delivered at a pace at least a little faster than slow, and possibly extending right through into medium pace or faster, the left-hand off-break will, because of the substantial amount of spin it is likely to carry, be an attacking delivery of the highest order. The finger action will probably be based on a first-and-third-finger grip (the reflection of the right-hand leg-spinner's grip), along with any amount of hand- and arm-rotation and wrist-hinging which is possible within the limited action time.

The opportunity for left-handers to become top-class off-spin bowlers, in the manner set out here, is nothing fanciful, but merely a reminder of the methods of successful bowlers of the past. We can now address the assertion that because most batsmen are right-handers, this form of bowling, in which the stock ball is an off-break, will be less effective than a leg-break. The basic idea is true, but in the context of a well-developed set of bowling skills, it is quite misleading. First it implies that an off-spin bowler, right- or left-hand, has not added danger to his attack by developing the ball that swerves in the air away from the bat. This ball will be delivered from over the wicket in both cases. Over-the-wicket is an excellent angle for the left-hander because his sharply turning off-breaks will not deviate so markedly to the leg side as they would from around the wicket. Just as the natural swerve of the right-hand leg-break bowler is from off to leg, so the left-hand off-break will swerve away before biting back off the pitch. Needless to add, the top-spinner from the left-hander bowling over the wicket will also be a very useful ball.

So far so good; but when we come to the ball that turns from leg to off we come face-to-face with Moyes' principal reservation. He implies that it is too much to ask the left-hand bowler to base an attack on bowling a great number of googlies and because this is so, the whole strategy is doomed to failure. We know enough about googlies now to be able to support the first part of that statement. As for the contention of inevitable failure, it is based on the erroneous assumption that the googly is the only means by which the bowler can turn the ball the other way off the pitch. If Moyes implies that no other variation but the googly can be disguised, then the history of bowling says otherwise. Plenty of googly bowlers have not disguised their intentions very well and plenty of non-googly bowlers have done so very effectively.

We looked at the possibilities in an earlier chapter – the off-break bowler adding the leg-break and the leg-break bowler adopting the off-break or the flipper – and saw the great rewards gained by bowlers taking these initiatives in the past. Our left-hand off-breaker developing the leg-break and accompanying swerve used by left-handers for a century or more, will have a formidable armoury at his disposal. The only difference required for this type of bowling, as compared to the classical left-hand attack, would be a requirement that it should almost always be delivered from over the wicket. But even here there is scope for variation around the wicket, especially if the leg-break is really turning.

For the bowler interested in following a new direction, what could be more intriguing than pioneering the left-hand flipper? In his hands it will be a quick, skidding leg-break, which may prove valuable, particularly as a straightening-up lbw ball when delivered around the wicket. Unless the pitch is lively it will not be expected to leap and take the edge for a slip catch. But it comes through quickly, usually low, and turns away, offering the chance that there may be some neat little snicks to the 'keeper's gloves fairly low down. Bowled over the wicket among inward-turning off-breaks, it could give batsmen some nasty surprises.

Spin is the essence of good left-arm bowling. Even though the pitch may not offer much grip, spin-swerve is a useful ally. As with right-hand bowling, spin-swerve – particularly when it is enhanced by the wind – can take the ball through on to the pitch at such an angle that turn, which intended to be in the reverse direction, is more than cancelled out. The appropriate response may be to accept the situation and adjust the field accordingly, while at the same time hoping that one grips the pitch occasionally. Changing ends is another option. Ideally, the combined machinations of spin, spin-swerve, wind and grip on the pitch should make a quick kill.

If I seem to have ignored left-hand bowlers of the fast variety in this discussion, it does not mean that they are not catered for, since I believe that the earlier chapters on swing and swerve allow for an easy conversion of those principles for use by the other hand. Everything I have said about spin in this section and in the earlier pages should be of potential value to bowlers of all paces, even though for the fastest bowler they are useful more for the slower part of their armoury.

REFERENCES

1 A. A. Thomson, *Hirst and Rhodes* (The Epworth Press, 1959), p. 183 **2** ibid., p. 183 **3** Chris Cowdrey, *The Cricketer* November 1987, p. 12 **4** D. Underwood, *Beating the Bat*, p. 29 **5** ibid., p. 30 **6** G. W. Beldham and C. B. Fry, *Great Bowlers and Fielders*, p. 288 **7** E. W. Swanton (ed), *Barclays World of Cricket*, p. 246 **8** A. G. Moyes, *Australian Bowlers* (Angus and Robertson, 1953), p. 141

Chapter 23

The batsman's point of view

THIS CHAPTER IS NOT REALLY ABOUT BATTING TECHNIQUE, but about entering the mind of the batsman. Apart from any intentions the batsman may have, what do we know about his basic capabilities? A few years ago scientists Bahill and La Ritz published a paper entitled "Do baseball and cricket players keep their eyes on the ball?"[1] Human performance was being studied by means of a sophisticated electronic arrangement which revealed exactly where the subject was looking as a ball approached. They concluded that baseball and cricket players do not keep their eye on the ball because it is physiologically impossible.

Using subjects who included amateur baseball players and one professional, tracking balls travelling at speeds between 50 and 93 mph, they found that it was possible to keep up with the ball only for the first 90% of its flight. Some were able to track the ball over the first portion of its trajectory, draw on their years of training to guess its future position, make a quick position-correcting, eyeball-rolling movement to this predicted location, and then resume tracking. The top subject, a member of the Pittsburgh Pirates, also used a little head movement during this process, prompting the authors of the paper to suggest that the old batting axiom "Don't move your head" should be expanded to "Don't let your body move your head, but it's fine to move your head to track the ball". He was also able to repeat his head position and stance most consistently as well as having smoother eye movement and the ability to track the ball for a longer time.

The inability to track the ball the whole distance arises from the fact that as the ball gets closer it is passing across the view at an increasing rate. A fast ball passing at a distance from the body equal to that between the eyes and the sweet spot on the cricket bat, will cross at about 500–1000° per second. Untrained people are unable to cope with this and cannot normally track targets moving faster than 70°/sec. The professional baseball player however had a smooth tracking speed of up to 120°/sec with his eyes and, coupled with a 30°/sec speed for his head, reached 150°/sec overall. Such is the value of a special natural ability coupled with years of training under conditions almost identical to those in which the scientific test was conducted. Top-class batsmen would also be expected to display this exceptional ability.

Since Bahill and La Ritz said little about cricket I have carried out some calculations to show what their work means for the game. The baseball player uses a cylindrically-shaped bat, demanding great accuracy in controlling the point of contact with the ball on a curved face. But he does not face the problem of coping with a ball bouncing off the ground. Although the cricketer has this problem, the greater chance of a controlled hit using a flat-faced bat more or less compensates. A baseball travels about the same distance as a cricket ball on delivery, and in both sports the point of impact with the ball is about the same distance from the eyes.

In what sense do both players line the ball up? Depending on whether the deliveries from both pitcher and bowler are left- or right-hand, to a left- or right-hand bat, and whether (in cricket) they are from round or over the wicket, and whether they are swerving or not, the balls in both sports are seen early in flight to be moving across the field of vision to some extent. The closer the ball is to the batsman or batter the faster it moves across the vision.

Baseball players are required to contact the ball within a fairly limited space alongside them, whereas for cricketers it extends on both sides from well above eye level to the level of the meanest grubber. A fast ball at 80mph travelling 17yds (15.5m) from the bowler's hand to pitch on a full length (2yds (1.8m) in front of the batsman) will travel towards the batsman and downwards (for 2.5yds (2.3m)), in 0.44sec. If we divide its trajectory into four periods we can find some of the problems faced by the batsman as the ball approaches. For the first quarter it crosses the vision at 17°/sec, the second 36°/sec, the third 61°/sec and the last, before it pitches, 183°/sec. Thus with 70°/sec as the normal limit, only in the last quarter is tracking outside the capabilities of the untrained. However, it is obvious that closer to the batsman a good deal of the rapid and unpredictable movement, which at this speed will be confined mainly to bounce, lies outside the limits of visibility. An 80mph yorker, pitching at the batsman's feet, presents an impossible tracking task of over 1000°/sec movement. However, because it does not bounce, the yorker (with its straight path) allows a trained batsman to make the anticipatory eye movements detected by Bahill and La Ritz. In other words, training allows the eye to move ahead of the ball to where it is expected to be. Tracking takes place by a series of such movements. The swinging yorker is a different matter! For a bowler of half the speed, assuming a straight line trajectory and pitching on the same spot, the above figures are halved.

If tracking was everything, then slow bowlers might never get the wicket of a trained batsman. Fortunately for the bowler, seeing does not necessarily mean doing. The sight of a batsman, bat raised, watching the ball hit his stumps is a common enough demonstration of the need to react in time.

Reaction time varies tremendously. The good news for batsmen and a stern warning for bowlers is that it can be greatly reduced by training. The bowler, who after bowling four inexpensive overs to a batsman thinks that he is on top, must not forget that whatever happens next he has been training that batsman. A painful shock may be in store. At worst, every ball was the same stock ball making the batsman so comfortable that the subsequent run-getting surprises nobody except the bowler. Just because runs were not being scored, there is no reason for the bowler to think he is on top to the extent that he can ease up or forget variety. At best the training was brilliantly designed to lead the victim into the one trap necessary for his demise, whether it was through being lulled, or frustrated and unsettled.

The scientific work we have been discussing has interesting things to tell us about this all-important learning process. The human eye, trying to track unpredictable targets, has a time delay of about 159 milliseconds before it gets into action at a new position. Such a delay in following a cricket ball could leave the eye several feet away from the ball, depending on whether the bowling was slow or fast. Predictable moving targets were a different story as the subjects quickly learned a high level of accuracy with no time delay. They did this by means of quick anticipatory eye and head movements. During a two hour period the best results were obtained when each subject was given 18 secs of training every 5 mins. Since a batsman cannot react rationally without first seeing the ball, the work discussed here demonstrated the vital part played by training, both within a game and before it. Reducing the amount of predictability and devising ways of manipulating all this training to the benefit of the bowler is the very summit of his art.

A century before the scientists moved in the Demon Bowler had worked out a few things for himself:

"What is the first duty of a bowler, Mr Spofforth?"

"To lead astray the batsman, to lead him astray by never allowing him to guess what is coming. So far as I am concerned I may send a very quick ball (I have never yet put all my strength into it), the next may be correspondingly slow. Therein, I consider, lies any power I may have as a bowler – this ability to vary the pace from the very quick to the very slow. Then I try to deceive him by break and variety of pitch. If you know your batsman from previous meetings, a good bowler knows his weak points. I am speaking of the best known men in the world of cricket. When I am bowling against a batsman whose peculiarities I am not acquainted with, I generally gauge him by his style, and have his stock in three or four overs. I dare say a batsman would tell you the same thing about a bowler. We try to lead each other astray, but the batsman is generally the first to betray himself. Having penetrated the armour, then I go for him, tickling him and tempting him. He fancies he has got my gauge by one style of break. Then I try another and suddenly revert to the first; or one puts, by the manner of holding the ball, a spin on that will not cause it to turn out of its course. The batsman may think by the action of the delivery that the ball will turn out of its course when it possibly finds its way to the wicket. But it is a difficult matter to explain. As I find a batsman is inclined to hit, to play back, or to play forward, so I tempt him, sometimes trying to 'beat the bat' – that is, going straight for his wicket, at others alluring him to hit so as to place the ball in the hands of one of the field".[2]

William Lillywhite, the star of the round-arm era, puts bowling firmly on an intellectual pedestal: "I suppose if I was to think every ball, they would never get a run."

Although the response of the batsman to each delivery may tell the bowler something useful, there are times when the bowler must be guided by principles rather than reacting to what happens at the other end. If things are not going in the bowler's favour and he has tried all his tricks – change of pace, variation of spin, flight and angle – to no avail, the temptation is strong to assume that there is no point in maintaining this variety. Such a retreat is based on a false interpretation of what the batsman has done. Even if he looks comfortable, he has been forced to solve one problem after another. The scientists we discussed earlier found that fatigue in problem-solving reduced the success rate in tracking experiments. Every new problem posed is a potential wicket-taker: persistence is necessary if the batsman is to be the one who capitulates, rather than the bowler himself.

Another type of misinterpretation of the batsman's situation by bowlers arises from timidity in a tense situation. Instead of bowling normally and employing his full complement of variations, the bowler "freezes up" and becomes highly predictable at the very time when variety would put more pressure on the batsman. Since the variations are not usually quite as reliable as the bowler's stock ball, the decision to forsake tidy but sterile controllability for the riskier option is nothing less than that faced by all good bowlers.

Selfishness, or at least lack of courage, lies behind another situation in which a bowler refuses to try variations in case they don't work. Although he may argue that the threat alone of these tricks is sufficient for the purpose, the real reason is more likely to be his own inability to face the risk of failure. In other words, he puts his own feelings ahead of his duty to his side. Only a captain with a thorough understanding of bowling and the powers and make-up of a particular bowler will provide the encouragement and reassurance required by a bowler in this situation.

Cricket has many situations of the swings-and-roundabouts type. The tall batsman looks downwards on the approaching ball more than does the short batsman. This means that the tall man suffers earlier from the problem of tracking, since the ball is moving across his vision to a greater extent. Tony Greig had much more difficulty with Jeff Thomson's yorker in Australia in 1974–5 than did John Edrich who was much shorter. On the other hand, the tall batsman is better able to deal with the bouncing ball. Where there is little bounce the shorter player is better off. We are dealing here with faster bowling. Now consider slower bowling, where better tracking is possible.

The average movement across the field of view over the last quarter of the flight of a slowish 40 mph delivery is only about 90°/sec. Both batsmen can now see it nearly all the way, except for the last few feet which they deal with either by moving forwards and destroying that part of the flight, or else going back for a longer look at it. But because he looks down on it to a greater extent, the tall man is in a better position to judge how far away it is. It is always easier to judge the speed of something from the side or top than by looking along its line of flight. Clarrie Grimmett's dictum stating that the longer the ball remains at eye level or slightly above it the better, is based on this principle and describes perfectly the mean trajectory for which he was famous. Tony Greig looked down towards Thomson's yorker but his eyes were unable to cope.

Role reversal – lion one day, mouse the next – is hard for a bowler to take. The batsman, now scoring freely at the other end, was all at sea the last time they met. Give him credit, he may have done some hard thinking in the meantime, but more likely every batsman looks better against him today. From all the possible reasons and excuses, we can extract one which holds useful lessons. Failure to adjust to the conditions prevailing on the day sums it up; a failure made all the more likely, almost inevitable, by the bowler failing to come down from that shaky pinnacle – success in the previous game.

That game was played on a fast pitch where the bowler did well by bowling short; today it is slow and he is being punished off the back foot. The wind helped his swing and swerve; today it blows from a different quarter. The light and the background are better today. The pitch took spin so that he did well by aiming his leg-break at the leg stump for it to take off stump or the edge of the bat; today it skids straight through and he is constantly being hit through the on side. The list could be longer. Just as a batsman, having made a big score, must start afresh to build another innings, so too must the bowler avoid any prior fixation on particular tactics, and be prepared to adapt to those required on the day.

A certain mysticism surrounds the subject of flight; language is inclined to soar into regions of scant practical interest to the bowler. What exactly is flight? Unless it makes the batsman falter or at least a little puzzled, it doesn't even warrant a name. We don't say "bad flight", we say "no flight". The cynic might suggest that flight is the last resort of the bowler who can't do anything with the ball, either in the air or on landing. One must agree that there is not much else to some bowlers.

For a newcomer unfamiliar with the game, it might be hard to accept that there could be anything subtle in tossing a ball to a certain area of ground about 17 yards away. Unless the bowler is clear enough in his own mind to be able to deal with this question, he has little chance of divining what the batsman might find difficult about it.

We will start at the very slow end, slower than Mailey. There have been a few ultra-slow bowlers in the game and some of them have been quite effective. Jack White (1891–1961) who played for Somerset and England was one such bowler. He bowled left-hand at a pace described by Jack Fingleton as "slow to stationary" and turned the ball only a little each way; yet he played in 15 Tests and took 49 wickets at 32.26 runs each. The steeply dropping ball bowled by the expert poses problems even for the best batsmen. Such bowling should not serve merely to provide a few laughs; it could well be worthy of revival, especially on pitches providing bounce. There is no reason why a subtle spectrum of variations should not be employed even at this slow pace. Only the quick-footed batsmen will be able to cope with it. A batsman interested in developing another string to his bow could find this type of bowling a particularly fascinating and rewarding endeavour. In yet another attack on slow bowling, designers of the all too common low-roofed artificial practice nets have ensured that such deliveries will never reach the batsman.

The use of the word "variations" in the above description has already answered our question. It means that although a batsman is not fooled by one ball, he may be fooled by another that looks like the first but is different. Here, in a nutshell, is the simplest and purest description of flight. We see that there is no such thing as a well-flighted ball on its own. If there is to be deception, it will only take place in relation to another delivery or series of deliveries: "a well-flighted group" may be a preferable phrase.

The case we have discussed involved deception in the air and nowhere else; so too with a fast or medium-pace bowler's change of pace. We don't normally use the term flight at that pace but it certainly is appropriate to do so.

Flight deception is intimately involved, not only with change of pace, but also with deliberate or fortuitous variations in swerve and/or swing, with or without the influence of wind. In other words, everything we have covered in this book is potentially useful in flight.

Extending our description further, we now include spin bowling of a pace and length which makes it difficult for the groping batsman to be sure of smothering the spin. Beating the bat may in that case have nothing whatsoever to do with flight; the batsman may have followed it well in the air only to be beaten off the pitch. Since that happy situation is not as common as the bowler would like, he must work for a little advantage from both directions; the turning ball may be enough to cap off a small mistake in picking up the flight. Again we have a situation where it would be wrong for the bowler to give up using one or more of his variations simply because the batsman seems to be coping. Although any one of these variations on its own may not worry the batsman, the sum total of small misjudgments of length, pace, angle and spin may be sufficient to bring about his downfall.

Flight variations can only be employed within a fairly narrow range of speed and trajectory if the deception is to succeed. Underwood, O'Reilly, Grimmett and Mailey all used flight superbly, but within a range appropriate to their methods. The suggestion that bowlers of any type should harness flight merely by bowling slower reveals a lack of understanding. One of Underwood's variations of flight was a ball slightly faster than normal.

The term "loop" carries a strong suggestion of slowing down. Bill O'Reilly regarded it as fatal:

> My advice to the talented tyro is to shun these words as if they were germ-laden. So often one hears them bandied about that one tries hard to assess the woeful damage they have caused in the bowling department. To me they are anathema. The young bowler who thinks that he must toss the ball high in the air to satisfy his claims for recognition as a promising spinner is a fool. Tossing the ball high should be regarded as an unfailing sign that the bowler is wasting everybody's time, and would be much better off if he turned his attention to batting, or feeding the chooks.
>
> I have seen looping bowlers never given the chance to hit the pitch when bowling to a quick-footed batsman free from the embarrassment of not knowing whether to go forward or back. A quick-footed batsman will always crucify a looping slow bowler.[3]

One bowler whom O'Reilly may have had in mind was Walter Robins (1906–1968), who Ian Peebles described as the best English leg-spinner he ever saw. He bowled at around medium pace, but after accepting advice to slow down, he was never as good again. Whether the term "looping" and all it implies is dangerous or merely useless, it deserves to be quickly forgotten.

REFERENCES

1 A. T. Bahill and T. La Ritz, "Do baseball and cricket players keep their eyes on the ball?", Proceedings of the 1983 International Conference on Systems, Man and Cybernetics (India), p. 79–88. See also A. T. Bahill and T. La Ritz, "Why can't batters keep their eyes on the ball?", *American Scientist*, 72, May–June 1984, p. 249–53 and A. T. Bahill and D. E. McHugh, "Learning to track predictable targets", *Investigative Ophthalamology and Visual Science*, 26 July 1985, p. 932–7   2 Interview in *The Pall Mall Budget*, 1886   3 W. J. O'Reilly, *Tiger: 60 Years of Cricket*, p. 211

Chapter 24
Wind and air resistance

A LONG THROW FROM THE BOUNDARY of 70 yds (64m), projected at 45° to the ground, would go about another 30 yds (27m) if there was no air. Cricket balls push the air aside, leaving a large turbulent wake. As we saw earlier, both swing and spin-swerve take place when this wake is diverted to one side or the other. Although drag slows a ball down very slightly in its flight towards the batsman, this slowing is of little consequence for cricket. But sideways deflection is of great importance where wind and drag may combine.

Until I carried out my wind-tunnel work it was thought that fast bowlers could break through some imaginary barrier into a region where both drag and swing suddenly decrease, but this is not so. In fact, the swing force at most seam angles used by bowlers increases steadily with speed, and the drag falls off only gradually. Drag is also remarkably unaffected by other factors and my results show that it does not depend to any significant extent on whether the balls are new or old, four-piece or two-piece, spinning or non-spinning.

Bowlers know that wind resistance causes the ball to be blown off track occasionally. Maurice Tate's only wide in his whole career was when a sudden gust of wind caught the ball at a seaside ground. Wind at ground level is usually far from steady; trees, buildings and other obstacles cause all sorts of changes in strength and direction. Used cleverly, wind is a valuable ally. But it can also ruin a well-directed delivery. The difference between a good ball and a bad one, when bowled to a good batsman, may be no more than a matter of inches. The slower the delivery the more it is blown off course; yet another reason why spin bowlers, not wishing to make life unnecessarily difficult for themselves, should, in the main, seek to push the ball through.

We saw earlier how air speed generally increases both the Robins Force and the swing force and the use to which an up-wind bowler can put this extra air speed. Unfortunately, an opposing factor operates for bowlers applying top-spin in any form and we noted earlier the fatal effect of loss of forward speed when the ball against the wind dips into a slow pitch. On fast pitches however, this down-dipping, high-bouncing delivery is an excellent combination for the bowler.

Into the wind, the swing bowler has a good opportunity of exploiting the extra air speed. Without the wind against him the swing bowler can only obtain higher air speed by bowling faster. Although the swing force increases with speed the flight time is shortened at the same time. There is also a probable delay at the beginning of the flight while the wake deviation develops. Against the wind the ball moves through more air in order to get to the batsman and therefore will swing more. The down-wind delivery passes through less air, making it more reliant on pace and/or turn, since both swing and swerve will be reduced.

Another important effect of wind is the way it slows or quickens the bowler's run-up and delivery. The human body has a very considerable wind resistance, as every cyclist knows. The effects of wind on the bowler are more likely to exceed those on the speed of the ball. Strength and stamina – always important, particularly for faster bowlers – are vital if long up-wind spells are to be sustained. Problems of balance and timing during delivery can arise for both fast and slow bowlers under these conditions. A slow bowler being pushed over a little by a strong wind from behind can find himself bowling short at a time when he expects the wind to make him over-pitch.

Since swing requires a smooth flow of air around one side of the ball, we must regard all wind as potentially destructive of swing; wind near ground level is usually turbulent. Turbulence will vary however, and may not always be destructive. The sideways push of the wind may also be in the same direction as the intended swing and will enhance it. If the wind blows against the intended swing, we have an unpredictable situation which depends on which force wins the contest. Good bowlers seem to be capable of swinging against moderate side winds.

Swing bowlers should be conscious of the way in which a cross wind can upset the seam angle they have chosen to use. A bowler sets the seam at a small angle – say 10° towards the slips for the outswinger – but because there is a strong cross wind from his left the seam is effectively pointing to the right of the air stream from the side and will be an inswinger. To counteract this problem a larger seam angle – say 30° – should be employed. The situation is somewhat unpredictable and will depend on the speed and angle of the wind, the bowling speed and on the amount of swing force the ball itself is capable of generating.

Chapter 25
Ground-spin

THE SURFACE OF EVEN THE MOST HEAVILY-SPUN BALL is moving around the ball many times slower than the ball is moving through the air. When it lands the bottom of the ball catches on the ground to some extent and is slowed down while the rest of the ball moves on above it (fig. 52a). The universal effect as discussed earlier, no matter whether the ball initially had back-, top- or side-spin, is that the tendency towards top-spin is increased. This does not necessarily mean that the ball will actually *acquire* top-spin; it may merely experience a decrease in back-spin. This situation would arise from a fast or medium-pace delivery which is given a fair amount of back-spin and lands on a "skidding" pitch. This same delivery on a "gripping" pitch may be turned over to come off with heavy top-spin. If the bowler has applied top-spin in the first place, then such a pitch will impart even more.

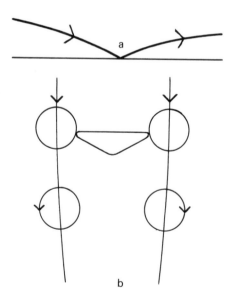

Fig. 52 *Ground-spin and spin off the edge of the bat.* By gripping the ground during contact (*a*), the ball acquires top-spin which makes it dip in flight after bouncing. By gripping the edge of the bat on either side (*b*), the passing ball acquires side-spin which makes it curve in behind the bat.

Ground-spin

Depending on the amount of off- or leg-spin applied by both fast and slow bowlers, the ball coming off the pitch may also carry a certain amount of rotation towards one side or the other. Fry mentions leg-spin from one bowler coming off the pitch with "a curious upwards curl". Nevertheless, on most pitches – particularly on a gripping pitch – the predominant spin acquired will be top-spin.

I will call this ground-induced spin "ground-spin". It has all manner of interesting consequences, not only for bowler and batsman, but also for the wicket-keeper, the fieldsman and the umpire. The fieldsman at point, reaching down for the ball only to find it spinning away to his left, or his team mate at square-leg, equally embarrassed on the right hand, are classic victims of ground-spin. Because the batsman has turned the ball square, the top-spin becomes spin on an axis pointing in the same direction as it is travelling. The ball rolls to one side as it travels along the ground, or worse, will kick sideways as it bounces.

The wicket-keeper, always under pressure, is more than ever deserving of our sympathy now that television has revealed what can happen between the pitch and his gloves. Movement after pitching is mentioned several times in cricket literature. This can include the most vicious antics where a ball can climb, dip or swing violently and unexpectedly. Ground-spin lies behind this behaviour, but its nastiness will be manifest in a witch's brew involving spin-swerve and possibly swing; in fact it is always likely to be confused with late swing.

The simplest of these gyrations is the Robins Force downward dip, resulting from ground-spin and causing pronounced top-spin on a gripping pitch. The rising ball seems to be drawn downwards by some invisible magnetic force. The 'keeper, standing back, seems to be in some trouble; perhaps the ball is dropping in front of him, or he is always having to bend to take it. The casual observer would simply say that he is standing too far back. The same problems worry slip fieldsmen and the hooking batsman who can't understand why he was caught behind off a *bottom* edge.

This accentuated top-spin and dipping flight resulting from the contact of the ball with the ground has two possible effects of interest to the fast bowler firing the ball in short. The delivery that fails to rise much and strikes the batsman's pad may be experiencing a dip or at least a flattening of trajectory which would increase the chance that a ball striking the pad fairly high would still be heading for the stumps; in other words, a justifiable lbw decision. The other consequence relates to the danger in attempting to dodge a rising ball which, because of the effect we are discussing, rises less than expected.

Less frequently a ball is seen to climb as it approaches the wicket-keeper because it has landed on the smooth leather, gripped less, acquired less top-spin and therefore dipped less than a previous delivery. An alternative explanation from my wind-tunnel work is an unpredictable negative Robins Force, where the top-spin causes an upward rather than the usual downward force.

Consider now what happens when that area of the ball that contacts the pitch, remembering that it may be an inch or more in diameter, catches more on one side than on the other. This could happen when the ball lands partially on the seam and partially on the smooth leather. As well as gaining top-spin, the ball is spun a little to the side. Two results are possible. One involves the ball being turned to a good swing angle and perhaps having a swing-killing fast wobble removed by acquiring a heavy non-wobbling spin around the seam. In this case the ball simply swings perhaps better than it did on its way down the pitch, or in a way which may not have any relation to its swing before landing. The other possibility is an induced partial side-spin, causing spin-swerve on the way to the 'keeper.

These problems facing the wicket-keeper will come and go depending on the amount of grip the ball obtains on the pitch. Both the ball and the pitch will affect this grip. If the seam is new, or if it is kept clean, and if it is not too flattened, it will grip better. If the bowler is getting a good deal of movement off the pitch, these effects are more likely to be seen, but I doubt whether wicket-keepers would complain; if they themselves are in trouble, then the batsman is being called upon to exercise real skill.

We can extend our discussion to what happens when a ball comes off the edge of the bat. This must have at least some effect, both on the path and the rotation of the ball. The ball coming off an outside edge will experience a sort of ground-spin effect, but in this case it will be side-spin (bat-spin!). The direction of the induced spin as the right-hand batsman looks down on it, on the off side, must be clockwise; therefore, assuming a positive Robins effect, it will curve from off to leg as it approaches the 'keeper and the slips. I wonder how many slip catches are dropped because of a combination of ground-spin and bat-spin, dip and swerve? Leg-side snicks, including inside edges thick enough to influence the rotation of the ball, will make it swerve from leg to off. In both cases the snick curves back inwards, justifying the old rule which says that if there is any doubt about who should go for the catch, it must be left to the wicket-keeper.

Umpires cannot take much comfort from all this because the ball off the edge of the bat swerves in the opposite direction to the deflection. Many of the classic umpiring controversies where batsmen have apparently been wrongly judged not out may have been caused by this side-spin. Whilst the thick edge will not cause any trouble because the deflection is greater than any opposing swerve, the fine edge, especially the one where the ball grips the bat with the seam as it goes past, places the umpire in an impossible position. Not only does he fail to see any deflection, he may well see the opposite – an inward curve past the bat. In this case we must sympathise with him when he assumes that the curve was the work of the bowler alone. Cricketers must accept that umpires will always be obliged to say not out under these circumstances. Will we now see devious batsmen applying a strip of gripping material along the outside edges of their bats?

It is worth noting that this same grip of ball on bat will allow the ground-spun top-spinner to grip and climb up off the face of the bat, making it generally more difficult to keep shots down.

Spinning balls from edges, or even balls carrying ground-spin, also add to the problems of out-fielders, especially catchers. All these problems arise from spin, but how often do we see fielding practice based on fielding the spinning ball? Bowling machines should prove useful in this area, but bouncing the ball off a gripping surface on to a bat edge would be a substitute.

Chapter 26
Practice

GOOD QUALITY CRICKET PRACTICE is not easy to come by. Quantity is rarely a problem, but cricketers too often settle for nothing more. Three bowlers queuing up to bowl to one batsman is a laughable rehearsal for actual play and it is obvious that cricketers have opted for nothing more than some sort of physical work-out.

Gary Sobers says he practised very little, and this should remind us of the greatly differing needs of cricketers. Players like Sobers, playing several days a week, may merely be wasting energy practising. If they need to brush up on technique, or even experiment a little, they are good enough to do at least some of it in the games they play. Most cricketers are developing at one level or another and usually require training of as high a quality as possible.

Since the bowler in the queue has no chance of developing his ability to deliver a series of six carefully related deliveries intended to lead the batsman astray in subtle stages, the basic design of such practice is incapable of educating bowlers beyond the cricket equivalent of the kindergarten. We will assume that a great deal of prior development has taken place when the bowler practised alone, as it did with many famous bowlers. Likewise, batsmen may have been using throw-downs or bowling machines. When they come together for practice worthy of the name, one batsman one bowler is the only rational way to improve both. After six deliveries from one bowler another takes over for his six and they continue to alternate. Time can be saved by having several balls available which the resting member of the pair helps to return.

Quality practice also demands that the bowler should not be treated as a sort of human bowling machine. Batsmen may benefit from bowling delivered in tired drudgery, but for bowlers it is nothing more than that, and a source of all manner of bad habits both physical and mental. Repetitive work is certainly necessary, but it should be strictly on the bowler's own terms. The risk of suffering from any number of repetitive stress related injuries, including crippling tendonitis of the shoulder, is too great to justify a bowler being a batsman's hack.

Today's coaches could learn something from Jack Massie, writing more than sixty years ago about practice for boys aged 12 to 18 years:

No boy should be allowed to bowl continuously for longer than ten minutes at a time at practice, and twenty minutes in all on one day.

Every boy should be taught to bowl at practice with some definite plan in view the whole time. He should practise some particular ball or some particular plan of attack, and should be able to say what he is practising at any time when asked. A boy, or any bowler for that matter, should bowl at practice exactly as if he were bowling in a match; that is to say, he should have a definite bowling crease of the correct width, and should pace out his run in the same way as he would do in a match, and he should be called for a no-ball should he go over the crease.

On no account should a bowler be allowed to bowl haphazard just for the sake of giving a batsman a strike.[1]

Synthetic surfaces are a mixed bag and the time is overdue for cricketers to reject some of them. Used outdoors they soak up water in wet weather and may not dry out until long after the surrounding grass has dried. The ball will not grip under these conditions. Practice wickets should be of a construction, both in the mat and the base, allowing quick drying. In spite of claims that these surfaces when dry behave like turf pitches, they are mostly quite disappointing. Some of them, because they allow very little turn, fail to provide the bowler with an adequate feed-back on his efforts. Ageing plastic strips often seem hard and gripless. Their boring predictability is basically at odds with the essence of the game. For practice nets their obvious usefulness has been limited to a great extent by poor design. They are still a long way from turf. Laid over crushed limestone they generally lack bounce, especially when damp; laid over concrete they generally bounce too much.

Modern practice nets are in most respects a backward step compared to those used thirty or more years ago. I refer to the damage inflicted by metal and concrete on balls, bats and on the frames of faster bowlers jarring down on the hard surfaces. Ian Peebles wrote vividly of the shock he experienced early in his career when he moved full of enthusiasm from months of highly promising indoor practice to playing outdoors on turf. Everything felt so different, and his bowling suffered as a result.

Good bowling is a matter of inches; only a bowler can appreciate the way bowling in boots fitted with metal sprigs feels different from bowling in synthetic-soled boots. Not only does it *feel* different during that crucial time in the delivery action when feet and ground are in contact to move the body into a precise position, it *is* different. The absolute requirement for a bowler, fast or slow, is to experience a firm and reproducible grip on the ground. Outdoors, the run-up to synthetic practice wickets should be turf, kept in good repair and on which metal sprigs should be worn. Limestone or other stony types of run-up are hard on the feet, are often dangerously unstable on the surface, accelerate ball wear and are unacceptable substitutes for earth or clay. I hope that no bowler, particularly of fast or medium pace, is forced into the dangerous situation of having to bowl using synthetic soles without metal sprigs on a damp synthetic mat.

Bowlers wishing to practise spin-swerve and accompanying break off the wicket, might wish to try the method used by the great M. A. Noble as told to S. F. Barnes, who used it with memorable results:

> I asked Noble if he would care to tell me how he managed to bring the ball back against the swerve. He said it was possible to put two poles down the wicket, one ten or eleven yards from the bowling crease and another one five or six yards from the batsman and to bowl a ball outside the first pole and make it swing to the off side of the other pole and then nip back and hit the wickets. That's how I learned to spin a ball to make it swing. It is also possible to bowl in between these two poles, pitch the ball outside the leg stump and hit the wicket. I spent hours trying all this out in the nets.[2]

REFERENCES

1 R. J. A. Massie, *Bowling*, p. 14
2 G. W. Beldam and C. B. Fry, *Great Bowlers and Fielders*, p. 232

Chapter 27
Captains

A CAPTAIN CAN MAKE OR BREAK A BOWLER. He either provides an acceptable framework within which a bowler feels free to operate at his best or, as sometimes happens, exerts a corrosive influence on all concerned and allows the game to seep away in forgettable time wasting.

Bad captaincy manifests itself in various forms: putting bowlers on and taking them off for no apparent reason; regarding any questioning of decisions as contrary to team discipline, selfishness on the part of the bowler and destructive of team spirit; acting alone in the absence of any mechanism for hearing complaints, and reacting to criticism by making life unpleasant for that individual; removing the bowler from the crease for periods longer than normal; exercising the power to drop that bowler from the team.

A bowler quickly learns that, under some captains, if he wants to bowl, it doesn't pay to speak out. Perhaps it is wise to regard the effect of power, or the dumb response of incompetence, as a potential problem with all captains, unless there is good evidence that for once a bowler has found someone with whom he can engage in constructive dialogue.

The work of the Test captain, or at least the visible results of this work, is for all to see, analysed and discussed down to the last wave of the finger. At levels below this the opportunities for captains to harm the game, and in particular the morale and development of bowlers, are legion. Clubs failing to take seriously the appointment of captains do harm to themselves and to cricket.

Many club captains don't understand the simple concept of bowlers maintaining pressure on batsmen from both ends, of working in tandem. A bowler may sink down onto the dressing-room seat at the end of the day without a wicket to his name, yet through his consistency and the understanding of his captain he may have pressured batsmen into rash shots against the other bowlers and into attempting suicidal runs.

Cricket would benefit from a sort of Captains Anonymous which puts to them the question "Do you really want to win?" If the question is too frank it can be rephrased as "I know that you would like to win, but are you doing all you can to bring this about?" The answers, if honest, would reveal no surprises to experienced cricketers: "I wanted to give everybody a bowl"; "An old friend of mine is captaining the opposing side and I regard this game principally as a social affair"; "We haven't won all season and it's no use trying now"; "Look at this team, a bunch of no-hopers"; "The committee just want me to keep everybody happy"; "I played cricket at a high standard earlier in my career, and I've got no real interest in this grade"; "Winning doesn't mean much to me, sport is far too competitive"; "I used to be keen to win when I was younger".

A bowler engaged in the long and absorbing task of developing mastery of his craft is powerless to change these attitudes and circumstances by himself. His own cause, and the cause of good cricket, are best served by a rapid and quiet move to another team or club, offering better prospects.

One aspect of that disconcerting and subversive attitude to the competitive element in sport was nicely put by a writer in *The Times Literary Supplement*:

> The ability to tap the boyhood sources of energy and illusion is essential in most highly competitive activities, and one would hesitate to back a fully adult person (should one exist) in any serious contest. There is nothing like a sudden upsurge of maturity to impair the will to win.[1]

Happy is the bowler whose captain continually brings out the best in him; no tension, no frustrations. Cricket is a complex game. For many field changes there is an equally strong case for the opposite course; do you close the gap, or feed the batsman's strength hoping for him to make a mistake? Out in the middle is not the time for extended discussion. If a captain has not taken the time to work out these tactics with the bowler before the game starts, then in the event of a disagreement on the field he must accede to the bowler's wishes. To do otherwise is to presume to know more about the bowler's craft than does the bowler himself, without giving the latter the chance of putting his case.

But in order to bring some balance to this discussion we need to consider what happens when the bowler's halo slips a little. Where better can a good captain display his qualities than in handling a chronically inaccurate bowler or a bowler with no guts? We will assume that the problem lies deeper than a day off form, or difficulty in coping with an unusually good batsman or two. Good captains might have a check-list which includes the following: suggest particular remedial work in the nets; suggest that fewer variations be tried; bring on bowler against less aggressive batsman, or at a time in the game when all batsmen are less aggressive; suggest to the bowler that he examine his own motivation. If these measures fail, then more is being expected from the bowler that he is capable of giving; in other words, he is in the wrong team.

This conclusion raises an important issue of greater significance to cricket than the fate of one inadequate bowler. I refer to the conflict between a bowler's continuing development and expectations placed on him. Consider a young medium-pace bowler, included at an early age in a squad from which will be selected a team to play a series of games for an elite group. Because he is young, let us assume about twenty, he has a range of ability limited to little more than the ability to bowl straight with good control at a brisk pace. At what stage does he embark on learning the skills which will take him above the hordes of straight-up-and-down medium-pacers? These new skills are not the skills which brought him selection in the first place, and their demanding and perhaps lengthy period of development, the outcome of which is uncertain, could require his removal, for a considerable period, from the ladder of advancement. In other words, the system discourages the very development that it purports to foster in the most promising material available. Common observation seems to indicate that more young bowlers should be showing some sign that they are grappling with the challenge of technical development. Instead of lavishing time and money on bowlers in the type of system described, we should seek ways of informing young bowlers about the full range of options available to them and then ensure that conditions exist in which they can develop. The large number of exceptional bowlers who have taken relatively lengthy periods to develop tells us that such expertise is not acquired overnight and raises fears that their early inclusion in a performance-based selection system might stifle such development.

Returning to our inadequate bowler, let us hope that he is placed at a level where he can experiment a little, overcome his problems and develop without embarrassment. Is it too revolutionary an idea to suggest that certain cricket teams should be selected, not with winning but with the development of every member of the side as their principal objective? I am not referring to the fine thoughts normally expressed by captains and coaches, but to the genuine requirement of every player – batsmen as well as bowlers – that they must reach out and try new techniques if they are to remain in the side. There need not be an age limit and the composition of the team could change quite rapidly depending on the needs of its members. In such a team bowlers would be charged with the exciting and demanding task of breaking away from the need to rely on uninspiring uniformity.

Our hypothetical captain, not only of the type of team suggested above, but of all teams, should be just as concerned with promoting attacking and penetrative bowling as with helping the expensive bowler. If he does not, then he and his team merely drift down into mediocrity along with far too many others.

No book on bowling appears complete without diagrams and notes on field placing. In my young days I copied them into notebooks and added more from important games I attended. Looked at now they remind me of nothing so much as the products of a group of racing tipsters making their picks for the big race and between them seeing nearly every horse as a potential winner. The possible range of variations in bowling skills, pace and spin, pitch conditions, wind and batsmen – from day to day, or even minute to minute – make a mockery of any attempt to lift predetermined plans from a book. If the precise positions used by famous bowlers are of interest, and it is *precise* positioning that good bowlers do require, the published diagrams, casually scaled down to the size of a printed page, are unreliable.

Trial and error, a flexible approach and a careful noting of the results obtained with different placings, is the way towards fields which will suit a particular bowler under particular conditions.

Jack Massie said it in 1926:

> The bowler decides where he wants his field placed and the captain places the men in these positions. Each bowler should be taught right from the jump to study this matter of placing his own field to the best advantage for his own bowling, and it is a matter which each individual bowler must study very closely.
>
> The most important thing to be borne in mind is that fieldsmen must not be wasted by placing them at random in order to stop the result of bad balls, but they must be placed where they will be most useful for good bowling and the bowler must see to it that he cuts the "loose stuff" down to a minimum. Further, because it is desirable to have a man in a certain position for one batsman, it does not follow that he should be in the same position for every batsman and a boy should be taught to study the batsman accordingly in order that he may make the best use of his field.
>
> It will not pay as a general rule to plug away at a batsman's weakness the whole time as this will have the effect very often of giving him practice in this particular point with anything but the desired result. It may be found far more effective to go through strength to weakness.[2]

Captains flushed with the success of a bowler and perhaps living out some boyhood fantasy, are at times prone to go overboard in bringing fieldsmen in around the bat. Whilst all concerned may imagine themselves as re-enacting Jim Laker's 19 wickets at Old Trafford, a little cool thinking should be directed towards the gaps in the out-field which, particularly for a spinner, will do his cause no good at all when desperate shots put balls in the air.

A captain worthy of the name, with a team employing a wide range of skills and enjoying competitive cricket, typifies the best in the game. Such a team is creative in deploying its bowling strength. But this approach is not possible in a good deal of the one-day cricket which is played at present. Draws are part of the essence of cricket. Eliminating the need to take wickets changes the game fundamentally and the restriction on overs per bowler reduces that flexibility which, along with declarations, gives the game its character.

The widespread problems arising from pitches lacking pace, bounce and friction have had their effects on captaincy. Because there are so few spinners about, captains are out of touch with spin. Those who are competent are likely to come under fire from spinners simply because they perceive that spinners are often not necessarily the most effective bowlers under the prevailing conditions. In other words, these captains are realists in getting the best from their team in the present deficient environment.

Whatever a captain does best, he must have faith in his bowlers and be neither excitable nor dull and apathetic, but cool, alert, adventurous and flexible.

REFERENCES

1 *The Times Literary Supplement,* June 26 1981 2 R. J. A. Massie, *Bowling,* p. 13

Epigraph

THIS BOOK HAS NOT BEEN TOTALLY PREOCCUPIED WITH TECHNICALITIES, historic and modern; various aspects of cricket philosophy have been given due attention. Concluding our exploration of the art of bowling, we can do no better than embrace the following attitude that embodies an ideal of sportsmanship going back at least as far as the ancient Greeks.

The summit of a bowler's art is to bowl a ball which the batsman thinks can be hit safely but which in actual fact gives the bowler a chance of winning the contest. Whether the bowler wins, or whether it is the batsman who wins is immaterial. The very essence of the game is to be found in those climactic moments when bat and ball move towards each other in a contest taking place at a level of the utmost possible skill.

Bibliography

Archenbach, E. J. Fluid Mech. 62 Pt 2 (1874)

Allen, D. R. (ed) *Cricket on the Air* (BBC, 1985)

Altham, H. S. *A History of Cricket*, Vol. 1. (Allen and Unwin, 1962)

Bahill, A. T. and La Ritz, T. "Do baseball and cricket players keep their eyes on the ball?", Proceedings of the 1983 International Conference on Systems, Man and Cybernetics (India) and "Why can't batters keep their eyes on the ball?", *American Scientist*, 72, May–June 1984

Bahill, A. T. and McHugh, D. E. "Learning to track predictable targets", *Investigative Ophthalmology and Visual Science*, 26 July 1985

Bailey, T. E. *The Greatest of My Time* (Eyre and Spottiswoode, 1968)

Barkla, H. M. and Auchterlonie, L. J. J. Fluid Mech. 47 Pt 3 (1971)

Barton, N. G. Proc. Roy. Soc. London A 379 (1982)

Bedser, A. *Twin Ambitions* (Stanley Paul, 1986)

Beldam, G. W. and Fry, C. B. *Great Bowlers and Fielders* (Macmillan, 1906)

Benaud, R., *Richie Benaud's Way of Cricket* (Hodder and Stoughton, 1969)
Willow Patterns (Hodder and Stoughton, 1969)

Bentley, K., Varty, P., Proudlove, M. and Mehta, R. D. Imperial College Aero Tech. Note (1982) and *Nature* 303 (1983)

Border, A. *Ashes Glory* (Swan Publishing, 1989)

Bowen, R. *Cricket, A History of its Growth and Development Throughout the World* (Eyre and Spottiswoode, 1970)

Bradman, D. *The Art of Cricket* (Hodder and Stoughton, 1958)

Brearley, M. *The Art of Captaincy* (Hodder and Stoughton, 1985)

Briggs, L. J. Am. J. Phys. 27 (1959)

Broadribb, G. *Next Man In* (Putnam, 1952)

Brown, F. N. M. 'See the wind blow", Dept. Aerosp. Mech. Eng. Rep. (University of Notre Dame, 1971)

Cameron-Lee, S. and McAuliffe, K. W. "Principles of Pitch Preparation", New Zealand Turf Management Journal (February 1989)

Close, D. B. *Close on Cricket* (Stanley Paul, 1986)

Cooke, J. C. Math. Gazz. 39 (1955)

Daish, C. B. *The Physics of the Ball Games* (English Universities Press, 1972)

Duckworth, L. *S. F. Barnes – Master Bowler* (The Cricketer-Hutchinson, 1979)

Fairfax, A. *The Science of Cricket* (1953)

Fingleton, J. *Fingleton on Cricket* (Collins, 1972)

Foot, D. *Harold Gimblett, Tormented Genius of Cricket* (Heinemann, 1982)

Gover, A. (ed), *The Lord's Taveners Cricket Clinic* (Graham Tarrant, 1986)

Graveney, T. *Cricket Over Forty* (Pelham Books, 1970)

Gregory, K. *In Celebration of Cricket* (Hart-David, Magibbon, 1978)

Grimmett, C. V. *Grimmett on Cricket* (Thomas Nelson and Son, 1948)
Tricking the Batsman (R. M. Osborne, 1932)

Hollowood, B. *Cricket on the Brain* (Eyre and Spottiswoode, 1970)

Ibbetson, A. *Weather 33* (1978)

Illingworth, R. *Spinner's Wicket* (Stanley Paul, 1969)
The Young Cricketer (Stanley Paul, 1972)

Imbrosciano, A. "The swing of a cricket ball", Project Report, Newcastle College of Advanced Education, Australia (1981)

Keating, F. *High, Wide and Handsome – Ian Botham* (Collins Willow, 1986)

Kelly, K. *Cricket Reflections* (Heinemann, 1983)

Lester, J. A. (ed) *A Century of Philadelphia Cricket* (University of Pennsylvania Press, 1951)

Lyttleton, R. A. *Discovery* 18 (1957)

Macartney, C. G. *My Cricketing Days* (Heinemann, 1930)

Macoll, J. W. J. Roy. Aeron. Soc. 32 (1928)

Mailey, A. *10 for 66 And All That* (Phoenix Sports Books, 1958)

Marks, V. *The Test and County Cricket Board Guide to Better Cricket* (Octopus Books, 1987)

Marriott, C. S. *The Complete Leg-Break Bowler* (Eyre and Spottiswoode, 1968)

Martin-Jenkins, C. *The Complete Who's Who of Test Cricketers* (Orbis Publishing, 1983)

Massie, R. J. A. *Bowling* (NSW Cricket Association, 1926)

May, P. B. H. *A Game Enjoyed* (Stanley Paul, 1985)

Mehta, R. D. "Aerodynamics of sports balls", Ann. Rev. Fluid Mech. 17 (1985)

Moyes, A. G. *Australian Bowlers* (Angus and Robertson, 1953)

Murphy, P. *The Spinner's Turn* (Dent, 1982)

Nyren, J. *The Young Cricketer's Tutor* (David-Poynter, 1974)

O'Neill, N. *Ins and Outs* (Pelham Books, 1964)

O'Reilly, W. J. *The Bradman Era* (Collins Willow, 1984)
Tiger: 60 Years of Cricket (Collins Willow, 1985)

Parker, E. *The History of Cricket*, The Lonsdale Library of Sports and Games, Vol. 30 (Lonsdale, 1950)

Peebles, I. *Bowler's Turn* (Souvenir Press, 1960)

Philpott, P. *Cricket Fundamentals* (Batsford, 1982)
How to Play Cricket (Jack Pollard Publishing, 1973)

Pollard, J. (ed) *Cricket – The Australian Way* (Landsdowne Press, 1961)
Six and Out (Jack Pollard Publishing, 1980)

Pridham, C. H. B. *The Charm of Cricket – Past and Present* (Herbert Jenkins Ltd, 1949)

Robertson-Glasgow, R. C. *More Cricket Prints* (Werner Laurie, 1948)

Robinson, R. *On Top Down Under* (Cassell, 1975)

Ross, A. (ed) *Crusoe on Cricket* (Pavilion, 1966)
The Cricketer's Companion (Hutchinson, 1979)

Rundell, M. *A Dictionary of Cricket* (Allen and Unwin, 1985)

Scovell, B. *Ken Barrington – A Tribute* (Harrop, 1982)

Sherwin, K. and Sproston, J. L. Inst. J. Mech. Eng. Educ. 10 (1982)

Smithers, P. *Melbourne Age* (17 November 1990)

Bibliography

Spence, P. "Bending the back", *Australian Cricket* (January 1990)

Swanton, E. W. (ed) *Barclays World of Cricket* (Collins Willow)

Taneda, S. J. Fluid Mech. 85 Pt 1 (1978)

Thomson, A. A. *Hirst and Rhodes* (The Epworth Press, 1950)

Trueman, F. *Freddie Trueman's Book of Cricket* (Pelham Books, 1964)

Underwood, D. *Beating the Bat* (Stanley Paul, 1975)

Walker, P. *Cricket Conversations* (Pelham Books, 1978)

Watts, L. *The Fine Art of Baseball* (Prentice-Hall, 1975)

Whitington, R. S. *Bradman, Benaud and Goddard's Cinderellas* (Bailey Bros and Swinfen, 1964)

Wieselsberger, C. "Der Luftwiderstand Von Kugeln", Zeitschr. f. Flugtchn. u. Motorluftschiffahrt, 5 (1914)

Williams, M. *Double Century* (Collins Willow, 1985)

Index